THE LOST DECADE

POLLY TOYNBEE & DAVID WALKER

THE LOST DECADE

2010–2020
and
What Lies Ahead
for Britain

First published in 2020
by Guardian Books, Kings Place, 90 York Way, London N1 9GU
and Faber & Faber Ltd, Bloomsbury House,
74–77 Great Russell Street, London WC1B 3DA

Printed and bound by CPI Group (UK) Ltd, Croydon, CR0 4YY

A CIP record for this book is
available from the British Library

ISBN 978–1–78335–171–8

2 4 6 8 10 9 7 5 3 1

Contents

Introduction

The Tory triumph in the 2019 general election, the fourth election within ten years, bookends their assumption of power in 2010, but for many it means that the pain and dismay of the lost decade from 2010 to 2020 will extend long into the 2020s. During the campaign, Boris Johnson grandly pronounced the end of austerity but said nothing about repairing the damage done; he was highly selective about which cuts might be partially restored and who would receive his largesse. The UK economy is in trouble, financial sustainability under threat. It may be only a matter of time before his government resorts, again, to slash and burn.

That's one reason we need the social accounting offered here. Another is that during Brexit and political party turmoil, amnesia was deliberate, with the past rewritten. Here's our bid to fill the role of recording angel. We can't understand what is happening now unless we consider all that led up to it. Such is the volatility of contemporary politics that much may have changed between the time this book went to press in December and you reading it. But we are not primarily concerned with the charivari of Westminster, the turmoil, deep-dyed cynicism and crass opportunism of parliaments. Our book records the effect of what the government did, what it spent and cut and who suffered as a result, how attitudes and sensibilities change, sometimes at pace, sometimes glacially.

We have tried to track the past decade methodically: employing statistics where appropriate; listing what was enacted and what was delivered; and presenting vignettes of the lives, experiences, attitudes, emotions and responses of people we talked to around the country. References and sources for our facts and figures are listed at davidwalkerassociates.wordpress.com.

Our 2010 book *The Verdict: Did Labour Change Britain?* measured the Blair and Brown years. We used it to benchmark what Tory ministers inherited. Here we record the fate of Sure Start, social security, inequality, the legal system, defence and support for research and industry. The decade from 2010 to 2020 saw a drive to renew and harden Tory anti-state, anti-tax individualism, testing them to destruction. The core beliefs of most of those around Johnson's Cabinet table were nurtured in Thatcherism, though much was opportunistically suppressed in the 2019 election to stay in power.

The decade was dark and fractious; will the next one be the same? Perhaps not. Empirical reality may force the adoption of more progressive policies. Electoral and practical necessity demands spending and repair to popular services, from social care to police and potholes. The climate emergency, demography and ageing, new technology: these are unstoppable, and require an active, interventionist state. Meanwhile, attitudes on gender, inequality and diversity will go on liberalising. Challenges from Russia and China, let alone any practicable Brexit settlement, make mending a broken foreign policy essential. This book is both a spur and a reminder of all that was lost and all that needs reclaiming after the lost decade.

1

Leaving It All Behind

What happened will scar the rest of our lives. Beyond the Brexit rupture, austerity will ricochet down the years ahead. The phalanx of predominantly older people who powered the 2016 referendum vote will pass on, but their works will outlast them. An April 2019 survey by the Hansard Society found 56 per cent of the general public judged Britain to be in decline, expressing a defeated hopelessness that jarred with both the patriotism promised at the start of the Brexit campaign and the restoration of national fortunes promised as a reward for belt-tightening. Just before he died, the poet Geoffrey Hill, with David Bowie's disappearance in mind, saw the spirit of the nation sinking low.

This was a decade of lost time when it came to the pressing national tasks of cutting carbon emissions, renewing roofs and railways, boosting technical skills and refitting national defence with cyber-capacity, or preparing for our inevitable ageing. It was a decade of hard work and lost earnings: real wages, adjusted for inflation, dropped by 5 per cent. The escalator that had carried successive generations to higher levels of affluence jerked, then stopped. Twenty- and thirty-somethings were worse off than their parents had been at the same age; ubiquitous avocado on toast was a myth, and many were still forced to live with their parents because they couldn't afford to move. People in their forties and fifties were worse off than people of the same age used to be. Such a prolonged period of stagnation had not been seen since wartime, perhaps even the Napoleonic era. But those at the top saw their pay rise, massively.

It was certainly a good time to have a few bob. During hearings at the European Parliament, the whistleblower who exposed the £200 billion money-laundering scandal at Danske Bank said that the UK was getting worse at combating corruption, letting limited liability partnerships be abused; UK shell companies were the preferred vehicle for non-resident clients, some linked to Putin and the Russian kleptocracy. Access to ministers was openly sold in exchange for party donations. It was fitting that oligarchs were made welcome in our oligarchy. David Cameron created new peers faster than any of his predecessors: membership of the House of Lords grew to 793. The only other countries with larger second parliamentary chambers were the People's Republic of China, Kazakhstan and Burkina Faso.

Who were *we*? The question forced itself more urgently than at any time since Great Britain was melded together in the eighteenth century. England, Wales and Scotland went their different ways in 2016. The Irish question was exhumed from the shallow grave where it had rested in relative peace for twenty years, to dominate politics in a way William Ewart Gladstone might have recognised. If Brexit was nationalism in action, whose 'mish-mash of myth, legend, history and wishful thinking' – as one historian defined the -ism – was it? Together with austerity's destruction of public spaces and services,

Brexit sharpened differences and distances, stretching the gaps between places, classes and ages, between degree-holders and those who had not gone to college, feeding mutual contempt and a growing suspicion that we no longer shared the same mental or moral space as our physical neighbours. At least we agreed we disagreed: three-quarters of the population thought Britain 'more divided'. The country had been cleft.

Us and Them

A television crew from the BBC – which itself suffered a melt-down of editorial control and journalistic self-confidence – went to Merthyr Tydfil to portray the Brexit Party's astute use of social media. When they tried to film a Nigel Farage rally, burly men approached the camera. 'Not wanted here,' they growled. 'British Broadcasting Conspiracy', 'left-wing scum', then something unintelligible about 'mainstream media', that cod phrase of the Trumpites and their British analogues. This was Welsh leavism, brutish and threatening, far from Nye Bevan's green-valley socialism.

But this story was about a cultural disconnect. The day after the encounter was broadcast, the Welsh government decreed that parents would no longer be permitted to hit their chil-dren. As in Scotland, smacking would be assault. Here was a parallel Welsh trajectory, this one revealing that around those burly Merthyr leavers social norms were continuing to liberal-ise. In which direction lay the future? By 2020 the signposts were pointing confusingly to more Toryism, but of a social democratic bent: Plaid Cymru on the rise; more Welsh language; remain improving in the polls; the Welsh economy fragile, as symbolised by the huge uncertainty over the Port Talbot steel plant, its government more dependent than ever on grants from Westminster.

'We have become an us and them society,' the Social Mobility Commission reported. Along with immobility they found alienation and social resentment: 'whole tracts of our country feel left behind'. But that could easily sound like *we*, the metropolitan elite, the governing class, pronouncing on what *they* felt. They were perfectly able to speak, and had done, in the Brexit vote and countless polls and vox pops. It turned out that many who had voted leave were not poor or northern or left behind or much afflicted by austerity. They were, nonetheless, resentful, yet the reasons given for that resentment often sounded suspiciously like an echo of the headlines that newspaper proprietors – non-British and resident in extra-territorial tax havens – had long been procuring from journalists who were more poisonously partisan than ever before.

'Whole communities feel the benefits of globalisation have passed them by,' said the commissioners. So why go on voting for MPs opposed to the active, redistributive policies needed to temper the negative effects of migration and globalisation? Why support a leave campaign whose instigators wanted the UK to become an unregulated tax haven? (Maybe it already was. The OECD found that fewer than a third of the fifty-six tax authorities it surveyed had dedicated units to oversee the tax affairs of the wealthy. HM Revenues and Customs (HMRC) claimed that it was focusing on the issue, with 375 staff locked on the tax owed by 6,200 people with assets worth more than £20 million. Yet, as the hyper-rich expanded, so did their willingness to avoid tax.)

'Listen to the leavers,' commentators kept insisting. But they constantly emphasised difference and discord, and it was hard to fashion a coherent response. For example, where was the sense in supporting a Brexit that was actively damaging research, productivity and growth while reducing the means to redress the inequities between groups and regions?

But beware Britocentrism, for this was also an age of anxiety in Hungary, Italy, Poland and the US, while insurgent right-wing parties in Spain, France and Germany dug up the old template rejecting immigration, protecting privilege and abhorring social change favouring women and the LGBTQ community, displaying a yen for authoritarian rulers, clowns and demagogues. Other countries, too, were engaging in painful conversations about identity, past and future. Germany struggled to define a role commensurate with its European standing; Emmanuel Macron rose meteorically before, battered by the *gilets jaunes*, old reflexes and incompatible aspirations, the stock of this epitome of centrism plummeted and the burning of Notre-Dame seared France's soul. Foreign observers were perplexed at the disappearance of those self-proclaimed British virtues of pragmatism, tolerance and humour, gone for good. Unlike France, Germany or Hungary, the UK wasn't unitary. Spain and Italy had their problems defining nationhood, but nothing like those facing a polity comprising Wales, Scotland

and, most anomalous of all, Northern Ireland. English nationalism stirred, disconsolate but unformed. The hard right in England, represented by Tommy Robinson and the assassin of the MP Jo Cox, did not even try to shake off its brutishness. It had no ideas, no theories of the kind that underpinned pre-war fascism. But themes and memes blew in from the US.

Sleeping Under Cardboard

The tone of public life coarsened. Precious institutions bore pockmarks from the flak. The dissolution of trust did not just enfeeble the political class, media and corporate chieftains; confidence in charities also tumbled into a ten-year trough. Meliorism, the taken-for-granted inevitability of upgrade, died with new statistics on longevity. Mortality had been in retreat, but now the long improvement in our life expectancy came to an abrupt end. Infant mortality rose in a pattern unseen since before the Second World War.

Both trends were hard to disconnect from poverty and the axing of social services. Psychiatrists estimated that one in five girls and young women in England had cut, burned or poisoned themselves in deliberate acts of self-harm, part of a rising trend. After deaths by crushing were reported, London binmen learned to check waste containers before emptying them: 'You can't spot people if they're sleeping under cardboard,' said one. A BBC interview with a nurse captured how it felt to be stigmatised and excluded: 'I see more misery and hardship for myself and my children. I have just been awarded a 1 per cent rise, and yet the cost of living continues to increase. The chancellor has cut tax credits in an underhand way. It seems as a single parent and a public sector worker I am an enemy of the state.' Foreign journalists who came to film the food banks found themselves tripping over sleeping bags in doorways. Welcome to the country of homelessness, payday loans, bedroom tax and zero-hours contracts.

But the era's winners won big. One in five of those born in the 1950s now owned a second property. The total wealth embodied by second homes, buy-to-let investments and those foreign gîtes, rural villas and flats on the Costa climbed to £941 billion. The old did well, the young badly (even if some of them will later in life become lucky inheritors). Top people coined it; recipients of benefits suffered. Jeff Fairburn of Persimmon was gifted a £75 million bonus, not for entrepreneurial heroism or risking his own money in clever investment, but for milking a scandalously loose housebuilding subsidy devised by Chancellor George Osborne with that characteristic mixture of dogma and administrative incompetence. The UK still had more very highly paid bankers than the rest of the EU put together. The dividends paid out by companies in the UK reached a record high of £99.8 billion in 2018. Growth slowed, but profits rose. The list of winners also featured vice-chancellors, who often pulled the strings of the university councils meant to hold them to account in order to put through substantial increases in their own pay, which were ultimately paid from the public purse.

Osborne himself was one of those who did very nicely, thank you, after being given a succession of handsomely rewarded jobs. As editor of the London *Evening Standard*, he first pursued a personal vendetta against his former boss, Theresa May, before returning the paper to Tory partisanship and savaging the Labour London mayor at every opportunity. His new boss was a pal of Boris Johnson's who had sold part of the equity to the Saudis; the *Standard* slathered the new prime minister in treacle.

The High Street Falls Low

Median pay stood pat. An average worker's total weekly pay fell in real terms from £525 in 2008 to £497 in 2019. As incomes idled and the use of contactless payments surged, people dealt with less physical cash. In 2006, 62 per cent of payments in the UK were made with notes and coins; ten years later, it was only 40 per cent, with over 300 cashpoints closing each month by 2019, stranding towns such as Battle in East Sussex. The Royal Mint stayed production of 1p and 2p pieces.

If consumption kept growing, it was partly because after 2015 households again started loading up with debt. Paradoxically, consumerism could no longer sustain its ancient creation, the high street. The collapse of friendly and familiar retail brands probably contributed to a pervading sense of loss and dislocation. Kinks guitarist Dave Davies tried to defend an ornate shopping arcade in north London against destruction, saying, 'Feelings are attached to things, not just people . . . little shops matter.' The upside/downside of that was the consummate ease of online shopping, with goods delivered by a dense network of competing, carbon-emitting vans and lorries, and lots of openings for gig-employed drivers, badly paid.

The fate of retail suggests a metaphor for what happened to the UK at large after 2010. Along the high street financial forces went to work unseen on the bricks and mortar. American online companies, unregulated and monopolistic, squeezed traditional commerce, their man in the White House threatening dire consequences if they were brought to tax justice. You could be in King's Lynn or Greenock, Coleraine or Wrexham, and the streetscape shows many of the same shop fronts. You can still find major brands – Clark's shoes, Thornton's, Primark, Holland & Barrett and Boots – but in between is dereliction. The 'n' and the 'h' in the sign for the Debenham's store in Banbury are hanging loose; it's been closed down, and a pop-up card shop has colonised part of the space, the rest empty or let to charity shops. Elsewhere, Marks & Spencer has downsized or gone; estate agents' signs tell of frontages to let, while marginal nail parlours and vape shops have moved in, along with the homeless and destitute. This is 2020's Britain. It hasn't fallen apart, but it's pockmarked, squalid and reeking of decline. Meanwhile, out of town, people with cars and money still flock to Asda and Waitrose, though those companies are not without balance-sheet anxieties, shutting up shops, too.

That word – anxiety – recurs. As ambiguous as the attitude and well-being data is, it shows worry, discomfort and tension; the gloomsters attacked by Johnson when he took office as prime minister had good reason to be uncheerful.

We Never Had So Much Control

Paradoxically, people had opportunity aplenty to express their feelings. The phrase 'take back control' was so rich in nostalgia and the promise of recovery, yet we had never had as much control, electorally at least. In addition to the cycle of council contests, in England new metropolitan or regional mayors were voted for in Greater Manchester, the West Midlands, Liverpool, Cambridge/Peterborough, Avon (Bristol, Bath, South Gloucestershire) and South Yorkshire. The inhabitants of the north-east who vociferously grabbed the 'left behind' badge had been given the chance of an elected assembly in 2004, but responded with apathy, largely voted no and would probably not be much keener now. Judging by turnout and local interest, better governance for cities and regions was not what people meant by taking back control, and interest stayed depressingly low. The gap between the size of the potential electorate and those actually on the register continued to grow: Democratic Audit said it could be as high as 8 million people.

The 2010 coalition deal specified a referendum on fairer voting for the House of Commons. This, too, turned out to be a form of control people did not want to take back. Opposing change, the demon team who won the Brexit referendum cut their incisors on this one and practised their dishonesty. Not that they needed to. Extraordinarily, in the light of subsequent party fragmentation, fairer voting was not what the people wanted and only two out of five bothered to turn out, with 68 per cent of those who did backing the status quo. A year later, in England, barely one in seven voted in the first elections for police and crime commissioners, a pet project in which Cameron and co. promptly lost all interest. A year after that, one in three voted for the UK's members of the European Parliament. But enough of them backed UKIP to frighten Cameron into conceding a referendum to the Tory Eurosceptics.

In 2015 the Tories won the UK general election with 37 per cent of the vote. Third in terms of votes cast, UKIP got only a single seat, which showed how much had been squandered by the failure of fair voting in 2011. On to June 2016, when 72 per cent took part in the referendum on EU membership; 51.9 per cent said leave. The people whose will was subsequently cited as being expressed amounted to 37 per cent of the voting population. A year afterwards, Theresa May asked for a Brexit mandate and – insofar as votes 'say' anything intelligible – was refused one, even though the number of people voting Tory increased. On a 69 per cent turnout, she was left dependent on a deal with the ten Democratic Unionist Party MPs. Seven Sinn Féin MPs continued to refuse to take their Westminster seats. Electoral enthusiasm drained away in the drear days of December 2019; we picked up the result of that contest in the Introduction.

Abstention is a reminder that most people are only intermittently interested in public affairs, which doesn't stop them expressing their views, however ill-informed. We get on with our lives regardless of politics, even when matters of life and death turn on political decision-making. We often said to the people we talked to for this book, 'But your job, your children's life chances, their housing, the things you cherish, they're all affected by policy, tax and political choices.' They don't necessarily believe it.

The Abyss

Jack London called his book about the East End *The People of the Abyss*, in that Victorian/Edwardian tradition of intrepid writers venturing into the heart of social darkness. Leavers tried to tar their opponents with the same brush: 'You talk as if we are troglodytes, blind political moles, when we are quite capable of trading off our economic interests against an expression of identity as anti-Europeans or proud Little Englanders. *We can and will self-harm if we want to, in the name of patriotism.*' Scholars once wrote books about the paranoid strain in American politics; well, it was evident here now. The attitude shone defiantly through polls during the Tory leadership contest in June 2019, when party members – an unrepresentative handful, predominantly white, male and old – said they would sacrifice everything – the existence of the UK, big losses to GDP and personal material well-being – in order to secure the great prize.

Shouting from the other side of the abyss, 'What is the prize?' did no good. Brexit was about profound, unbridgeable differences in understanding how the world works. There is no healing unction for a cognitive wound. Possessing a university degree marked out and divided us; the clash of view and value started with schooling. Liberals (tending to be tolerant, opposed to censorship, the death penalty and so on) had long been far apart from authoritarians. Now those divisions mapped closely the leave/remain divide. But left–right remained, meaning for or against government, tax and market interventions. A great Brexit puzzle was how, having won the vote, leave pushed and got pulled further and further rightwards on this scale, too, eventually creating in the Johnson government the spectacle of committed small-staters being forced to announce big spending in the name of leave. Nearly 100 per cent of Labour Party members thought austerity had gone too far, against 11 per cent of Tories; 15 per cent of Tories thought the government should redistribute income, against 94 per cent of Labour members. Authoritarians and liberals split between Labour and Tory in the 2017 election, though it was the first where age was a stronger predictor of voting intention than social class.

Crumbling and Crumbly

This era was always going to be pressured, because an ageing society is more likely to be tense and divided: demography is destiny. Between 2010 and 2020 the population aged sixty-five and above grew by 25 per cent to over 12.5 million; by contrast, the number of children under sixteen grew by 8 per cent. Single-person households rose sharply to 7.7 million, with surveys suggesting they tended to be less happy and saved notably less. As the proportion of senior citizens keeps growing, choices have to be made about resources, taxes, health and care. Except that society doesn't make 'choices' in that reasoned sense. Decisions are fragmented, people grumble and adapt, the noisiest dominate, and things are allowed to happen. More older people needed care, but it wasn't provided, and the quality of their and their families' lives diminished as a result. Austerity and failing social supports went some way to explaining why the Office for National Statistics (ONS) found that life expectancy in the UK had stopped improving for the first time since 1982, when such predictions were first made.

To age is to crumble. You can't keep putting sticking plasters on infrastructure, said the chair of the commission supposed to be reviewing it; he could just as well have been talking about our senescent constitution as the national patrimony. The home of the UK parliament was falling apart, physically as well as politically. The Palace of Westminster was a Victorian pile that had not been built to accommodate computers, miles of wiring and central heating, which is why fire safety teams had started to patrol 24/7. Old buildings can be renewed: look at the marvel of St Pancras Station – but that was resuscitated before 2010, when spending flowed. What was now characteristic was indecision, an unwillingness to spend, to plan or to undertake bold collective investment. At Westminster, rabbits in the headlights, MPs dithered and cowered in fear of the public reaction to big spending on their own workplace.

What a paradox: if Brexit was about control, wouldn't the nation want to celebrate the locus of sovereignty, parliament? No, disclosures about MPs' expenses, so mercilessly exploited by right-wing newspapers, had a lasting effect, stocking already deep pools of dislike and suspicion, giving leavers their pretext for repeatedly trying to ignore, sideline, prorogue and denigrate parliament. Eventually, a decision about the fabric was made, but Westminster is not to be vacated until the mid-2020s, when MPs and peers are supposed to disperse to nearby sites (they failed to take up radical proposals for upending the rule of the south by decamping to York, Manchester or Birmingham).

The need for physical renewal was visible everywhere. A mid-morning train from Sheffield to Barnsley sets off late, the ancient rolling stock wheezing and shaking, the electronic station indicator on the blink, the franchisee, Northern Rail (owned by the German state railway company), a byword for decrepit and unreliable service. The transport interchange at Barnsley is smart, joining bus and rail, and wheelchair accessible, but it was opened in 2007 thanks to Labour-era largesse, which Osborne, Cameron and unfathomably large numbers of the public called excessive and wasteful. There is no Yorkshire public transport authority to ensure buses and trains connect.

These could, and should, have been years of renewal, building on what had been done, pulling the UK faster out of recession by refreshing physical infrastructure. But for that to happen, the public had to will the means. Resources needed to be mobilised (through taxation or long-term borrowing), big and bold decisions made, projects tightly managed. Instead, citizens were fractious and carping, distrustful of collective authority, except when it came to Brexit, when they insisted that collective will did exist and must prevail.

Austerity was a double whammy. Even spending at 2010 levels would mean less per capita when the number of people was growing – and it was, mightily. In 2020 the total population is 67.3 million, compared with 62.8 million in 2010. The 34.5 million licensed vehicles on Great Britain's roads in 2010 grew to 38.4 million, but road space increased by only 1 per cent. That gap translated into congestion and slower journey times. Meanwhile, it will take councils in England fourteen years and £9 billion to clear the backlog of overdue road repairs. Making life harder for motorists might have been willed and welcome had it been part of a concerted, justly administered response to the climate emergency; instead, we had a kind of anarchy, bits of policy running hither and thither amid rigid spending reductions.

Astonishing

'We should never stop reminding ourselves just what an astonishing decade we have lived through,' said the Institute for Fiscal Studies (IFS), ever honest and reliable. 'The UK economy has broken record after record, and not generally in a good way: record low earnings growth, record low interest rates, record low productivity growth, record public borrowing followed by record cuts in public spending.' There was also record employment and remarkable growth in jobs, at least until 2019, with 'help wanted' becoming a familiar sign. But the new jobs paid indifferently at best, and often badly. Meanwhile, the gap between those in work, especially the young, and the retired grew into a chasm. For many, home ownership used to be an unmissable step on life's ladder; it went into decline and precarious private renting increased. Those born in the 1980s and 1990s were spending longer and longer as tenants.

The 2010s began with bust as the financial crash and recession pushed public debt high. It's still hard to get a true measure of the consequences of the banking collapse and its display of greed and market failure, along with political and civil service incompetence and misunderstanding. As the tide went out, what emerged naked was a bloated financial sector beached far apart ethically and functionally from the 'real economy'. How much of our destiny was now dependent on this whale, financial services having come to supply such a hefty proportion of the Treasury's revenues?

Who Won?

One story tells of transition after the crash, which looms over the decade. Post-war, up to Margaret Thatcher, the UK was mildly social democratic; after her, Tony Blair attempted a rescue focused on the NHS, schools, welfare and Sure Start. In a brilliant book, *The Rise and Fall of the British Nation*, historian David Edgerton argued that Labour briefly stole the Tories' clothes by positioning themselves as the party of UK unity, which devolution was meant to strengthen. But what happened during and after the financial crisis showed how strong the individualist, anti-social democratic reflex was; how easy it proved to strip away the edifice of policy interventions built by Blair and Gordon Brown.

Through one lens, the 2010s saw Labour marginalised. Perhaps the die was cast before 2010, when too many Labour ministers bought into the untruth of fixed limits on state borrowing during economic crisis, including the hapless Liam Byrne, author of the infamous bare-cupboard note to his successor as Treasury chief secretary. Brown and Alistair Darling failed miserably at explaining the causes of the crash or turning circumstances to the Left's advantage. Had Labour been elected in 2010, it too would have implemented austerity. But measures would have been less harsh, the poor and helpless would not have carried the main burden, nor would towns and cities in the north of England, Wales and Scotland have taken the heaviest hits. Had Labour won there would have been no referendum on Europe. Part of the story after 2010 was Labour's ineffectiveness as the principal opposition party at Westminster, and in Scotland, the SNP becoming what the Tories had forever been in England: the natural party of government. Labour lost in 2015 and made only marginal gains in 2017, followed by Jeremy Corbyn's failure to seize the initiative during the national crisis over Brexit.

Writers scratched national itches but were curiously out of the loop. In *All Together Now?* Mike Carter tramped the land, angry at what England now was but also upset with himself for letting 'it' happen. Blame the anti-collective turn, the politicians who pushed it (and the people who voted them in) – or should that be the amorphous forces of globalisation and finance capitalism? Forty years of Thatcherism, strong or lite, had weakened the capacity to act collectively. Protests, marches and campaigns were mounted but were thematic and brief.

Yet through another lens Labour won posthumously. Market idealism had been rent by the crash, and intellectually Thatcherism was spent and anachronistic; the Right had run out of ideas. Consciousness of the climate emergency was now growing and, sooner or later, we'd have to return to the active state as the only answer to national failures in productivity, transport, the environment, fairness, social mobility and ageing. Come 2019, and Labour's 2010 Equality Act was still a fixed reference point, causing the government deep embarrassment over social mobility and poverty. More shame could have been piled on the government had everything smacking of 'Blairism' not been so resoundingly denigrated by the Corbynites, refusing to give New Labour credit. Outside the Corbyn cult, welfare, education and health in 2010 were taken as the benchmark against which decline had to be measured. Our book *The Verdict* was written as a tally of what was and wasn't achieved by Blair and Brown, as this book aims to do for subsequent years.

Floreat Etona

The 2010 Tory manifesto had deplored child poverty and, addressing social justice, had not dared to diverge from the era's dominant, mildly egalitarian ideas. But in office the Tories saw their chance, camouflaged by the Liberal Democrats and succoured by holy fools from the Left – Labour MPs Graham Allen and Frank Field – and political chancers such as Alan Milburn and John Hutton doing projects and studies at their behest. Reality soon dawned: bipartisanship was one-way, austerity the priority, and the Tories retained their core identity. Within weeks prime minister and chancellor washed off the soft soap and plunged back into the Thatcherism they had marvelled at as adolescents. They pushed the free-market line in social policy, schools, the NHS, probation, prisons and transport. Cameron's casual pretence that he had no strong beliefs was a fairy tale sold by sycophants and gullible reporters. He personally pushed privatisation and public service outsourcing, exhibit A being the ugly report he commissioned from a party donor called Adrian Beecroft, who advocated firing staff at will, Victorian levels of employment protection and an end to trade unions. The report asserted that deregulating the labour market would increase GDP by 5 per cent, a figure which, said the LSE economist John van Reenen, had been plucked from the ether as if by witchcraft. So much for evidence.

In his book *For the Record* – lots of mea and little culpa – Cameron just about admits that he consistently put the Tory party before everything; what was good for his party was, of course, best for Britain. Toryism remained the governing default, more a tic than a philosophy. However much of a minority their electors were, the Tories exuded the bogus confidence that they owned, represented, *were* the backbone of England, if not Britain – a sociological absurdity that could never have been sustained if the media had been differently configured and the biases of the press matched voting preferences rather than owners' prejudices. It's important to see the continuities between Cameron and Boris Johnson, their easy assumption about this natural order and its fixed electoral props across England, north as well as south, where sufficient numbers would always back them, come what may (except May), in Witham, Tarporley, Aylesbury, Maidstone, Howden, Horncastle and scores of other places outside the cities. Their support was guaranteed, despite the rush rightwards – indeed, middle England willed it, asking why it took so long for the Tories to become the sadistic, authoritarian, nationalist party they were by 2019.

Cameron, May and Johnson represented an identifiable class – possessors, aspirants to possession and the deferential – at a time when, paradoxically, resentful class consciousness was advancing, though a big effort was made to cloak it non-threateningly as 'social mobility'. Etonians ruled just as we became more acutely aware of the UK's (or should that be England's?) rigid social selection. The stage was stormed: too few working-class actors were playing alongside Benedict Cumberbatch (Harrow) or Eddie Redmayne (Eton). Access to universities, the arts, consultancy, journalism or the law was found to be barred to those lacking the correct background and education.

Sociologically speaking, none of this was new but, attitudinally, the plates seemed to be shifting, with more grudging complaints against posh supremacy. That did not stop Cameron practising government by school chum. His resignation honours list was 'so full of cronies it would embarrass a medieval court', said Tim Farron. Jeremy Hunt, head boy of Charterhouse, slugged it out with Bullingdon Johnson to lead the party. It wasn't just the Tories. Jeremy Corbyn attended the kind of prep school where, as a former pupil put it, a boy could be flogged for 'having your cap at a rakish angle'; Momentum media strategist James Schneider was privately educated, as were Labour apparatchiks Seumas Milne and Jon Lansman. Author Robert Verkaik said these schools produced inflated egos with 'an innate sense of entitlement and . . . an almost pathological willingness to risk everything', which explained much in recent politics.

Toryism Triumphant

The 2010s demonstrated the extraordinary staying power of the Tory party: battered, fractured, its leaders vainglorious and downright incompetent in varying measure, its ideological commitments rejected in poll after poll, yet its core support was sufficient to keep a grip on power, abetted as always by the media barons, money men and the individualist inertia that kept so many on the right side of the road, time and again. The money men performed indifferently. For all their rhetoric, Tory ministers presided over an economy that did not grow much; entrepreneurs did not miraculously step up and innovate, whatever the would-be titans of free enterprise such as James Dyson kept promising.

Tory rebels showed the party at once fissuring and solid. Yes, Johnson expelled Brexit refuseniks. But consider Dan Poulter, a doctor who, after meeting Cameron in 2006, was persuaded to enter politics and became a minister in 2010. He later resigned, having woken up to 'chronic underfunding of mental health and social care services, a shortage of social and appropriate sheltered housing, together with a benefits system that does not always adequately recognise the needs of people with severe and enduring mental illness'. He concluded that tax cuts were wrong, that truly governing for one nation also meant recognising the role of the state in changing the lives of the most disadvantaged for the better. None of that stopped him remaining a Tory MP, standing again in 2019, demurring not at all as he trooped through the lobbies behind Johnson. The prime minister's brother, Jo Johnson, vowed in the 2015 election to outspend Labour on the NHS and 'reach out to parts of society that had shunned us'. He became a minister, before resigning over Brexit, then, whistling 'The Vicar of Bray', becoming a minister again, before resigning again and then standing down as an MP, apparently now woke to his brother's true character. Myopia, inconstancy and prevalent cynicism were part of the rich mix.

Some of the Tories expelled in the great Brexit purge were from the one-nation faction, but ironically, others, such as the former chancellor Philip Hammond, were dry-as-dust anti-tax and anti-government-intervention disciples. This ideology had been an expanding element of the Tory presence. During these years, the Thatcher revolution was ratcheted up in a sort of second phase, 1917 compared to 1905, the Jacobins succeeding the Girondins. Dogmatic small-state Toryism was boosted by Brexit, capturing the castle when Johnson succeeded. His was 'the most right-wing government we have had in my lifetime, probably including Thatcher', said Nicola Sturgeon, and she was right, though her implication that Scotland could hare off down a social democratic path tomorrow was contradicted by harsh fiscal facts. It's true that before Theresa May submerged, for a brief interlude her speeches tacked towards intervention and a more pragmatic line on the state. Her speechwriters invoked the activist Tory mayor of Birmingham Joseph Chamberlain and the plight of the 'just about managing'. But Hammond remained chancellor, and in his budgets more was taken from benefits and austerity was deepened.

Alongside nostalgia and nationalism went dogma and disarray. This generation of right-wing politicians had rigid beliefs but was also incompetent. Amyas Morse, head of the National Audit Office (NAO), said ministers saw themselves as chief executives but lacked the qualifications that ought to go with the job. Pundits asked how it could be that with so little in the way of workable ideas, talent, administrative nous or electoral support, the Tories were able to change society so much. 'In the gentleman-dilettante tradition, many Conservative politicians leave boring detail to civil servants,' wrote Simon Kuper of the *Financial Times*. 'When you know that your class will always prosper, you can afford airy gambles. Hence Cameron's bet that a referendum would put the European issue to bed, reunite the Tory party and see off the threat from Farage.'

Perhaps if you despise active, socially minded government, you are fated to run it badly. Perhaps at some deeper level, ideological commitment was veering even further away from what the system could ever deliver. Later, we will look at Universal Credit; what Tory ministers wanted from this gigantic measure was undeliverable on the timescale, budget and policy assumptions they were making. All roads led back to austerity and their determination to diminish the state's size and significance, yet in their departments they tried to rule as firmly as if they had the managerial capacity of earlier times. Public sector employment fell to 16.5 per cent of total jobs, its lowest level since 1945. The last-minute rush to fill the civil service cavities exposed by Brexit did nothing to counteract the effects of diminishing the payroll.

Spending cuts weren't the only line of attack. Downsizing was accompanied by wilful fragmentation. Public service managers were told to snarl and fight with one another, to transfer their work to private companies. Take the fire that broke out at Grenfell Tower in North Kensington in 2017, killing seventy-two. First responders showed the ethos of public service: they were courageous and dedicated, whatever the questions later asked about the protocols of evacuating a high rise. The follow-up, especially on the psychological consequences for residents, showed NHS staff at their best. But Grenfell also exhibited the disjointed, uncommunicative nature of public services and the downdraught from outsourcing. Fire officers connected only haphazardly with council housing departments; no one looked at the emergency services in the round. The Department for Work and Pensions (DWP) passed the welfare buck to underfunded councils. They in turn were suspicious of the NHS.

Insouciant ministers could be both ignorant of and indifferent to the rules; with Brexit this tendency worsened. Johnson's and Michael Gove's backgrounds in journalism explained a lot: their vocation was sensationalism, saying, not doing, posturing in print, not providing. They played fast and loose with public money. Johnson's tenure as London mayor, which ended in 2016, had seen him adopt the wheeze of a new pedestrian bridge across the Thames. It would be privately funded, he promised. The project fell apart, costing the public purse an estimated £53 million in futile fees. The *Architects' Journal* spoke to a commercial property developer who had donated £50,000. 'The money was pissed down the drain by a bunch of incompetents and I feel conned,' he said.

The bridge was an example of an old trick: keeping the public domain ticking over, but at threadbare cost. Another age-old Tory trick was appearing to be the party of English/British nationalism while promoting full-blooded market capitalism, which will always tend to weaken the nation state, diluting its capacity to tax, regulate or confine companies; international giants could make engines just as well in Bratislava as Bridgend, and it wasn't for them to worry about the social consequences. But nationalism was about order, hierarchy, restriction (on migration, for example) and control. The Tories had long managed to ride both tigers, even when, as under Thatcher, they jerked apart, as they did in defence procurement and energy policy. English nationalism never had cruder or clearer expression than when Tory party members said they wanted a no-deal Brexit, even at the expense of the economy and harm to their own finances. Business had always preferred the Tories, largely out of the callow self-interest of executives who did not want to pay more tax. But now the nationalist Tories – voiced by Johnson – were saying out loud, 'Bugger business.'

We sort through the tissue of contradictions in the next chapter: how the leaders of Brexit did not actually believe in the barriers their voters wanted to build high; how their companies shifted outside the UK to compensate for the anticipated losses from Brexit; how their bulletins to investors urged them to short UK stocks before the post-Brexit downturn. The Brexit voters wanted a return to the 1950s, when businesses were home-owned, when men were men and women knew their place, before black people arrived in any number. What they usually failed to add was that the 1950s were when Tory governments led large-scale public interventions: a colossal public housebuilding programme and expansion of the NHS and social security.

Decrepit Thatcherism

Just how much of the Tories' intellectual capital still came from Thatcher was seen in the utilities. Take water. Regulation of the private companies that supply it in England was 1980s vintage and the system leaked like a colander; investment, profit and the public interest all needed rethinking. Research by Greenwich University found aggregate cash flow from payments by householders for water and sewerage after operating costs exceeded by £36 billion what the companies spent on maintaining reservoirs and pipes. And they weren't maintaining them very well, as the leakage showed. Since 1990 water industry revenue had grown by 34 per cent in real terms. Professor Dieter Helm, no friend of public ownership, called it a major regulatory failure.

Energy prices and pointless competition provoked public indignation; rail franchising failed. Labour plans for renationalising became popular even among Tory voters. However keen ministers were on outsourcing, the companies let them down by either failing to perform per spec or pulling out because they could not turn a profit. They could make the former chief executive of outsourcer Mitie, Ruby McGregor-Smith, a Tory peer and non-executive Whitehall director, but that wouldn't stop Carillion crashing with an almighty thump, leaving contracts high and dry, and Serco and Capita coming close to the edge. Austerity, it turned out, was not good corporate news.

Thatcher hated state ownership but exulted in her 'brutally activist state' (David Edgerton's phrase), whether to repress trade unions or project force thousands of miles away in the Falkland Islands. That dualism lived on, with Cameron's state reaching into the bedrooms of social security claimants, and May's chartered vans, emblazoned with messages, telling migrants to go home. But Cameron was lackadaisical about law and order, breaking with Tory tradition, forcing Johnson to scramble for excuses when he tried to pick up the old refrain about Tories being tough on crime. Ever the electoral calculators, they spent whenever the public outcry hurt their ears. They turned to the subsidy state when the Scots appeared likely to vote for independence, bunging extra money their way, just as May and Johnson bought support from the DUP. Their talk of industrial policy and Osborne's new-found interest in the north of England sounded heterodox but was merely confused. Spending on scientific research and development, which was broadly sustained in the midst of austerity, was directed towards the priorities of 'UK plc'. This made little sense, David Edgerton commented. How could they believe in UK plc when for thirty-five years Tory ministers had sold national assets and allowed companies to be taken over and dismantled? Equities listed on the stock exchange were largely foreign-owned. Suddenly promoting UK companies and production made no sense when the Brexit-induced collapse in sterling stoked a fire sale of UK assets.

When the Sun Shone

A lot of people did go on having disposable income, especially the baby boomers. When the sun shone, they filled the pavement cafés and consumed. The press of holidaymakers at Stansted Airport on an August morning, relaxed campers round a fire on a balmy September evening in Dorset, boaters on the Norfolk Broads on a half-term break, a traditional panto at the King's Theatre, Glasgow – pleasure was still affordable for many. Add your own vignettes from holidays or family life, birthdays, exam successes, a new baby, a Mohamed Salah or Harry Kane goal and memorable moments such as the 2012 Olympics, and even a grim span of political history left many relatively content. New things happened in the nooks and crannies of social life, such as the sudden passion for gin. The number of trademarks registered for spirits and liqueurs in the UK grew by 41 per cent in 2017, when thirty-nine artisanal gin distilleries opened. And more people danced. Or, at least, they wanted to see it, and not just on television – dance show ticket sales were up half a million a year by 2017.

It's hard to be definitive about mood. Apart from Brexit, people did not devote hours to reflection on the state of the nation; attention was intermittent. People went about their daily lives, worrying about household finances, driving to work, thinking about sex, looking after children and relatives, watching television, going to the gym, drinking, seeking fun and earning their living. Opinion polls can exaggerate the sharpness of views. The proportion of life devoted to public affairs is exceedingly small, perhaps only four minutes a week. If we ask about well-being, the answer has to be partly impressionistic, and in the age of volatile, pack-hunting social media, impressions are fallible. We will devote a chapter to asking how far crime, disorder and international tensions have fomented a sense of unease or insecurity. Crime fell, at least in aggregate, to 2016, but anxiety about crime and some categories of offences then soared. Riots and episodes of disorder were infrequent, which is puzzling if we are right about growing insecurity and the incidence of austerity.

When they were asked, many responded positively to questions about their happiness, registering both satisfaction with their lives and dissatisfaction with the state of things. The number of those who thought things were OK in their own lives remained buoyant even when optimism about the economy took a nosedive. People's views were not always informed. In his book *The Perils of Perception*, Bobby Duffy of Ipsos MORI showed how often they got things wrong, wildly exaggerating migrant numbers, for example. Only 19 per cent believed the homicide rate was lower than previously; 55 per cent thought there was or could be a link between vaccines and autism. What people thought important varied and did not always reflect what the political class was focusing on. In 2017 two of the biggest stories, by volume of online attention, were fox hunting and the ivory trade. Neither were big political issues, though Tory ministers promised action on the latter before dropping the subject. When May, courting the shires, suggested eviscerating the ban on fox hunting in her manifesto, the instant furore forced retreat. Chastened, as one of her last acts (and a filler for the great hole in parliamentary business) May moved to ban the use of wild animals in circuses.

The Centre for Social Investigation reported a lower proportion of positive responses to the question 'Do you feel close to your country?' than in comparable countries. Increasing numbers thought empathy was on the wane. A shelf full of books was published on the unhappy present and dark future of democracy, amid worries about public ignorance and, inversely, the perils of 'epistocracy', a coinage meaning rule by people who know or think they know better. But trust had long been on the slide. Governments were among the least trusted institutions in France and Germany, as well as the UK. In other countries, too, confidence was split along class lines: those with higher levels of education and income tended to trust other people and the state more.

People were prepared to change attitudes or behaviour on certain issues. Councils encountered little resistance to tougher rules on sorting recyclables. Supermarkets began to cut plastic packaging. The relationship with drink was changing, with pubs closing at an accelerating rate, their number dropping from 52,500 in 2001 to 38,000 by 2020. Cameron built on Labour precedents to enact a right for community groups to bid for village shops that would otherwise close, libraries, pubs and recreation grounds. In fact, most pub closures were on the edges of towns and cities, where community spirit was least visible. 'Public spirit' was evanescent. The Tories ended their brief flirtation with voluntary action with a harsh crackdown on charities, turning the Charities Commission from a beneficent supervisor into a hammer of organisations daring to speak up or lobby over austerity. Then, in another turnaround, charity was hailed for setting up food banks.

On Your Bike

If some aspects of behaviour changed, on others we hunkered down, refusing to shift. Out of our cars, for example. In 2010 total UK bike sales amounted to £1.49 billion; they fell to £1.28 billion by 2016. But bike sharing expanded in some places; in Manchester, too many ended up in the canal. The number of people working in the bicycle trade in the UK dropped from 15,000 to a low of just over 12,400 over the same period.

Among them was Andy Brooke, whom we first met in 2014, just after he opened his shop on busy London Road, near Derby railway station. It seemed the perfect spot, near where the council was about to build a new velodrome. It felt like a good time for cycling commerce. The Tour de France came through Britain in 2014, starting in Leeds. Bradley Wiggins, Chris Froome and Geraint Thomas had become new national sporting heroes. Although only 5 per cent were cycling at least once a week, that was over 2 million adults, and they were cycling more miles than in 2010.

The Bespoke Bike Shop was high-end, specialising in machines for serious and well-off contenders, particularly triathletes. 'We're a destination shop. People come from far and wide,' Andy told us proudly. He and four part-timers built and fitted bikes to precise specifications.

In the shadow of the crash, and despite official cajoling to lend to small businesses, banks were hoarding money, refusing loans. Andy struggled to get finance. He moved the shop several times, but the last time 'it coincided with Brexit. That seemed to have an instant effect, with an overnight drop-off in sales. Before the referendum we'd been selling two bikes a week, but now it was down to two a month.

'A lot of people in Derby work for the big companies – Bombardier, Rolls-Royce and Toyota – but Brexit left them not knowing if they'd still have jobs, or if factories would close. Overnight people became very, very careful with their money.' His company filed for insolvency, his investor lost £20,000 and the banks lost more. He managed to avoid personal bankruptcy, though he is still being chased by banks. Derby council's velodrome suffered a similar fate: it was built but made a heavy loss. 'This has been a hard time for me,' said Andy. 'I got married, and I

was busy organising the wedding at the same time as I was deal-
ing with the shop's bankruptcy.'

Andy went on doing the specialised bike fitting, but now for
another company. He was seeking to sell a niche bike part manu-
factured to his design in China. Looking back, he was rueful. 'I
was so uplifted by the 2012 Olympics. That showed us off as a great
multicultural hub, welcoming everyone. Then came the referen-
dum, so many political lies. It was frustrating they weren't ques-
tioned. Now the country's creeping in the wrong direction. We're
going to leave. We nearly bought a home and took jobs in France,
but now I've been offered something in sports science in the US –
and that's where we'll go. We want children, but we don't want to
bring them up here any more, not in this atmosphere.'

That's one vignette on the UK economy. Andy's business
was post-post-industrial, making things at a small, specialised
scale in a sort of symbiotic relationship with the big producers, increasingly Chinese. Brexit disrupted everything, shaking
out people, attitudes, expectations – and, of course, decoupling
from the EU had only just begun. During these years, the basic
health of the UK economy was not sound, despite the slow
recovery from recession. It relied on household consumption,
fuelled by borrowing on credit cards. If you were too poor to
have a credit card, you could borrow from the payday loan
company Wonga – until it went bust. The plight of the north-
east was symbolised when Newcastle United's players ran out
displaying Wonga's name on their chests. But buying brought
pleasure. Poor families bought their sofas from BrightHouse

– another company making money from immiseration – at 69.9 per cent interest.

People and skills were out of balance. In the most obvious of market failures, companies large and small would not train staff either because they did not rate skills (another congenital disease) or because it was cheaper to buy them in from abroad. If migrant labour were stopped from arriving – the Brexit promise – the economy would shrink and there is no guarantee employers would bother to seek, let alone train, 'natives'. Some evidence suggested jobs were created by migration itself. The skills deficit grew, but Tory ministers denied the remedy – government taking over and paying for the training – as they cleaved to the doctrine of markets. Their apprenticeship scheme, paid for by a levy on larger employers, was doomed to fail, and quickly did.

'This is a very unhappy country,' said the Liberal Democrat leader Vince Cable, adding that 'having a greater sense of fairness around wealth would [help create] the kind of country people want to live in'. Polls certainly picked up unhappiness about equity and just rewards, but respondents did not necessarily want to adopt the remedies, such as taxing wealth and property more fairly. But was Cable right? Across the decade fell Brexit, which engrossed, enraged and made many unhappy, on both sides. As we revisited the same people we had talked to for our books *The Verdict* and *Cameron's Coup*, the question about tribal identity became inescapable. Andy Birks in Rotherham was a Brexiter, Andy Brooke of Derby a strong remainer. Our steel stockholder was a Brexiter, like the fisherman we spoke to on Hastings beach, but our prison governor was a remainer, like the doctors and teachers we met, though nurses and teaching assistants less so. Class and education did not stop being the great national dividers; Brexit even concentrated their influence. Large generalisations about place and people were erected after Brexit, myths and exaggerations among them.

Up North

The wind was gusting through Wakefield's old market square when we talked to passers-by, the market stalls mostly gone – another sign of disruptive, disturbing, regretted change. A majority in this constituency voted leave, but as elsewhere that still left many (including many Labour voters) strongly in favour of remaining. What large numbers of people said to us that day was that they had switched off, were fed up, wanted rid of this thing; politicians were a gang of clowns and unlovable rogues. These were proud Yorkshire people, yet what exactly did that mean when they were so passive about the fate of their own county?

Proposals to create a new Yorkshire in a structure embracing the old county's west, the Leeds region and the Sheffield conurbation had been airily dismissed by the communities secretary, but his rejection aroused no Tykes. (The perpetrator was James Brokenshire, whose seat was in the deep south of England, in Old Bexley and Sidcup.) The indifference of Wakefield's shoppers to what was happening – and not happening – on their own doorsteps pointed to an underlying, debilitating phenomenon: a deep-seated failure to engage. Except over Brexit, when engagement solidified into stilted, formulaic mantras on both sides.

Andrew's Yorkshire Butcher in Effingham Street in Rotherham survived the high street's decline, and owner Andy Birks is still minding a gleaming, white-tiled shop. When we last met in 2010, he felt custom was draining away; the giant Meadowhall shopping mall is only a couple of miles away. Since then more shops had gone. Andrew's itself moved out of the Riverside precinct to an improved location (thanks in part to a council grant).

But there the pies remain in perfect rows, their glazed crusts filled with home-cooked pork, venison, game and cranberry, alongside his prize-winning sausages. It's not the showy produce that kept the business going. 'Supermarkets don't sell the cheap cuts that a lot of people want from a local butcher.'

Rotherham's recent past didn't sound good. His income had dropped. 'We manage, nice house in the countryside, but everyone's finding their money doesn't go so far, so they can't buy so much good food from us as they did.' In the town centre there were more beggars and homeless people, fewer police. Environmental health inspectors didn't come round any more. 'Don't think there are any left. Haven't had an inspection in ages.' A litany of discontent unfolded. 'All the fat young people. Girls especially, they seem to think it's the norm to be really big. They don't eat well. Well, you look at the rows of fast-food places all round here, who's surprised?' Presumably they would be slimmer eating more pork pies.

Since we last met Andy, he had moved online. 'I used to spend £1,000 on newspaper or radio ads, but no more. I do it all on Facebook and Twitter because it's free.' RIP the local press.

Another recent development touched him closely: fracking was set to begin not far from his home. 'They closed the mines that gave people good work. Now they're drilling in this beautiful place, and they'll ruin the water table.' So he didn't like the free market? Yes, he did – less government at every level is his instinct – but with fracking he wants maximum intervention in the market. (Johnson got that message and suspended fracking for the duration of the election.) For Andy, Brussels and the EU were just the furthest point in a long continuum of official interference and tax-taking. 'Not government, not the council, not the prime minister, they do nothing for me, never helped me or my business. It's all a battle.' He complained about paperwork, officialdom and the minimum wage: 'I take on some blithering young idiot and I have to pay him £7.50 an hour, not that different to an experienced butcher, who isn't best pleased, so I have to push his pay up, too.'

This tone had been clearly audible in 2010. We revisited others from *The Verdict* to see how they were faring, to give a human face and voice to the facts, statistics and political decisions. People do get on with their lives, and many, all too many, never discuss government or politics, or wish to be involved. Yet, like it or not, they are involved, unavoidably touched by the events and policies we record here. We listened to remainers as well as to people of no fixed view, but Andy Birks's outlook was distinctive. This was more than a Poujadist, small-business gripe;

this was the authentic voice of middle England, querulous, nostalgic, individualist, contradictory . . . and dominant. We had heard it, too, in 2010 from the family we met in Sydenham, in south-east London. The Hatts, chosen as examples of median earners – mother and father in jobs, children employed, recent homeowners – were committed working-class Tory voters, but Labour had been good to them, we wrote, and they could have adorned a Labour election poster. Instead, these *Daily Mail* readers offered itchy discontentment about migrants, public services, crime, the NHS – a bleak outlook. 'This country's been dragged down. It's not a country I can be proud of any more . . . Our country should be for our people. It's not our country any more.' We heard it; policy-makers and politicians must have heard it, too. But they did not act. Six years later, it boomed out and won a great victory.

2

Brexit and the Break-Up of Britain

Eggleston Steel, a Derby steel stockholder, is unperturbed by the forecasts about Brexit's impact on industry. Turning over £3 million a year, its clients all within a forty-mile radius, the firm sees itself as a redoubt. Chief executive Richard Hewitt is a Brexiter of the 'just want out' kind. A lifelong Tory, he sees it as natural that he should want to be free from the bonds of Brussels.

In his warehouse steel is laid out in rows and racks, under a great gantry for loading and unloading. It was (of course) subject to the vagaries of world price movements. Thanks to a £90,000 EU grant, Hewitt could afford a laser cutter, so Eggleston could deliver L-shapes, C-shapes and whatever sizes were wanted for gates, fences, lintels and beams; personal service is the company's watchword. Since we last met, his son and daughter had joined the family firm.

The recession had hit them hard. No one was moving house, no one was doing DIY; there was no need for steel. He laid off four staff. But by 2014 the business was recovering and workers were re-engaged. Profits, Hewitt reckoned, had been static for ten years. Slashing spending had hurt: 'Our deliveries are taking a lot longer. The council's got no money for road repairs. I see schools and hospitals are badly squeezed.'

None of that, recession included, coloured his expectations around Brexit or his Toryism. He shrugs. 'It'll be OK.' Derby's

*car-makers were threatened, but he did not supply them. Surely
the building trade and many of his customers would be affected
in one way or another, especially if the UK crashed out? It was as
if he parked Brexit in a different part of his brain from his plans
for his business. 'I just think it'll all be OK,' he says again.*

'It' isn't over and isn't OK. Perhaps aeons hence there will be a
new normal for exchanges with our neighbours in Europe, but
it feels a long, long way off. The former ambassador to France,
Lord Ricketts, said trade negotiations to establish a solid base
for UK–EU commerce would make the toing and froing since
the referendum look like a simple, straightforward affair.

Brexit divided the UK by region and nation, age, education,
occupation, aspiration and tradition, and the tears in the fabric
may never be repaired. It cut across party allegiances and split
generations. It posed existential questions: who are *we*? Are we
the same people as *them*, spouting their vile or idiotic views?
It was, more than anything, a celebration of what Professor
Christopher Hill called the 'sheer unfamiliarity, even ignorance' of so many, remainers included, about the institutions
abroad in which the UK had participated for half a century.
And, it turned out, the institutions at home through which the
UK supposedly exercised democracy and the rule of law.

Until required to mark that ballot paper, most respondents
barely mentioned relations with Europe in answer to pollsters
asking what concerned them. The EU registered as a hot topic
for only 4 per cent. The referendum flicked a switch. Once
tapped, resentment about Europe poured out like bile, but

there were great lumps of other matter in it. Anti-European feeling must have been festering in the gut, nourished by tabloid headlines and mendacious reporting by Boris Johnson and other Brussels journalists. EU advocates went missing in action or lost the power of speech. Since the 1975 referendum, successive prime ministers had sooner or later echoed the nationalist line; attempts by John Major and Tony Blair to say or do otherwise were either short lived or as stuttering as the latter's bike ride during the Amsterdam summit in 1997. Margaret Thatcher's Bruges speech had its parallel in Gordon Brown's shameful attempt to sign the Lisbon Treaty in private so no one would notice. But it wasn't just anti-European feeling. The switch tripped resentments: against MPs, judges, 'the liberal elite', London, but also about the north, the old, fostering harsh contempt for fellow citizens.

Filling in that 2016 ballot paper turned out to be only a preliminary. The aftermath has marked the country permanently and has made the UK's existence even more precarious. The genie can't be stuffed back into the bottle; words can't be unsaid, broken conventions superglued back together or revelations covered up. Historians may coolly observe that Great Britain, its constituent nations and Ireland have suffered fits and seizures before, in 1688–9, 1707, 1801, 1846, 1911, 1931, 2014; those confident they have their finger on the pulse of time may say, 'The crisis will ebb,' or 'We'll adapt.' Many kept their heads down after the referendum and got on with it, only glancingly aware of public events. Looking at them, we might even dispute the idea of crisis; after all, millions of voters didn't bother to express a view in the ballot, and firms – look at Eggleston Steel – and people have since then largely gone about their daily lives as before (MPs, non-UK citizens of the EU, exporters, importers, exchange students excepted). The multitudes who marched, took to social media or did that unusual thing of discussing political events with friends, relatives and colleagues add up to only a minority. On the evening of Johnson's suspension of parliament we went to a West End theatre, where Phoebe Waller-Bridge, to the delight of a rapt audience, spent eighty minutes talking about her vagina in character as Fleabag.

Extraordinary events convulsed the UK's public life, but as 2016 recedes into the distance, it gets harder to recall what exactly the exam question was. Focus groups and polls showed not only that people's views were not always linear (or consistent), but also that after deliberation or acquiring new knowledge they could change their minds. Brexit is polymorphous: it's simultaneously about England and the UK, about the UK and Europe; about attitudes, instincts, sensibilities, places, races, self-image, reputation; about institutions, not just parliament. It's a long list.

Did Austerity Do It?

Austerity drove it. Had social spending been protected and public services not been ravaged, leave would have lost. Research linked less welfare to increased support both for UKIP and for voting leave. Economic buoyancy linked to remain, joblessness to leave. After the event, people in deprived areas of England said things are bad; Brexit can't make them worse. It wasn't true, but you could see what they meant. However, materialist explanations rapidly run out. Brexit was not – or wasn't entirely – about money, jobs, things; the EU was not the only aspect of modern Britain many leavers despised. It was the interplay of belief and ideas with the practical conditions of life (often comfortable and moneyed) that made the phenomenon. Substantial numbers of leavers were well enough off, reasonably well educated and lived in the south of England. Resentment, unease and frustration at changed local and social circumstances had swirled through the interviews we did in 2009 and 2010. Mass immigration had been mishandled (by successive governments) and was an electoral accident waiting to happen.

'Well, it's not quite as simple as that,' said Ken Clarke, the Tory remainer, when asked what he would say to leavers. Brexit 'isn't going to make the faintest difference to most of the things that so annoy you. What I will take on board is that you feel so angry about the ruling class and politicians and the Establishment and so on.' Those feelings were palpable but inchoate. They were probably no more acute in 2016 than before, but this vote offered an outlet, a chance to say, 'A plague on both your houses' – and let someone else worry about the consequences.

The City of London also did its bit. 'Brexit is a legacy of the banking crisis,' said Professor Nicholas Crafts of the University of Warwick. Financial meltdown led to austerity, which both boosted support for UKIP enough to frighten Cameron into promising a referendum and antagonised sufficient voters to tip the balance in the referendum.

Brexit: A Potted History

This was, of course, the second membership referendum. Joining enjoyed a fair measure of popular assent in 1972, which was formalised in 1975, when Margaret Thatcher wore that fetching Euro-jumper. Harold Wilson's use of the referendum device created the bad precedent of taking decisions of national import away from parliament. He had used it as a way of dealing with his recalcitrants, especially Jeremy Corbyn's mentor Tony Benn. Labour subsequently warmed to membership, while the Tories became sceptical, though not until after Thatcher enthusiastically endorsed the principle of a single market in goods and capital flows (and people).

UK membership was never wholehearted; the practice and institutions of the union interested few minds and touched fewer hearts. Despite the creation of the European Parliament, the EU enjoyed no gut-level support. Few leaders since Ted Heath championed membership; for example, Tony Blair, who spoke good French, never made a speech about Europe on British soil. Business stayed aloof, never praising the gains it made thanks to membership. Neither Whitehall nor town hall made the effort to educate voters or sell them on Brussels and Strasbourg. Media-spun nonsense pervaded the national psyche, though not until 2016 did it become evident how deeply. Newspapers knowingly published lies, which suffused the

Brussels reports from Johnson and others: Scotch whisky to be labelled a dangerous chemical; thatching and zips to be banned; Waterloo and Trafalgar stations to be renamed by EU diktat. Max Hastings, Johnson's editor at the *Daily Telegraph*, later admitted he knew they were lies at the time. But they were published nonetheless, and were compounded with residual feelings about the world wars and imperial greatness into a default English Euroscepticism that was dressed as a shouty man with a beer gut waving a Union Jack. Defeat at the hands of the Germans – Dunkirk – had long been transmuted into island-alone victory. 'We won' was the sub-theme of the First World War centenary celebrations from 2014 on. The UK's negativity towards the EU grew. Yet researchers found attitudes towards the EU derived from views about *national* politics and policy, and what Brussels actually did barely mattered.

An Accidental Vote

Scepticism did not make exit inevitable. By 2015 a recovery from recession was under way and people were telling pollsters that they were most worried about pollution and the gaps between generations and between rich and poor. The EU was not loved, but polls rarely detected widespread active revulsion. Asked about the most important issues facing Britain, respondents pointing to the EU had only risen above 30 per cent in the late 1990s, and it hardly registered as a concern during the noughties. It was the referendum itself that pushed concern higher, up to 60 per cent, where it then stayed.

The immediate cause of Brexit has to be David Cameron. If you think history revolves around personalities, then note his complacency and laziness. Seekers after deeper explanations might see in him a long-running decline in the calibre of the English upper middle classes, their governing party no longer up to governing (but remarkably adept at holding on). Like Blair, he imagined that airy speeches about modernisation could replace the hard slog of remaking local constituencies and renewing the base of sympathisers. Norma Percy's brilliant 2019 documentary, *Inside Europe*, showed how time and again Cameron sought to appease and put the preservation of party unity first; in his memoirs he had to admit it.

In 2011 UKIP showed that being anti-Europe was a mobilising force within the confines of the European parliamentary elections. Instead of responding strategically, Cameron was merely tactical: he promised an in/out referendum based on a simple majority, to be held, he also pledged, after he had won 'far-reaching' changes to certain European treaties. Opposing Jean-Claude Juncker's election to the presidency of the European Commission was a blunder, but one consistent with successive UK prime ministers' unwillingness to learn how European governance worked. Either their civil servants were similarly unaware, or they just weren't listened to.

Cameron had tried to buy off his anti-EU fanatics by withdrawing Tory members of the European Parliament from the mainstream centre-right grouping, weakening their influence as he aligned them instead with the nationalist far right. He apparently thought his referendum promise was a cheque that would never be cashed because the coalition with the Liberal Democrats would endure. After winning the 2015 election, he made successive errors of judgement over the timing, wording and conduct of the campaign and vote. Among them was his analogy with the 2014 Scottish independence vote. The many differences included the Labour Party's role: in one Gordon Brown had been muscular; in the other Jeremy Corbyn was absent, more saboteur than saviour, dismissing remain as histrionic, myth-making and reliant on 'prophecies of doom'.

A Motley Crew

Europe did for Cameron, then for Theresa May. But we are little the wiser about the anti-Europeans: were they really as incoherent and superficial as they appeared, while still able to pull off such a coup? In the sub-Nietzschean person of Dominic Cummings, the Svengali of leave, the exercise of will – exit – *was* the purpose. Columnists talked about Brexit as a cult, but it was baggy enough to embrace a motley crew of English nationalists, neo-fascists, small-staters and sentimentalists. The 'lexiters', with Corbyn in their ranks, were parochial (socialism in one country) but simultaneously super-internationalist. All variants of leave, we subsequently learned, were backed by money and by both US interests and Vladimir Putin. Their destabilisation agendas weirdly overlapped. The Electoral Commission proved underpowered and half asleep. The media, especially the BBC, were cowed; most of the printed press, foreign-owned in large measure, had always supported the aims of those foreign interventionists.

Brexiters straddled a contradiction. Many worshipped free markets; control by government was what they had worked to lessen; Thatcherism was their apotheosis. Sovereignty resided only with individuals, as preached by the oddly fashionable guru, the novelist Ayn Rand (Sajid Javid said he re-read *The Fountainhead* every year). William Rees-Mogg, father of the foppish MP Jacob, had co-authored a book called *The Sovereign Individual*, arguing for enclaves where the super-rich could escape taxation, democracy and anything resembling the national sovereignty apparently espoused by the leavers. A strong thrust in leave was deregulatory. The Open Europe website listed the EU regulations to be burned: an end to controls on water and air quality, asbestos, pesticides, food flavourings. This ideology, American, freewheeling and uncontrolled, surely could not attract little England nationalists, yearning for an imagined 1950s world of deference and order. Only a strong state could barricade the borders or bail out fisher folk. The point of sovereignty was less, not more, foreign trade, and a clamping down on free movement by citizens of nowhere. These contradictions melded into a generalised 'make Britain great again' yearning.

The same right-wingers who populated the leave campaign had been active destroyers of the signs and symbols of national identity. What said 'British' more than Royal Mail? Yet its privatisation in 2013 turned a public institution, with all its trappings of common inheritance, into a private business, to be chopped and changed as its owners maximised their profit. In the Fenland town of Wisbech leave got more than 70 per cent; in December 2018 the Tory-dominated town council passed a resolution insisting the government pursue 'no deal'. The same town council went ahead and chopped the grant that had kept open the Wisbech museum, a fine building, opened in 1847, that was dedicated to the town's proud past and distinctive present. If antagonism towards Europe were motivated by a sense of injury to place and belonging, why so little regard for repairing the former and sustaining the latter?

When it came to the vote, leave was cynical, opportunist and effective, deploying foreign money and data manipulation, committing crime (breach of the election laws) and lying barefacedly. Leavers claimed impossible savings. Admonished for their '£350 million a week wasted on the EU' lie, they simply repainted their bus with '£50 million a day' – no less mendacious. But they could rely on friendly journalists, a collective failure of nerve on the part of broadcasters and – it has to be admitted – the public's receptivity. Two-thirds of them heard about the claim painted on the big red bus. The UK Statistics Authority intervened to condemn this 'misuse of figures'. Its impotence was another facet of the age.

The Etonians and Nigel Farage of Dulwich College whistled racist and xenophobic tunes. Johnson, of Turkish extraction, warned direly of impending invasion by 80 million Turks, at the same time as the leave campaign gulled citizens of Pakistani and Bangladeshi descent with the promise that exiting the EU would mean more visas. (Non-EU immigration did increase after the vote.) Michael Gove, the white-tied ex-president of the Oxford Union, mocked 'elites' and uttered the epigraph of the era: 'The people of this country have had enough of experts from organisations with acronyms saying they know what is best.'

As orchestrated by Cameron and Osborne, remain put income and the economy first and assumed the two-thirds of voters classed as sceptical or hostile towards the EU would count both their pluses and minuses in the same way as Treasury economists. Remain was amateurish, polite and complex in its messaging, dumbfounded when confronted with leavers' lies. It failed to shake off the charge of 'project fear' that greeted its every warning of consequences. Afterwards it scarcely bothered to pursue and prosecute wrongdoing in the leave campaign, uncovered thanks to the dogged journalism of Carole Cadwalladr and others, for which they were mocked and vilified. Something had happened to the immune system of public life. Lies were condoned; liars lionised.

June 2016

23 June 2016 saw a striking turnout, which would have been higher had the EU citizens living, working and paying taxes in the UK been included. Myths quickly took hold. Far from a revolt of the dispossessed, victory was swung by Tory voters – further evidence of Cameron's inadequacy – who were relatively prosperous. And older. Age tipped the outcome everywhere: retired people in strongly pro-remain London backed leave in

similar proportions to the retired of Yorkshire, the north-west and Wales. When you had left school mattered. Exams passed predicted where you put your cross. The more students in an area, the smaller leave's vote; the more older people (who were less likely to have degrees), the larger it was.

Commentators ran with the two nations metaphor. Remain had the majority of those in work; leave most of the retired and unemployed. Half of those retired on a private pension voted leave, against two-thirds of those who relied on the state pension. Among private renters and households with mortgages, a majority voted remain; those who owned their homes outright (again, tending to be older) voted leave. Around two-thirds of council and housing association tenants voted leave. A majority of professionals and managers voted remain. The two tribes were also neighbours, workmates and relatives. In deepest leave territory, such as Sunderland, a quarter of voters backed remain; in strongly pro-remain Hackney, nearly a third said leave. A majority voted remain in affluent suburban Surrey. But that's also a reminder that, earthquake though it was, Brexit has yet to disturb the deep geology of England's politics. In Gove's Surrey Heath constituency – around Camberley – leave edged it by a thousand votes; in the general election a year later, Gove's majority increased substantially.

After their victory, leave campaigners were lauded for their brilliance, even being awarded a sycophantic Channel 4 docudrama, with Benedict Cumberbatch playing Cummings as deranged genius. The actor's earlier impersonation of Julian

Assange had the same manic, unhinged quality; ditto his take on Patrick Melrose in the adaptation of the Edward St Aubyn novels. Madness was in the air, with Brexit as national psychosis. Neither Melrose nor Assange were likely to get anywhere near Number 10; Cummings did.

WTF

After the vote, collective breakdown. No pause for reflection. Stiff upper lips trembled. The House of Commons, the civil service, the government, the BBC all failed to grasp the situation, failed to see that this was a gigantic, nation-changing project demanding the most skilful management. In his farewell summing up, the NAO's Amyas Morse scythed through Whitehall's lack of technical capacity, before, during and after Brexit. Tolerance, keeping calm and carrying on: those self-ascribed British characteristics gave way to panic, intolerance and twitching.

Cameron skipped away, singing a little ditty as he retreated into Number 10 from the Downing Street lectern. Had Johnson or Gove or another leave leader won the race to replace him (so the president of the EU Council Donald Tusk mused), they would have had to confront reality straightaway, and so perhaps would have avoided the subsequent descent into extremism. As it was, Theresa May treated Brexit as a Tory preserve, shrinking in stature and perspective every day until her defenestration. She blanked cooperation with the other parties, ignoring her small margin of victory in the election, and resorted to rhetoric – 'citizens of nowhere . . . jumping the queue' – that could only dismay and inflame. She consistently bent towards the hardliners, ceding the initiative to ludicrous figures who were pumped up by media attention, such as Jacob Rees-Mogg; this poseur would later become leader of the House of Commons. May's first instinct, shared by many MPs, was to have ministers run the show. It took a courageous outsider, Gina Miller, to organise a court case in order to secure a role for MPs in approving the start of the leave process, for which she paid the price of being targeted by the *Daily Mail* and having her life threatened. Here was one of the unleashed genies. Harsh language in the media was now matched by physical threats and actual violence.

Having acquired a role, the MPs' performance won few BAFTAs. A great majority approved the official notice of leaving the EU, Article 50 of the 2009 Lisbon Treaty, oblivious to what that entailed and on what timetable. Later protestations about the integrity of parliament rang hollow as a result. Delivering a letter to Brussels by train on 29 March 2017 was the easy bit; now where was the plan? Journalist Robert Peston was so shocked by the way May threw away any bargaining potential that he wrote a book called *WTF?*, a choice of title that also exemplified the coarsening of public English. Later, the attorney general said plaintively that they hadn't realised how complicated it all was. A common failing of commercial managers, attested to by the productivity figures, was replicated in politics: decision-making as short-term whim.

Since the 1970s the UK had been a member of an organisation that only a handful of officials – often an ostracised minority in their own Whitehall departments – few MPs and virtually no journalists had bothered to study, let alone sympathise with. The EU's interests were clear and clearly stated. Angela Merkel, the German chancellor, said time and again that the four freedoms – of movement of goods, services, capital and people – were indivisible, with no cherry-picking. Leaving the EU had to be seen to carry costs in order to discourage other potential escapees, as the camp commandant in a Second World War film might have said. (In Brexit, wartime symbolism and victimhood were inexhaustible.)

May pivoted to the right and adopted her rigid and self-contradictory red lines. The narrow margin of the vote pointed to compromise; instead, in her provocative Marlborough House speech she went for the extreme of leaving both a customs union and the single market, while promising frictionless trade, piling up trouble over the land border between the EU (in the form of the Republic of Ireland) and the UK. Despite the Troubles and the Good Friday Agreement, this had been largely ignored in the Brexit campaign.

Brexit then went AWOL in the election that she called for May 2017, which suited the Corbyn camp, even though Labour's clandestine association with remain improved its vote. In hindsight, the next two and a half years were a barely comprehensible welter of Tory faction and leaver impossibilism, a spectacle from which no one else could quite avert their gaze, the stakes being as high as they were. Later, Tory MPs who vowed to die in a ditch before accepting May's deal mumbled their assent to the even worse terms secured by Johnson. For thirty months politics and policy-making were hijacked.

Having lost her majority, May allied with the Democratic Unionists, without assessing the likely effects of the Irish border on potential Brexit deals. Until ditched by Johnson, this tribe within a tribe ruled the Westminster roost, inadvertently focusing attention on the multiple deficits in Northern Ireland's society and government. May committed heresy by accepting a line of trade control down the Irish Sea, causing ructions among the extreme Brexiters in her Cabinet; this became a central element in Johnson's deal. In July 2018 a showdown was arranged at the prime minister's official country house at Chequers, in Buckinghamshire; ministers were even told that if they wanted to leave the O.K. Corral, they would have to phone for their own minicabs. Brexit, more than ever, had become a Tory party psychodrama, in which the players were am-dram, not the Old Vic. 'Student politics,' the Tory grandee Ken Clarke harrumphed. During subsequent months, political burlesque unfolded, as secretaries of state and ministers peeled off, positioning themselves for May's inevitable demise.

A draft withdrawal treaty was finally displayed in November 2018. Europhobes formed a voting bloc with the DUP and obstructed May's efforts to gain assent. The opposition largely did what an opposition should, without having to exorcise its own demons or, in the case of Labour, alight on a coherent position. Meanwhile, for all the dissension, Tory MPs (including those who actually left to form the new Independent Group) made no stir over austerity, public services or addressing the alleged causes of popular discontent. Then, suddenly, in the scramble to replace May, they threw off the hair shirts and went for spend, spend, spend.

Come What May

The Brexiters' eventual success in ridding themselves of May put all the huffing and puffing of the interregnum between general elections in the category of wasted breath. May's deal was a 'hard' exit, the worst of both worlds: to have friction-less trade Britain would have to obey European rules and reg-ulations, yet would now have no veto and no say in those rules. Cabinet discipline had long given way as it became clear that May's deathbed task was to beg for a postponement of the 29 March 2019 exit deadline and face the humiliation of holding UK elections to the European Parliament in June. May's next desperate ploy, which she might usefully have tried in June 2016, was to talk to the Labour leadership in search of a parliamentary compromise. By then, with the European parliamentary elections ahead, it was too late, and so May's position in her own party became untenable. On 24 May she announced she would step down after the Tory party elected a new leader.

The candidates sucked up to a narrow group of elderly, ferociously pro-Brexit party members. Inevitably, the leader-ship finalists vied to take harder-line positions. Exit with no deal on 31 October, 'come what may' and 'do or die', pledged Johnson, echoed every step of the way by Foreign Secretary Jeremy Hunt, who was supposed to be the 'sensible' alternative.

31 October then came and went, without Johnson's political demise. With his elevation to prime minister, politics became about naked power play: he had it, Labour was nowhere near it, and the countervailing forces on which we had once relied – the civil service, business, 'innate decency' – fled the field. The Tory party was now the Brexit party, its single focus, leaving. Austerity was suspended for the duration of the exit process, and norms of economy and effectiveness in public spending abandoned. Everything was haphazard, with no one quite 'in control' of pathways and pipelines; for a national emergency, there was precious little 'national' and, despite panicking businesses, a striking absence of public alarm.

Labour's tactic had been prevarication: if it could straddle the two horses, it could profit as it did in the 2017 election. But essentially it made Labour another Brexit party, albeit with members who were overwhelmingly anti-Brexit. Labour voters, too, were in the majority anti-Brexit. Distraught Labour MPs floated alternatives, including a confirmatory vote – or second referendum – on whatever deal Theresa May presented. In the febrile parliamentary circumstances of spring 2019 several Labour MPs left. The Corbyn caucus's calculation had been that Labour voters backing remain would stay loyal to him, allowing him to tack towards leave. But the shocking results of the May European elections proved him badly wrong: Labour voters deserted in droves to the Lib Dems and Greens, far fewer to Nigel Farage's new Brexit Party. Labour won only 14 per cent of the vote, beaten by the Liberal Democrats, on 19 per cent, with the Brexit Party coming out on top, at 30 per cent. The only compensation was the Tories falling to under 9 per cent, behind the Greens.

Johnson eventually emerged with his version of May's withdrawal treaty, which he then shelved in favour of a general election. The period since June 2016 had been a trip to the desert, an endless parade of ministerial incompetence, parliamentary prevarication, fruitless trips to Brussels, unchallenged and unevidenced assertions, a relentless display of obduracy by the leavers. Constitutionalists argued that MPs had eventually done their duty and tied down a malfunctioning executive, before it rose again, tore up convention and suspended them – until the courts stepped in. Brexit exposed a deep strain of laziness and mediocrity, the press, broadcasters and journalists rarely doing any homework that would allow them to debunk magical assertions about 'World Trade Organisation (WTO) rules', vox pops allowing the public to keep on shying away from complexity. Perhaps May's mind-numbing repetition of 'Brexit means Brexit' conveyed a mindless truth: the vote was the act, in and of itself; the practical consequences could take care of themselves. The deed had been done; the rest was unicorns or project fear. That's what made Brexit so mystifying and maddening for remainers. In Brexit Britain something bad had happened to rationality.

That old (and sadly misquoted) Zhou Enlai crack about it being too soon to tell the impact of the French Revolution applies to Brexit in spades. Contemporary history is imperilled by the onrush of events. Here's a provisional audit, offered provisionally.

The UK's International Standing

Reputation may not be immortal, as Shakespeare had Cassio say, but quickly destroyed it may take for ever to rebuild. The national self-image was dealt a heavy blow in terms of how others saw us. The observation by the Dutch prime minister Mark Rutte that Britain was 'a waning country, too small to appear on the world stage on its own' might have been made before Brexit. The referendum result then accelerated a (some would say necessary and overdue) process of belittlement. Yet, after the vote, repeated ad nauseam was the boast that the UK would rise again, entering glowingly advantageous trade deals across the globe. In the world of Trump and China, this was psychiatric-grade delusion.

The Brexiters failed to spot the paradox. They had helped destroy any lingering reputation the UK had for diplomacy, trustworthiness and political stability; they savaged the very people – the Foreign Office and its diplomats – who would necessarily carry the burden of rebuilding our national standing. Negotiations with the EU were cack-handed and technically incompetent, as personified by David Davis. If they could not handle Brussels, how would they suddenly access the negotiating skills required to deal with the US or the WTO? Hunt, a candidate for the Tory leadership, was the same petulant minister who compared the EU with the Soviet Union and used threatening language about the Russians – who presumably would not be among the new global Britain's trading partners.

One of the great counterfactuals is how the Brexit vote might have transpired had Donald Trump become president in January 2016 rather than a year later. He capsized the rocking but just about seaworthy vessel of UK diplomacy, which had been able simultaneously to back the US line (on Iraq, the Middle East, China) while keeping in with the EU. Together Trump and Brexit robbed the UK of leverage on both sides of the Atlantic. The Foreign Office's reputation for *savoir faire* suffered a devastating blow with the appointment of Johnson as its head, in another example of May putting party tactics before the national interest. The UK's policy goals had become unintelligible; the country's ambassadors could tell no convincing story about where it was heading. Their despatches to London became tales of woe. The UK ambassador to the Republic of Korea, refreshingly frank, said: 'I have encountered a spectrum from mild bemusement to really quite serious and deep incredulity.' No serious decision-maker or opinion-former in that country thought leaving was a good idea.

Taking back control applied to the EU but not, apparently, to the US. On his departure from Washington DC, the French ambassador sought to correct any illusions entertained in the UK about friendship. 'When the British come for a free trade agreement there will be blood on the walls, and it will be British blood. It will be GMOs [genetically modified organisms] breakfast, lunch and dinner.' On his embarrassing state visit in June 2019 Trump confirmed that allowing American firms access to the NHS would be up for negotiation. Leave had been promoted by US right-wing interests who wanted their pounds of flesh: mainly they wanted an EU damaged by the UK's departure; the lonely UK would then be a US supplicant. Trump's hawkish adviser John Bolton smarmed over Johnson as if he were another pliant right-wing Senate Republican. Johnson reciprocated by sacrificing the UK ambassador in Washington, in a further blow to national diplomatic standing.

A country famed for its humour, tolerance and irony was suddenly displaying fanaticism, xenophobia and all-round nastiness. It was now a country where MPs got shot and public figures were menaced; where extremists were garlanded and hate speech had become everyday. German and French humourists now had a ready supply of material, and the British prime minister became a stock target of *Saturday Night Live* mockery.

The EU's Future

During Brexit, solipsism ruled. That is to say, a fixation on us and an absence of concern for *them* and future relationships. The effects of leaving on NATO and on European defence, let alone on our land border with the EU and our allies, were almost entirely ignored. Leave rejoiced in the EU's troubles, as if they were not the UK's to share. The Eurozone has deep and abiding flaws, and the European Commission's difficulties in enforcing common action on migration and upholding the norms of judicial independence and political pluralism in eastern Europe had been all too recently demonstrated. By November 2018 the EU's negotiator, Michel Barnier, was warning that there 'is now a Farage in every country' seeking to 'demolish Europe' – though the 2019 European parliamentary election results diminished these fears. Inside or outside the EU, the UK could never emancipate itself from how these questions would be addressed and resolved. Practical and incremental propositions for cooperation – on the environment and climate, energy, transport, research – were an ongoing and never-ending discussion (not least between Merkel and Macron) in which the UK had an inalienable interest but, now, no voice.

The UK was not the first member state to hold a national referendum on Europe. But in no other country was such a large slice of the ruling elite (which is what Tory ministers, the European Reform Group and its fellow travellers of course were) so committed to smashing their way out. Brexiters were aligned, by accident or design, with American nihilists and nationalists, and a global right keen to pull down post-war international institutions. Trump exhibited his instinctive animus against the United Nations and NATO, and the US was now demolishing the WTO. Those famous trade rules the Brexiters kept praying for were almost defunct.

Brexit proved to be an occasion for demonstrating the efficacy of EU institutions, the rule of its law, its unity and concern for smaller members (especially the Republic of Ireland). The lesson was not lost on the tiny Baltic states, with Putin on their border: what reliance could they now place on the UK's guarantees to them as a member of NATO? The spectacle of Britain's contortions and divisions may have warned off others. 'The Brits have probably inoculated others against trying to pursue the same path for at least a generation,' said Charles Grant, director of the Centre for European Reform.

The facts of life were exposed time and again, despite the leavers' lies (there was no substitute for that chilling word). Of all UK exports of goods, 47 per cent went to the EU; of all EU exports, 15 per cent came to the UK, producing an overall trade deficit of £64 billion. The UK's net contribution to the EU was 1.1 per cent of public spending. If the UK was to trade with the EU, given its relative size it would have to adopt EU standards. The penny dropped, for some, too late: leaving the EU demonstrated just how dependent on it the UK was – for the food we ate, medicines, prospects of scientific and techno-logical advance, disposal of yesterday's atomic waste. Viewing the UK with growing distaste, international investors piled money into the EU. In the three years after the referendum, the total capital invested in the EU27 grew by 43 per cent compared to the preceding three years, including UK compa-nies investing in other EU countries. It was clear 'neighbouring countries are beginning to reap the benefits of the uncertainty caused by Brexit', said Christine McMillan of the fDi database. Inward investment was falling markedly in 2018 and 2019, with a sharp drop in the number of jobs it created.

'Fuck Business'

Yet what Brexit disclosed about the economy was far from straightforward. Adam Smith's line about there being a lot of ruin in a nation held good. Capitalism depended on states (and unions of states) but was markedly indifferent to their well-being and fate. When 'business' spoke, it croaked, spluttered and rapidly fell silent again. Markets did not plummet on news of the 2016 vote; the value of the pound fell, stabilised, then fell again, but not enough to stop millions exchanging it for fewer euros on holiday. Confidence was sapped, as we just saw with the effect on inward investment. Had the decision to leave not been taken, by 2020 the UK's GDP would have been 2.5 to 3 per cent higher, but as it was economic activity was down by £40 billion a year, or £700 million a week – a resource that 'would never be recovered', the National Institute of Economic and Social Research noted. The calculation excluded the costs of preparing for crashing out and any estimate of what doing so would entail in terms of trade and growth. Both the state and business diverted billions of pounds' worth of resources into stockpiling and mitigation – the stockpiling having the paradoxical effect of boosting growth slightly in the quarter before March 2019, before pushing it back when orders were run down. The conjunction of leaving under ominous clouds from Trump's trade warfare and a German turndown led analysts to mark up the prospects of recession. Crashing out would make it even more likely.

The idea that leaving would uncork the champagne of enterprise was a drunk's daydream. Once, the Tories had believed that *joining* the EU would jerk companies into competitiveness. EU membership was a fillip, but nonetheless productivity remained relatively disappointing. 'Faults have not been the result of constraints imposed by EU membership but rather the consequence of domestic government failure,' said Professor Nicholas Crafts. 'There is no reason to think that EU exit will lead, either directly or indirectly, to improvements in UK productivity outcomes.'

The Brexiters demanded to know what business leaders knew about business. Boris Johnson's 'Fuck business' comment, made at an event for EU diplomats in June 2018, displayed how far the Tory party had wandered from its old identity as the party of UK plc. The Left used to think that Tory governments did what business told them. If so, Brexit snapped the link. The CBI bleated and the Institute of Directors grumbled, but they had no traction. After he resigned, Boris's brother Jo Johnson said that business had been 'thrown under a bus' (of which he took the steering wheel when he briefly joined his brother's government). One of the oddities of the 2010s was how marginal business was, especially over Brexit. Perhaps the tribal loyalty of business people to the party promising less tax – the Tories – triumphed over any principles or concern for the economy at large. Indeed, as Prime Minister Johnson asked, who had stuck up for bankers as much as him? In the week of his anointment, Standard Chartered's shareholders revolted, and the High Pay Centre was reporting that bank remuneration was higher than before the crash. In 2019 average chief executive pay was £5.2 million.

Economic and material interests did not dissolve, which led to astounding hypocrisy. Brexiters scrambled to insulate themselves against loss, and one of their own, John Redwood, advised them to squirrel their money safely outside the UK.

Jacob Rees-Mogg set up a new Dublin headquarters for his company, Somerset Capital, on the grounds of 'considerable uncertainty' in Brexit Britain. Perhaps the Brexiters were rational after all, their destructiveness reflecting a capitalism in which finance had become so strong, seeing opportunity everywhere, even in disaster for manufacturing and exporting firms.

Yet the City as a financial district was being damaged. Firms were relocating, and people would lose their jobs. The City tried to exempt itself from the consequences: why couldn't Brussels just assume nothing had changed for the financial sector? 'We failed to recognise the absolute unassailability of the four freedoms,' said Stephen Jones, the chief executive of UK Finance. 'Our mutual recognition ask was seen to be cherry picking.' That being the case, the City was curiously mute, perhaps reflecting its assessment that overall profitability would not necessarily suffer if banks were in Frankfurt or Dublin rather than Canary Wharf. In response to Johnson's constitutional coups, fantasists on the left talked about a general strike; in truth, the market-makers in the City had the power to stop him in his tracks, and never used it.

Merry England's Fish and Farms

Farmers and fishermen believed romantically that by escaping from the EU, they would shake off regulation, allowing them to restore their ancient prosperity. They plugged into Merry England symbolism (Scottish fishermen and Welsh farmers were vocal, too), its landscapes and seascapes. Farming constituted barely 0.7 per cent of GDP, fishing 0.5 per cent, but plangent nostalgia trumped numbers and gave them audiences. 'Newlyn fishermen deserve better', said a sign on a lamppost in the Cornish port, but so did car- and plane-makers, who would suffer if trade with the EU were damaged. The EU's fisheries and agricultural policies were flawed, but Brussels could not be blamed for changing consumer preferences, the destructive exploitation of stocks or national policies on land and taxation; and besides, the club rules could be changed, provided the UK were an actively involved club member, which it wasn't. Amid the swirl of Euro-myths floated straight cucumbers and fishermen's hairnets, along with misplaced masochism. 'It will do the country good to go without food,' interviewers were told. In reality, sealing the UK's borders would reduce the amount of fresh produce and increase the consumption of processed food, which was already high. Besides, austerity had not exactly engendered a collaborative spirit of unity in which rich and poor (all in it together?) would swap tales of privation.

On a brisk morning on Hastings beach we talked to Paul Joy, head of the small fishermen's association. Now winched up on the shingle, his boat had been out at dawn. 'My father, born in 1906, made an adequate living with a boat smaller than mine. Now I can't. I'm lucky to get a Tesco shelf-stacker's pay. Everyone subsidises fishing with other work.'

Fishing quotas and the Common Fisheries Policy were to blame. Joy drank deep of the elixir – the simplicity of blaming everything on Brussels. Forget consumers' dislike of mackerel, forget the logistics of getting fish to market, forget the pitilessness of small-business balance sheets. The twenty-seven small boats fishing out of Hastings amounted to nothing economically, but those picturesque old salts with their nets, huts and fresh fish stalls were a £5 million tourist draw in a struggling town.

Joy thought they would wrest back control. After all, Gove had promised instant freedom from fishing restraints. Later, when environment secretary under May, he changed his tune: the issue was how to preserve precarious fish stocks. A coastal truth was the policy of successive governments, including Labour and Tory, to allow the sale of fishing quotas, often to non-UK companies. Most of the UK's quota was held by a handful of large ships, leaving only 4 per cent to ten-metre boats such as Joy's, although they made up 77 per cent of the fishing fleet.

'Get rid of quotas,' said Joy. But his focus was on the small boats. Some 80 per cent of the fish landed in the UK (mainly on big boats) was sold to the rest of the EU. 'Our' fish headed for tables across Europe; 'our' fish (what we ate) was mainly imported. Nothing was as simple as the tales Brexiters told. Fishing was an emblem of the clash of domestic interests, as well as the inevitability of European cooperation – but not to Paul Joy. The idea, the emotions, the concept of Europe overshadowed inconvenient reality.

As with the fishermen, six out of ten farmers voted for Brexit.

On Exmoor, on a beautiful sunlit evening, 1,200 feet above sea level, on land fit for little other than grazing, Robin Milton contemplated a non-EU future for his thousand ewes. His income was tiny. 'But you can't know the pleasure it gives me, the pride I take in my sheep, the landscape, my hedges and stone walls.'

He voted leave, influenced by his son, who thought ending production subsidies – 55 per cent of UK farm income came from the Common Agricultural Policy – would see agricultural land prices fall, allowing younger people to get into farming. But again, it was a complicated story: the steep rise in the price of farmland had been driven by rich investors, attracted by the fact that farmland was inheritance-tax exempt. Among them was arch-Brexiter James Dyson, who was reported by Farmers Weekly *to own 33,000 acres, more than the Queen. This most conservative of innovators squealed at the prospect of losing his own farming subsidy from the EU.*

The leave campaign promised cheaper food, neglecting to add that that had to mean less income for farmers. Anxious, Gove promised that the UK would maintain all the farmers' subsidies post-Brexit, at least until 2022. But markets would collapse since meat exports to the EU were tariff-free, and under the vaunted WTO rules the price of selling Milton's lambs in Europe would rise 60 per cent. Also, once the UK had 'taken back control' of subsidies, they would be scrutinised as part of the general expenditure, along with farmers' perks, business rates exemption and tax-free diesel. Membership of the EU usefully obscured a great deal, which was why Brexit farmers appeared to be saying, 'We want a subsidy, but not their *subsidy.'*

Contradictions came tumbling to earth from leave's airy fantasies. The Tories had been the farmers' friends, yet here were Brexiters promising farmer-destroying trade deals. So why did Milton, a leading light in the National Farmers' Union, hold firm? *'I still believe leaving is best, mostly because Europe needs reform, and Britain going will shake them up. They'll have to change.'* Then, uncertainly, *'I still expect that we shall rejoin during my lifetime. We shall have to.'*

Within weeks of that interview, forward sales of feed and animals were falling, as prices of imported supplements and vitamins rose in line with sterling's decline. European buyers of lamb started making alternative arrangements, fed up with uncertainty about the UK's supply. Perhaps Milton's son will get his wish and land prices will fall, but quite what he will do with his Exmoor acres when he can't make money from sheep farming is unclear.

Farmers had political clout, which was what the forward-facing and considerably bigger digital sector oddly lacked. During Brexit, no one mentioned the EU digital single market, launched in 2015, covering data regulation, privacy and copyright. The UK had had a hand in shaping it, and now faced exclusion. Berlin, Grenoble and Rotterdam were eyeing with intent the technology clusters of Cambridge, Manchester, Newcastle and Dundee. Mike Butcher, of Tech For UK, said, 'The tech world is a sort of canary in a coalmine. Technology isn't stopping: people will just up sticks, pack their bags and go wherever they're most welcome. And the optics of Brexit are not about welcoming. They're about closing doors.'

The list of Brexit-afflicted sectors was long: pharmaceuticals (after the vote the European Medicines Agency upped sticks and departed), advanced engineering, battery technology, aerospace, robotics, vehicles, architecture, art and design . . . In all of them intra-EU networks, often supported by EU policies, were robust and extended. Motor manufacturing in the UK had been revived thanks to access to European markets. Now, changing technology (electric propulsion) and consumer concerns (pollution) were forcing large-scale restructuring. Brexit compounded threats to UK plants, some of which were already marginal to the plans of the multinationals. Cutting off supply chains and export markets tipped them over the edge. Honda announced the end of manufacturing in the UK from 2021, when production of the Civic would cease, with huge consequences for (leave-voting) Swindon, with 3,500 direct redundancies, and further thousands of jobs lost among suppliers. The UK's biggest car-maker, Jaguar Land Rover, started to cut 4,500 jobs across its European workforce, with the impact concentrated on the UK. Nissan had first cheered the Brexiters by announcing it was going ahead with a new factory in the north-east; as the first exit deadline neared, the company's calculations tightened and it reversed direction.

'Business' had no single view, and many smaller concerns, like Eggleston Steel, were pro-leave. Tim Martin, the founder of the Wetherspoons chain, put anti-EU beer mats in his pubs; it would be Chapel Down Bacchus for his customers instead of wines from the Loire or Abruzzo. But Wetherspoons went on enjoying buoyant sales, which showed the loyalty of its Brexiter customer base, or perhaps it was just inertia. Martin went on supplying, and they went on drinking Hoegaarden and Burgundy regardless.

The British Hospitality Association said a third of hotel workers and 75 per cent of waiting staff came from the EU; most versions of Brexit would affect them deeply. But not yet. Surveys found consumers were not altering their spending habits, despite the uncertainties. PricewaterhouseCoopers said that in December 2018 people in those parts of Britain with higher proportions of leave voters were more likely to say they would not change their plans. Kien Tan, PwC's retail strategy director, said, 'All this stuff is going on politically but, in terms of people's day-to-day lives, it really only affects certain groups.' For a vaunted PwC consultant, this was a superficial analysis. Any growth in UK productivity depended on investment, and Brexit had chilled that to freezing point. The UK economy was already permanently scarred, as the Bank of England's governor Mark Carney put it, even before any exit. In tight conditions, with unemployment low and wages starting to rise, investment in labour-saving equipment was the order of the day. But Brexit uncertainties were too large. The UK's low productivity growth, which was down to 0.5 per cent a year from 2010, fell in 2019 to 0.2 per cent. Offhandedly, the Treasury said it would put £200 million into the Cameron-era British Business Bank to compensate businesses for losing European funding.

Acme Whistles survived, though its owner had seen one neighbouring firm after another close in the Birmingham metal-bashing district. Tool-making, paintbrushes, jewellery . . . Acme Whistles' owner, Simon Topman, pointed out the factories that had gone.

But he had kept going. Whatever the travails of local industry, his business was expanding: his workforce was up from fifty-five to seventy. About 85 per cent of production was exported, 40 per cent to the EU.

Founded in 1870, the Acme workshop feels almost untouched since, its wooden walkways and outside staircases offering a Dickensian scene. How well it suits Acme's products: eighty-three types of whistle – train, bird and dog whistles, crow scarers and even a pig grunter; whistles for the Royal Navy, scouts, women's self-protection, orchestras, comic pantomime whistles, megaphones, hunting whistles and whistles for referees of every sport. Making them is old-fashioned work, the men and women at the benches manufacturing small runs of each type by hand, the process not worth mechanising.

With Brexit, says Topman, 'I worry most about losing the level playing field in health and safety, regulations and rules on plastics. I use a lot of plastic. Any kind of divergence, any barriers at the frontiers will make life very difficult.' He fears swimming alone in shark-infested waters. Chinese counterfeiters steal his designs, flogging knock-off versions on eBay, Amazon and Alibaba. 'We sue about six companies a year, and each case costs us £25,000 or sometimes £200,000. We really do need international muscle within the EU to enforce our patents and designs.'

He had to prepare. 'I don't want to move any bit of the company, but I might have to use an offer from a German client for space to open a foothold in the EU. I have always employed people from around here. It's a deprived area, and they stay with me for twenty and thirty years. I let them flex their hours to suit family

*and outside activities, and we have a waiting list for jobs here
long as your arm. What kind of madness is this?'*

Unfree Movement

One minute immigration was overwhelmingly important,
the next it sank down the pollsters' list of salient subjects.
Economists kept saying that overall it had brought economic
benefit and added to growth, that incomers had not replaced
British workers in British jobs (to echo Gordon Brown's clumsy
lapse in 2008). But the subjective experience of migrants – and
reports about migrants in the media – left a host of overlapping,
often negative impressions. 'The public,' the National Institute
for Economic and Social Research confirmed, 'base their opin-
ions on other sources than economic evidence and government
statistics and instead rely on their personal experiences and
local narratives.' Indeed, migration often translated as Muslims,
changing streets and neighbourhoods, new arrivals, Polish
shops and television pictures of migrants in the Mediterranean.
Perhaps the two versions were incommensurable; experts and
the public talked at cross purposes. Additionally, the immigration data was far from robust: successive governments had failed
to check who was leaving the UK, and they ran away from the
admittedly touchy question of identity documentation.

In areas where migrants arrived, attitudes changed. While
the overall proportion of an area's population born outside the
UK did not have a significant effect on the leave vote, the *pace*
of change after 2004 did. All areas that experienced at least

a 7 per cent increase in the proportion of migrants voted to leave. White voters voted leave by 53 per cent to 47 per cent, but two-thirds of people describing themselves as Asian voted remain, and three-quarters of black voters. Six out of ten of those describing themselves as Christian voted leave; seven in ten Muslims voted remain.

Eurosceptics succeeded in eliding the EU and migration. The anomaly became even larger after the vote, when migration into the UK by EU citizens fell and migration from elsewhere (often the very migrants most disliked) increased, yet migration dropped down the list of public concerns. Movements into or out of the UK were huge. In the year before the vote, net immigration was 333,000, with the overall churn more like a million either arriving or leaving. Migration had destabilised particular places. In one Sheffield ward there were more than six thousand people of eastern European heritage, half of them under seventeen, with obvious effects on schools. In 2010 we recorded the dense concentration of Roma people in the streets of Gorton, in Manchester; the city voted remain, but the unhappiness we noted was replicated elsewhere. One in five homelessness acceptances in 2015–16 were foreign nationals – more than double the number in 2009–10.

Migration was in part a class issue. Bank of England research showed that the bottom 10 per cent in the income distribution, often unskilled, had lost out, if only marginally. Labour had opened the door to unlimited migration from Bulgaria and Romania, when other EU countries had delayed the admission of nationals from those two countries to their labour markets.

Expansion to the east and into the Balkans had been an EU goal based on plausible but abstract geopolitical notions. No one had bothered to tell Gorton or anywhere else a convincing story about the long-term security of the continent or about how decisions were made in the EU, not least when the UK's participation in it had been so hesitant, unengaged and spasmodic. Neither Labour nor Tory governments had done enough to protect the unskilled in the areas most affected by migration, but the unskilled also used public services – health and social care especially – staffed by migrants. (An estimated 100,000 of the UK's 1.4 million social-care staff were non-UK EU nationals.) Cameron and Osborne had said they would toughen migrants' entitlement to benefits. They did, for people already in Britain; they failed to utilise the powers available under European law to deter the small number of EU migrants who were not working. They ignored trade union requests for tougher wage inspection and the controlling of gangmasters. Austerity diminished councils' capacity to plan and provide.

Popular sentiment bundled together recently arrived workers, job-seekers, refugees and ethnic minorities who had lived in the UK for generations. Labour home secretary David Blunkett had wrung his hands ineffectually about asylum-seekers massing at Calais, and since then pictures of its camps had often appeared in the press. 'Control' seemed to have been lost. Asylum-seekers had been dispersed on the cheap, which meant they ended up in places with spare housing, most of which were already deprived. Many of the 1,500 asylum-seekers placed on Teesside ended up living in the Gresham area of Middlesbrough, which was already highly mixed, partly because that was where the company to which the outsourcer G4S subcontracted its commitments to the Home Office owned property. 'Look how many they send to Rotherham. They don't put them in Kent, do they?' said Andy Birks, the butcher. What disturbed that town most were the Romanians and the Slovakians. 'I can tell you that the Asians round here – very good people, been here a long time – they feel the same about those East Europeans as we do. Some of them are just here for a free ride.' Polls found people emphasising the 'contributory principle' negatively, accusing migrants of undeservedly getting housing and social benefits, taking out more than they put in.

Still, the numbers could be exaggerated. Pupils in one Sheffield school, many themselves Asian, were found to believe that the UK population was between 50 and 90 per cent Asian. The irrelevance of Brussels to previous Commonwealth migration was clear – except to a significant proportion of Brexit voters. Some migrants had to cross the Channel; therefore, it was the EU's fault. Millions were on their way, said the leave campaign. By June 2019, 71 per cent of people from ethnic minorities reported having faced racial discrimination, compared with 58 per cent in January 2016. But was overt racism 'new' or an old brew uncorked? The *Windrush* scandal stirred some consciences, and a warm stream of approval flowed towards Britons of Caribbean descent as ministers sought to atone for the persecution and expulsion of their grandparents.

When Home Secretary May paid for vans to tour the streets with placards effectively saying, 'Go home,' no one made any connection between migrants (illegal, unwanted, usually black or brown) and the Greek surgeon to whom you were sent for a consultation about your hernia – but the referendum result had the effect of lumping them all together.

In 2016 the lives of the 3 million non-UK EU nationals living in the UK were suddenly turned upside down. Their status remained unresolved, and became even more threatened when the Johnson government announced that the borders would be sealed on 1 November 2019, potentially marooning hundreds of thousands of them if they were prevented from returning to their homes here (a decision that would also jeopardise the status and rights of UK nationals living in the rest of the EU, a fifth of them over pension age). These people were not brown or poor but white, many of them educated people doing middle-class jobs. A deputy director at Ofsted found his application for settled status rejected because the paperwork was not in order. Emmy van Deurzen, a psychoanalyst with dual UK–Dutch nationality, reported EU patients losing their appetites and becoming subject to mood swings, their anxiety made acute as the prospect of no deal came, went and came back again. 'The British character has been turned upside down,' she said, adding that EU citizens 'were the canaries in the coal mine. Now British people are in the same position, affected by the constant stress of politics and not being able to plan their lives.' To stay in the UK, EU nationals (except Irish citizens) would have to provide evidence of five years' residence. The deadline was 30 June 2021 – or earlier in the event of no deal. Those who had not successfully applied by then would become, in the ominous language of the Home Office, 'immigration issues'. At first, the online applications were over fifty pages long, requiring extensive and sometimes hard-to-access documentation. In a demonstration of stupendous incompetence, the app through which applications could theoretically be made did not work on iPhones.

'When I came here I was like: "Wow, the English are so tolerant,"' Sławomir Kaczyński told a reporter. (He worked in catering in Dartford, and after the vote took up a job offer in Iceland.) 'But after five minutes they start crying that they pay for everything and that foreigners steal their jobs. After Brexit the country showed its true face.' By 2016 there were an estimated 900,000 Polish citizens in the UK, the largest group of foreign nationals in the country. The Brexit vote caused a sharp fall in EU immigration; as a result, there were the predicted labour shortages in those sectors where Poles had previously been so welcome, especially construction and hospitality. (Net migration to the UK from the EU in the year up to March 2019 was under a third of the level it was in the twelve months preceding the vote.) Some said they suddenly felt unwelcome; some talked of returning to Poland. Bartosz Kowalczyk of Polish Business Link said, 'The mood is very tense.'

Belligerent Isolation

'But we don't mean the Poles,' leave voters would tell reporters in vox pops. So who did they mean when the same interviews captured their belligerent, isolationist tone? Here were people in Dronfield, near Sheffield: 'Europe needs us more than we need them' – a supermarket worker; 'I don't want anything to do with Europe' – a retired office worker; 'We were a mighty country once, and now we bow and kowtow to everybody' – somebody in a frame shop. Journalists seek colour and accentuate marginal and extreme views, but there were too many such expressions not to conclude that the referendum had either unleashed dormant but strong beliefs or conjured severe views into life. People were specific in their dislike of the EU, often exaggerating its size, resenting its complexity. They felt, in an inchoate but passionate manner, that their Englishness (or, for a smaller proportion, their Britishness) was impugned or threatened. Some were merely confused: 'There was this logo on a red bus saying our money should remain in the UK. That's why I voted for remain.'

Fantasy and superheroes were doing good business. Melissa Pirbudak, a leave voter from Kent, said fellow Brexit supporters thought some 'magical force field' would cover England and something wonderful would happen. The EU was apostrophised as an evil superpower, conspiring now to stop salvation. It was responsible for the disappearance of shipyards and collieries; it had closed the A&E department in Burnley. As the difficulties mounted, good old stoicism transmuted into masochism. We can take it. 'We'll have a difficult twenty-four or thirty-six months,' said Alex Johnson, another Kent leaver, 'but we've got to tough it out.' They had been persuaded, Irish columnist Fintan O'Toole argued, into the joys of self-harming, choosing between shooting themselves in the head or in the foot. But how thick would the phlegm prove when the Blitz began? This was a country where the slightest hint of shortage – an accidental blip in the supply of chickens to KFC in 2018, for example – caused a national outcry.

A neat piece of research suggested the absence of the *Sun* from Merseyside bore some responsibility for the region's strong-ish remain vote (the Murdoch paper had tried to blame Liverpool FC fans for the Hillsborough disaster, and as a result had been boycotted). But the corollary was that anti-European reporting and opinionating, day in, day out, had worked. Many voters in 2016 had absorbed a view of the EU crafted by the Australian–American press owner and the other tabloids. If they had succeeded with Europe, then how many other dimensions of public opinion had been pushed and pulled by the mass-selling right-wing papers? In no other European country is ownership so concentrated or national politics so intertwined with newspapers. Some say this is too simple, too linear; that people think for themselves. Alternatively, in 2016 the ideologues who owned the press secured another triumph.

The Compromised Constitution

Brexit subjected core institutions to the ultimate test, and they failed. Examined on their knowledge of an institution to which the UK had belonged since 1972, 'the political elite have gone on being ill-informed, not to say deluded, about [its] nature', declared an expert from the London School of Economics. Permanent secretaries admitted – privately, of course – to 'not understanding the EU well enough', and that after the vote 'notes on a fag packet became plan A'. If there was such a thing as the 'deep state' – an imagined entity jumbling Le Carré, vague memories of 1970s coup talk and the old deference to generals and permanent secretaries – it proved remarkably ineffective. Parliament (which for practical purposes meant the House of Commons) consistently put party loyalty ahead of allegiance to the House as the ultimate authority in our system of government; few MPs had read any seventeenth-century history, and even fewer cared that they were treading over fundamental questions about the distribution of legitimate power and lawful rule. MPs seemed to practise odd indifference to their constitutional position. Dominic Cummings had cocked a snook at them, refusing to give evidence to a House of Commons committee; he was in contempt of parliament. It was later discovered that the Commons – ostensibly run by MPs – had unquestioningly issued him with a parliamentary pass.

Confident parliamentarians, the MPs elected in 2015 might have declared the referendum vote a giant test of opinion, advisory only, and, moreover, one that offered no guidance about how or when leaving was to be effected. Instead, they retreated, fertilising the growth of the plebiscitarian myth that only the vote, once, conferred legitimacy. It took a third-party application to the Supreme Court to give MPs the right to decide on Brexit – a right they had refused to claim for themselves. By a majority of eight to three, the justices held that a new Act of Parliament was needed to authorise the triggering of Article 50, on the grounds that Brexit would change basic legal rights. The MPs elected in 2017 had stopped executive government (in the shape of May and her ministers succeeding in their carve-up) but were at a loss when it came to agreeing on what to do next. They failed to anticipate the ruthlessness of Johnson and Cummings, and cavilled when those two bared their fangs.

The checks and balances that are supposed to keep government honest failed to check and balance. Statecraft became corrupted by falsehood and deceit, at home and abroad. Civil servants and diplomats failed to demand evidence backing up the decisions they were instructed to carry out. A few walked out or were fired – among them Sir Ivan Rogers, one of the handful of mandarins who understood how the EU worked. The government, he said, was peddling fantasies and delusions. The head of the civil service, Sir Jeremy Heywood, was ill; he died in 2018. None of his fellow permanent secretaries made any public show of leadership; none chose to examine the threadbare doctrine that said they were answerable solely to ministers and not to the wider public interest or idea of the state. Like the BBC, the civil service was supposed to be neutral on policy. But Brexit, as the courts had said, was an existential issue, and going ahead as if the 'will of the people' had in fact been disclosed in a narrow vote was a categorical error. The NAO, an honest watchdog, expressed its alarm at the departmental mayhem and wasting of money, but futilely.

An uncomfortable truth was disclosed by Brexit. Despite the passage of time, devolution wasn't a permanent fact after all; its institutions were contingent, to be dropped or ignored as UK power-holders thought fit – as when the European Union (Withdrawal) Act was passed without Scottish consent and Article 50 was triggered without consulting Cardiff or Edinburgh. They received courtesy calls from Johnson, and were then cut out. Devolution's future is one of the multitude of bits of unfinished Brexit business. In Northern Ireland, Brexit foregrounded a mess of anomalies and unfinished historical business. Civil servants and the public alike had simply forgotten that a land border existed between the EU and the UK. The DUP's enjoyment of bribery and deference after the 2017 election was temporary; what will last is the realisation that Northern Ireland is a problem no one now wants to have, perhaps not even the Republic of Ireland. Tory party members said it: they would rather have Brexit than maintain the union. Brexit had exercised the Irish government before the vote, and 'Dublin outplayed its former colonial master', wrote the *Guardian*'s Rory Carroll. While London dithered, the Irish forged an alliance of member states. It was a case of solidarity with the member that was staying in. By early 2017 the Irish government and the EU were convinced there was no 'technical solution' to keeping the border open. The Europhobes still went on playing with the notion, but only an agreement binding both sides in a customs union would keep trade frictionless.

After Brexit

The constitution was thrown into the air, and the pieces are still landing. Some kind of reckoning on representation, partisanship and the legislative function was overdue before June 2016, and is now even more urgent. Renewal will be hard, self-hatred and mutual contempt being the principal products of Brexit, along with a stunned realisation of how many citizens are indifferent and lacking in basic civic knowledge.

Indeed, the literature around Brexit expressed revulsion at what it revealed about modern Britain. The culturati did push back: for example, in the British Library's unexpectedly successful Anglo-Saxons exhibition. We are them and they are us, was the message. These islands were once physically joined to the continent; in the Dark Ages, European culture, expressed in Latin, was a unity, and had to remain so; Marion Turner's biography of that English icon Chaucer unmasked him as a consummate European. But all this implied reintroducing the UK to Europe, and vice versa. In the *Lancet*, its editor-in-chief Richard Horton argued that Brexit could be mitigated by 'intensification of our European collaborations, deepening our European associations, and strengthening our European sympathies. If we think of ourselves as European, we need to act like Europeans.' It was a distinctly minority view.

Brexit has far to run. The Institute for Government (IfG) has said the 1972 negotiations to join the EU were a walk in the park compared to what comes next. The four years from 2016 were more a psychodrama or sort of national ad break; they were not actually about borders, lorries, documents and finance. They elapsed somewhere between body and mind, between material interest and belief; they kept flummoxing those who took an instrumental view of voting or said people's principal interests were materialistic. Brexit was never wholly, or even largely, about its ostensible subject – the UK's relationship with the EU. The very word 'Brexit' pointed to a truth. It did not include or allude to Europe. A British exit was the point, not what it was exiting from. The tautologous slogan 'Leave Means Leave' said it: the meaning was in the leaving, not in what was being left or how.

3

Austerity Britain

Nearly all the people approached for Brexit vox pops, all those attending Farage rallies – and remain marches for that matter – either had jobs or were over working age and lived well off their pensions. Here was a key to the 2010s. Joblessness in the sense of dole queues largely disappeared. Perhaps at some level of consciousness the availability of work, however badly paid, made for a sense of security, encouraging some working-age voters to take the risk of Brexit. But the bulk of leave voters were retired and now had reasonable pensions. It was those in work who formed the core of remain voters and were more likely to grasp what Brexit might do to their industries and their futures.

Unemployment had always been the great driver of discontent, distress and political upheaval, but now Beveridge's 'giant' of idleness had slunk away. Economists used to say it could never drop below a minimum of 5 per cent – certainly not without triggering inflation. Now it did, without pushing up wages. After the crash, unemployment spiked, then rapidly fell; after the Brexit vote, 'Nobody seems to have told the labour market,' consultant John Philpott sarcastically remarked. Grim warnings about the consequences of Brexit lost credibility when the 'help wanted' ads multiplied.

But despite all the jobs, nobody became much better off – except in boardrooms. The work that was available often paid badly, taking the form of 'gigs' done by harassed delivery drivers and Deliveroo cyclists. The trend was not confined to the UK; across the developed world the rewards from paid work were falling. The great nostrum of politics and policy had always been that in order to escape poverty, you must work. Now jobs often paid too little for working parents to feed their children. They accepted it, perhaps having no choice. Unions were weak or absent; employers cracked the whip; staff jumped or moved on, to be replaced by employees on the same or less money. Companies kept a larger slice of their revenue for directors and shareholders, and the share of GDP going to workers fell. All this linked with the loss of solid jobs in the public services and the long-running move away from skilled and better-paid manufacturing employment to (often unskilled and less well-paid) jobs in the service industries. The trend also helped explain why inflation didn't rise: in services prices changed much less regularly than for goods.

We don't say that everything was bad; rather it's the counterfactual, that things could have been so much better than they were. People got by; with the exception of the poorest, it wasn't so much a desperate decade as an endurable period of little or no growth and relative stability. We saw in the last chapter that neither Brexit nor the rightwards lurch were emanations of economic discontent, at least not directly, but they can't be dissociated from the way austerity, as a deliberate policy, stripped out public services, jobs and social supports.

Signs of revolt and resentment co-existed with passivity, even fatalism, around jobs and pay; expectations stayed on the floor. In our interviews we picked up a pervading lack of curiosity, let alone knowledge, about what was going on: why board-room pay was shooting ahead when theirs was not; why voting leave in Scunthorpe or Glamorgan would have dreadful con-sequences for the steel mills there; why rationalising property taxation made sense for the vast majority who were never likely to pay inheritance tax (fewer than 25,000 estates paid it a year, less than 5 per cent of all deaths). Perhaps this was when com-plexity won: people gave up trying to fathom things out and surrendered to reflexes and simplistic formulae, which were replayed to them by Nigel Farage and Boris Johnson. It was populism at its worst, the triumph of the inexpert.

National Income

The crash shrank the economy by 6 per cent, and it took until 2015 before it returned to its pre-recession size. Earnings from overseas turned negative, forcing the UK to depend on the 'kindness of strangers', as foreign financing of UK liabilities grew. The slow speed of recovery was the result of the specific choice made by George Osborne, David Cameron and their Liberal Democrat backers in the coalition: their austerity was a direct assault on demand and economic activity.

When the cake grew again, it was at nothing like previous rates, with the result that by 2020 the UK's GDP was only about 12 per cent bigger than before 2008. Over the same time span the UK itself grew; it had more people. Per head GDP amounted to £6,545 at the onset of recession, took a hit, then began growing slowly to reach £6,730. That's a gain of about £200 a head in real terms over the twelve years, historically puny and just about enough to pay for one Nokia 7.1 handset, SIM-free.

Adjusted for inflation, what people took home from work declined as the effects of the crash and recession were compounded by austerity. Things got better in 2015–16, worsened after the Brexit vote (which knocked down the value of sterling and increased the cost of living), then recovered a bit during 2018, before falling back again amid Brexit uncertainties. But incomes never got back to their pre-crash level, taking nine years to grow as much as in one 'normal' year before the crisis. It was the Bank of England that gave us the title for our book, calling this a 'lost decade' for wage growth. The Resolution Foundation reckoned it would be 2024 before average earnings attained the giddy height they reached in 2007, meaning seventeen years of lost pay growth.

The picture is similar for households, which might have more than one earner. Median household income (after taking into account housing costs for non-pensioners) grew by £1,000 to about £24,000 a year. That worked out at less than 0.5 per cent per year, or 4 per cent in total for the eight years from 2010. Median household net disposable income after housing costs was £420 a week in 2010 and barely more, £437, by 2018. To understand how remarkable this flatlining was, compare it to growth of 35 per cent in the decade to 2003, and 33 per cent in the ten years after that. If epochs take their 'feel' from how much money people have, then the story is one of stasis: people in working-age households had as much as they had before, but no more. In a consumer society, the signals kept saying, 'Spend, keep up, acquire,' and it was perhaps not surprising that to keep going, many households had to borrow.

Here was a paradox. Osborne and his successor, Philip Hammond, made a great fuss about the state's indebtedness. Under them consumer debt expanded, so that by 2019 each UK household owed on average £15,385 to credit-card firms, banks and other lenders, not including mortgage debts. Debt as a share of household income was now 30 per cent higher than it had ever been. Rob Kent-Smith of the ONS noted that by early 2019, unprecedentedly, households had spent more than their income for nine quarters in a row. An optimist might note that some households were buying new homes, acquiring assets with future value; a pessimist would cite those high rates of indebtedness. Every sector of the UK economy – households, companies and government – was in deficit at the same time.

The Jobs Miracle

Many borrowed to bridge the gap between salary and living costs. An old shibboleth had crumbled: families could be 'hard-working' but still not have enough on which to live decently. Households did what politicians of the right and left had long demanded, what moralists, pundits, the CBI and social-security officials had insisted on for ever: they found work. The recession had made it more difficult: by the end of 2011 the jobless rate reached 8.4 per cent, higher than at any point since 1995. But then unemployment fell, returning to its pre-recession level at the end of 2015, and kept on falling. In April 2019 the ONS recorded it as being lower than at any time since 1975, at just 3.8 per cent. Over 76 per cent of people of working age (those between sixteen and sixty-four) were counted as being in paid work, with many of the remainder students. Those above the official working age kept going: the number aged seventy and over in full- or part-time employment rose to a peak of nearly 500,000 in 2019, up 135 per cent. But many of the new jobs were less secure and mentally and physically harder to do. The intensity of work increased. One in four said they had to work at high speed all the time and were worried about being treated fairly, a lack of influence over their job, no training and the incivility of their bosses. People worked because being unemployed meant less money to live on, whether you were claiming disability or not.

It wasn't just the UK. Vacancies reached record highs in Japan, the US and across the European Union. Dire predictions about robots rang hollow when, ten years on from the recession, 2.7 million more people were counted as being in work. Around two-thirds of the extra jobs were taken by migrants. But economists kept saying that migrants had not come into the UK and taken pre-existing slots that home-grown workers could or should have had a first shot at; that wasn't how the labour market worked. Many jobs were only created because employers knew that migrants, already in the UK, were available. Besides, British workers' participation in the workforce also rose to record levels. But be careful, said Professor David Blanchflower, the author of *Not Working*: if there's such a demand for labour, why aren't wages rising? These aren't *good* jobs, meaning secure and decently paid.

The number of sixteen- to twenty-four-year-olds not in education or employment also fell, from 958,000 in 2011 to 783,000 by 2018 – still a worrying number lost and nowhere, many of whom were suffering from mental illness or depression. Though Northern Ireland and the north-east of England still had the highest proportion of young people thus classified, much of the growth in jobs happened in 'left behind' Britain, places where unemployment had traditionally been higher. The strongest rates of growth were in Merseyside and South Yorkshire, though total employment levels remained lower than in the south.

Not all work was welcome. More women in their early sixties took jobs because they had to. Stuart Lewis of the charity Rest Less reported that nearly half of the women who planned to work beyond state pension age said it was because they simply could not afford to retire. More disabled people were now working, though some of them were already in jobs and had just been reclassified as disabled. Still, the proportion of 'workless' households fell steadily, especially those containing single parents and people aged over fifty-five.

One reason pay did not rise was because the balance of power had shifted in the labour markets to employers. The *Guardian* talked to Brian Dennis, who lost his job at the Redcar steel-works when they were shut in 2015. He had applied for fifty positions, to no avail. Staff at the Department for Work and Pensions commented on the CV he had been sending out: 'They told him to take off the fact he was a union rep and a Labour councillor – and he got the next job he applied for.' His pay dropped by £15,000 a year. So, jobs growth, but no collective bargaining, thank you.

Young people were less likely to have spent time out of work than those of the same age ten years previously, but – here's the rub – they were more likely to have spent their early careers in low-paying jobs. Two-thirds of the growth in employment was in precarious work: part-time, self-employed, on zero-hours contracts or at the beck and call of agencies working in health and social services. Self-employment could leave work-ers with no rights to pensions, sickness or holiday pay, and it was a status often taken on by single parents and people with disabilities. In what the Resolution Foundation called 'the Wild West', conditions were pitiless: staff were not paid for travel time and given no work despite turning up. Theresa May, in her brief 'red Tory' phase, asked Tony Blair's former adviser Matthew Taylor to investigate. He found that most workers were still directly employed on permanent contracts. In the gig economy there were possibly 900,000 agency workers, with only about three out of every hundred workers on zero-hours contracts. Taylor's recommendations for (mild) re-regulation of the labour markets sits on the shelf.

Bank Crash and After

The welfare of one group of workers, bankers, never ceased to be an official priority. The Bank of England, Number 10 and the Treasury had mobilised to rescue the banks following the crash. (The state also bailed out their retail customers, then got blamed by them for being too big. It was an augury of a period when the public willed and wanted incompatible things, then lashed out when they couldn't get them. Johnson's cake-ism caught the spirit of the times.) The authorities lowered interest rates, making money cheaper, which pumped up the price of shares and houses. Inequality trailed in the wake of quantitative easing.

But no one counted the winners and losers. In hindsight, a banker-punishing crash – had it been short and sharp – might have made Brexit less likely. Letting rip would have hurt property dealers and the wealthy, and might, just might, have provided a kind of national catharsis. Professor Nicholas Crafts of the University of Warwick argued that the UK economy was up to 16 per cent of GDP smaller than it would have been if bankers had not gambled and been bailed out. But bankers were incorrigible and learned no lessons. Later, on the day Deutsche Bank announced 3,000 job cuts in London, tailors from Fielding & Nicholson walked into the bank's offices to fit senior managers for suits. 'Our timing was not great,' said tailor Ian Fielding-Calcutt. 'We just went ahead as normal with our clients, who obviously weren't affected by the cuts.'

Cameron had talked of jailing criminal bankers; nothing more was heard about incarceration, and the strong recommendations from Sir John Vickers's review were watered down. Perhaps the realisation that the bankers got away with it did fuel resentment and a desire to give the Establishment a kicking, except that some of the loudest proponents of that were themselves fat-cat financial dealers. Gargantuan payouts continued; no prosecutions were mounted. Fred 'the Shred' Goodwin, destroyer of RBS, lost his knighthood but not his £17 million pension. No other honours were retracted. Osborne did introduce a levy on banks in 2011 (which lasted in a significant form until 2015, when the government capitulated to HSBC's threats to move its headquarters from the UK), but banks were also allowed to offset their tax bills against losses on loans, and the government exempted a chunk of their overseas income from UK tax. Much banking remained both unsupervised and hazed in unaccountability. It's still unclear whether the Bank of England or anyone else knows what the finance sector is up to or what banking balance sheets really say. The impotence of the Financial Conduct Authority was laid bare when Neil Woodford, a year after paying himself and his business partner £36.5 million, refused to waive the gargantuan daily fee paid by the investors whom he was barring from withdrawing their money after his funds plummeted.

It may sound extraordinary to suggest the Old Lady of Threadneedle Street was cognitively impaired, but the evidence comes in the shape of 'quantitative easing'. Neither its governors nor the Treasury fully understood what they were doing and certainly did not anticipate that it would plump up the feathers of the rich and turbo-charge house prices. Perhaps

Osborne did grasp how the latter spread good feeling (and a tolerance of austerity and a willingness to vote Tory) across the land. For all his would-be orthodoxy, Osborne readily clung on to a policy started under Labour that, in defiance of immutable rules, gave the green light to printing money, billions of it. This was only OK if the bank lent the freshly printed pounds to business, however, not to councils or the NHS to invest in buildings and infrastructure. It wasn't OK for the bank to use its credit to lend to the government, but it was OK for it to lend – on ridiculously easy terms – to equity financiers and bankers.

Confusion and public misunderstanding followed Labour's inability to give a politically convincing account of why the public finances had been drained. If Brown had saved the country from economic disaster, he lacked the nous to explain why. Osborne had it. To the drumbeat of the right-wing media, echoed by the Liberal Democrats, who confessed later they knew better, the Tories exaggerated the seriousness of ballooning borrowing. Labour had spent profligately on public services and a recession had occurred; therefore, excessive spending was to blame, and prudence now demanded cutting and culling. Osborne successfully reframed the crisis as a result of the size of the public sector rather than wild over-lending and risk-taking by financiers.

Perhaps that message was easier to grasp because it was simple and binary. For *The Verdict*, we were surprised that many did not believe that public services had improved sufficiently or else took improvement for granted, forgetting the leaking school roofs and Nissen-hut hospital wards that had been fixed.

Osborne's political triumph was to capitalise on this and secure public support for retrenchment, with 47 per cent saying in 2010 that they were willing to accept less from public services in order to pay off the national debt. By 2018 that figure had fallen to just 15 per cent. Approval of Tory economic management rose until 2015. Austerity appeared to satisfy a public mood, and until Brexit the Tories remained well ahead of Labour in polls on whom the public would trust to run the economy.

After the event, economist Simon Wren-Lewis claimed a majority of his profession saw austerity as politics, not fiscal necessity. At the time, a dominant chorus of economists and pundits gave Osborne cover, repeating the verse that urgently demanded cuts, and deep ones, too, if the UK economy was to be halted at the cliff's edge. They did not ridicule his preposterous comparison between the UK and Greece. The expediency of austerity was demonstrated when Johnson arrived, and it was as if the 'rules' adumbrated by Osborne had never existed: government could borrow as much as it liked, or at least as much as ministers needed to secure re-election.

In 2010 the state could safely have borrowed more, keeping welfare and public services going until the economy recovered, at which point growing tax revenues would help repair the deficit. After the event, economists' models put the upper bound of UK state borrowing at 95 per cent of GDP, well above the level in 2010 or ten years later. But instead of the Keynesian case for spending in a downturn and borrowing to finance it, what won out was Osborne's everyday metaphor of that 'maxed-out credit card'. Whether he believed it or was merely being cynical, the image reinforced the idea of specific predetermined limits to state borrowing, even when interest rates were preternaturally low.

It quickly became apparent that the credit card was remarkably elastic. National debt rose by 72 per cent between March 2010 and March 2018, to 83 per cent of GDP, or £1.8 trillion. There were no ill effects; in fact, the interest rate paid on the debt fell from 3.9 per cent to 2.2 per cent in 2016 (and rose slightly after that). The IFS commented that despite national debt being 50 per cent higher than before the crisis, debt interest was 'actually less of a burden . . . the fact that debt is set to fall only slowly is less of a concern'. So size did not matter. The state could safely have borrowed far more. Austerity, on the timing and scale at which it was practised, was unnecessary . . .

The Politics and Economics of Austerity

. . . except politically. In *Dogma and Disarray*, we paid tribute to the Tories' opportunism, as they used the financial situation to shield their political ambitions. Choices made in 2010 shaped the era, and still do. Retrenchment would have been hugely less damaging if it had been paced, but it was deliberately rushed. Tory values drove the policies of reducing the deficit by cutting spending rather than raising taxes, together with targeting welfare.

If the melody later changed, the bass line remained the same. May entered Downing Street in 2016 bemoaning the plight of those 'just about managing', but nothing much changed on the fiscal front under Hammond's stewardship. Later, two things were apparent. The basics of Tory policy since 2010 – hitting benefits for the poorest hardest – were not touched, even when Johnson splurged in order to try to win the 2019 election. Yet austerity could always accommodate party interests and, subsequently, Brexit. Restraint was abandoned to pay for the fabled ferries that never were. Austerity never touched favoured projects, including HS2, or interest groups that voted. Osborne invented £10,000 pensioner bonds just before the 2015 election, paying a whopping 4 per cent interest; they were closed to new investors straight after. Revenue was foregone when he increased the inheritance tax threshold for couples to £1 million; proposals were floated to allow parents to pass on tax-free gifts to their children five years before their death rather than seven.

The era's definitive move was to cut spending rather than increase revenues. Cuts bore 89 per cent of 'fiscal consolidation'. A mix of higher borrowing and tax rises would have been both fairer and economically more efficient. The former was ruled out, until political desperation later demanded it; the latter were forbidden because higher taxes would affect the Tories' core vote. Cutting spending and, specifically, the incomes of poorer families had a strong and immediate downwards push on demand, which continued through to 2020. Public investment was slashed; the rebuilding of schools and hospitals was stopped in its tracks. This hit GDP growth directly. Any pick-up after the recession was delayed, and the annual rate of growth never got above 2 per cent. Austerity had continuing effects, too, which after 2016 were compounded by Brexit. The UK fell from top of the G7 countries for growth in 2015 to bottom.

No sooner was a key 2010 promise realised – nine years on, public sector net borrowing (the budget deficit or gap between receipts and revenues each year, allowing for investment) fell, to 2 per cent of national income – than its political pain proved too great and it was promptly abandoned. So the great achievement of, in the year to March 2019, borrowing only 1.2 per cent of GDP, compared to 10 per cent in 2010, did not last long. Of course, any comparison between the two years was meaningless, given the scale of the financial crisis and the urgency of the state's response. In 2010, as in 2019, the significance of any given level of borrowing and deficit depended on the prevailing interest rates and willingness to lend: throughout the decade the former remained low enough and the latter high. The drama of 2010 – the necessity of immediately bringing annual borrowing down – was exposed by the Tories' own later actions as a fetish. That this was about borrowing on the revenue account, separate from what government should borrow in order to invest in and construct long-lasting assets, was a salient point that went unheard in the noise generated by ministers and their claque in the media.

Taxing Times

The UK is relatively under-taxed: at 34 per cent of GDP, revenues are much less than in France (46 per cent) and Germany

(38 per cent), though more than in the US, on 27 per cent. Other countries in Europe had increased the proportion of national income spent on public services as GDP grew. But the shibboleth said the UK had reached a limit in terms of taxes on income. Perhaps there was a political limit, polling results suggested. Among the reasons the Tories succeeded in both 2010 and 2015, and became the biggest party in 2017 despite continuing austerity, was a public reluctance to pay more.

By 2018 tax as a proportion of GDP was almost exactly the same as in the last of Labour's 'normal' years, 2007. Because there had been a small amount of GDP growth since, this meant that people and firms were paying more tax in total at the end of the decade. Average earnings, while not rising much, tipped over the threshold, so that a rising proportion of income was taxed at the higher rate. Even though millions paid tax day in, day out, it was not much understood. In successive budgets the Tories raised the personal allowance threshold for income tax. It sounded like they were being generous to low earners, who by 2019 would not pay income tax until they were earning £12,500. Hammond boasted that 'since 2015 we've taken 1.7 million [people] out of tax altogether'. But everyone got the allowance, so the principal beneficiaries were in the upper half of earners: setting the threshold at £12,500 meant higher earners *saved* £860 a year, while those on the £12,500 threshold only gained £130. But only tax aficionados would have grasped this injustice. Theresa May misspoke when she tried to claim the top 1 per cent paid 28 per cent of *all* taxes: they paid 28 per cent of all income tax, which is only about a quarter of the total tax take. Meanwhile, Tory chancellors went AWOL over the taxation of petrol and diesel. A movement called Fair Fuel UK, which claimed to have 1.7 million supporters among the UK's 37 million drivers, hovered threateningly. Philip Hammond admitted they had foregone £46 billion by not going ahead with scheduled increases in fuel duty.

Tax revenues from employment reached an average of £3,538 per person in 2018. This was the highest amount ever recorded and stemmed from the fact that more people were in work, contributing income tax and National Insurance (NI). Some employers, including public bodies, avoided paying taxes for their staff by calling them self-employed, even if all their time was spent working for one outfit; the revenue foregone by the Treasury was estimated at £11 billion. The number of self-employed small tradespeople rose by a remarkable 25 per cent after 2007, partly through choice, partly through employers and agencies avoiding NI, sickness and holiday pay. The new generation of the self-employed did not do well: their average turnover fell by a fifth.

If income tax remained broadly progressive, the picture was different when you looked at all taxes. Once VAT was taken into account, the poorest 10 per cent were paying a tax rate of 49 per cent of their income, compared to the 34 per cent paid by the richest 10 per cent. VAT, condemned by the IFS as a treasure trove of silliness and inconsistency, accounted for a growing proportion of tax (20.8 per cent) as corporation tax was cut from 28 per cent in 2008 to 17 per cent in 2020. This amounted to a £170 billion gift to the corporate sector, pocketed without producing extra investment. Further giant reductions were bandied about during the Tory leadership battle in 2019, even though the UK already had one of the lowest corporation tax rates in the developed world. Even business lobbyists had become sceptical. That was partly because there was a tax they wanted something done about, which was business rates.

Here was an old sore turning septic. The valuation of commercial premises was out of kilter with economic reality. Huge Amazon sheds paid less than corner shops; the online transactions they fulfilled were seriously undertaxed, while rateable values on shops failed to adjust as the high street was battered. Small businesses could end up paying a large proportion of their revenue in property taxation. It wasn't just that the Tories failed to reform business rates; Cameron proposed using them as the new base for council funding, which would exacerbate regional disparities. Westminster's business rates raised £2.2 billion, while the Wirral's raised only £70 million. Under Thatcher, business rates had been taken out of council control, but now they were to be returned, allowing central government to slash grants on the grounds that councils had their own revenue, though the amounts they could levy were severely restricted.

Tax Havens

The bullying power of the wealthy swells the more wealth they control. The rich and their representatives continually frighten chancellors with threats to offshore their money. But the facts of tax injustice became more glaring during the lost decade, and public indignation grew. When panjandrums met at Davos, they bewailed the inequalities of income and wealth but turned shy and retiring over their own tax-avoidance schemes. UK businesses, including railway companies, banks and consultancies, widely used 'arrangements', the result of which was to deprive the exchequer of revenue. A government genuinely concerned with fiscal consolidation would have squeezed them, along with the Googles and Amazons who played the jurisdiction game, hopping their corporate accounts between countries to minimise tax. Half the foreign profits of US multinationals were booked in tax havens (which included the Republic of Ireland and the Netherlands).

Some 8 per cent of global wealth, $7.6 trillion, was thought to be hidden in havens. The 2016 database leak from Panama lawyers Mossack Fonseca made the fiscal wound gape gangrenously, and the Treasury tentatively turned towards naming the clandestine companies behind the discreet nameplates in St Helier, Nassau and Douglas. Those incorporated in the UK were required to declare their beneficial owners, as well as their shareholders. The government introduced unexplained wealth orders, which could be used to force high-value property owners who claimed limited income to explain themselves. Much hinged on enforcement. It was thought some 6,800 UK citizens controlled 12,000 firms from within low-tax jurisdictions. They were as tax-resistant as ever, with some 30 per cent of the UK's estimated ninety-three billionaires having moved to tax havens.

Backbench Tory MPs collaborated on legislation to force the UK's own offshore tax havens in the English Channel and the Irish Sea to make their registers of company ownership fully searchable. But, at the very last moment, despite Brexit distractions, the May government withdrew the crucial clauses. Lobbying by the territories (or their clients) had evidently proved effective. The government then allowed banks implicated in wrongdoing to help run a new Economic Crime Strategic Board, which would supposedly hold companies to account. Sue Hawley, policy director of Corruption Watch, said it didn't pass the sniff test, even to a nose with heavy catarrh. The government chose not to implement a 2009 law that would have banned large donations from those resident abroad for tax purposes. Tax-exile donors went on being given honours and titles, and they gave more than £1 million to the Conservative Party just before the 2017 election.

The Taxman Doesn't Cometh

Much more could have been done to secure revenues. The bright idea of pushing vehicle excise duty online meant cars, vans and lorries no longer displayed tax discs on their windscreens; the number of untaxed vehicles leapt by three times in the three years after, forfeiting £107 million a year in revenue. Meanwhile, HMRC cut 15,600 staff and closed 157 local offices. Its ability to bring in money was affected, along with the quality of service. In 2018, 4 million calls to HMRC went unanswered, or one in ten, according to the NAO. Though it eventually got round to pursuing staff who masqueraded as self-employed, including broadcasters and senior medics, the tax gap – the difference between tax officially calculated as owing and what actually got collected – had risen since 2010, with a walloping £35 billion denied to the state to spend. Some put it much higher.

Hawsons Chartered Accountants had looked after business in Sheffield for 160 years. Chris Hill, the senior partner, had seen the local effects of the HMRC pullback. 'There were five offices; now there's just one big hub for the whole area. And if you call that one, you can't speak to anyone. You're kept on hold for long periods, and no one has a clue what you're talking about. They say they will pass it on and get a decision, but you never hear back. Before, you could have an intelligent conversation with someone you knew, who knew your clients, who knew the area and could resolve the problem efficiently.' The upshot was that the tax authorities no longer had eyes and ears in the community. Before, staff would hear when someone was driving a flash car or living in a house beyond their apparent means while claiming they made no profit.

The accountant's clients struggled with Making Tax Digital. This programme was of a piece with changes at the DWP and the Ministry of Justice, pushing transactions and processes online in pursuit of staff shrinkage and lower spending. Making Tax Digital required everyone, even small businesses, to fill in complex online forms. When there were local tax offices, a perplexed manager could go to a counter and ask for help; now they had to turn

*to accountants. 'Good for our business,' said Hill, 'not good for
theirs. We have to do the Revenue's work for them now.'*

Accountants used to be trusted to provide solid numbers, but
company accounts began to read like racy fiction. 'Not our
job to police fraud,' they said, as Patisserie Valerie collapsed
like a soggy eclair. 'Happy to sign off fantastical figures,' they
said, just before the bells tolled for Carillion. 'Oops, forgot to
pay tax,' they said at depressed Conviviality. BHS, Mitie and
Ted Baker were among the companies whose shareholders and
pension fund investors were kept in the dark until too late.
Corporate trust waned.

The regeneration of accountancy honesty has begun with the
remaking of the regulator, the Financial Reporting Council. It
still has some way to go and must involve tackling something
that ministers have failed to address: the overweening, anti-
competitive power of the Big Four consultancy/auditing firms.

The Axe

Under Blair and Brown, public spending had grown exuber-
antly, but so did population, expectations and need. After 2010
those three kept growing, but at best the money flatlined. What
that amounted to, the IFS said, was 'an unprecedented period
of spending restraint'. The economy grew by 18 per cent from
2010, population by 6.8 per cent; social, housing, health and
other needs also grew, often disproportionately, during and
after the recession. To get by, modern Britain depended on

flows of public money, income support and the 'social wage'; public services were the glue in an increasingly fissiparous society. But the volume of public spending was roughly the same in 2020 as in 2010, though how it was made up changed dramatically.

Bailing out the banks and coping with the crash sent spending to 44.9 per cent of GDP. The austerity plan aimed to push it down by a fifth to 36.3 per cent. In the event, the plan backfired, targets were missed, and by 2019 spending reached 38 per cent of GDP, a sixth less than in 2010. But that total includes pensions, which were protected. Spending on public *services* excluding pensions and social benefits dropped from 16.2 per cent to 14 per cent of GDP. For every £100 spent per person on public services in 2010, £86 was being spent in 2020.

Public sector staff paid the price. Their pay was cut – which is what the 1 per cent cap imposed in 2010 amounted to – at least until 2017. Their pension rights also diminished, and many faced retirement on amounts lower than they had been promised. Posts were deleted, 600,000 of them, or 10 per cent of the total. A quarter of all local government jobs went: some as straight redundancy; others outsourced to private companies. At Northampton Borough Council half the staff disappeared. By 2019, 16.4 per cent of all workers were in the public sector, back to the level it was when Tony Blair took office. It was almost as if the period of Labour government were being extirpated. These were not just jobs, but functions. Especially vulnerable were services that prevented things happening, which often disappeared, invisible until sudden crises in child protection or crime exposed the missing support. Cuts in youth workers surfaced when knife crime exploded and the police became more and more worried about the expanding networks of drug dealing, nicknamed county lines, which exploited young people. Natural England, which looks after national and country parks and long-distance footpaths, had its budget cut by a half and staff numbers fell by a thousand, resulting in less conservation work, sites of special scientific interest going unmonitored, the register of trees not being updated and payments to farmers being delayed or missed. In its 2015 manifesto, the government pledged to plant 11 million trees in England by 2020, but by 2018 just 1.4 million had been planted.

Where the axe fell reflected political sensitivity and ministerial heft, not real-life effects or the risk of social damage. The wish to keep one good behaviour badge meant the foreign aid budget was protected, as Cameron and later May stuck with the pledge to meet the UN's target of 0.7 per cent of GDP, despite assaults from the right-wing press and Tory MPs, including Priti Patel, who was appointed international development secretary by May. (She self-immolated, later to rise from the ashes as Johnson's draconian home secretary.) Meanwhile, the Foreign Office shrank and 270 diplomatic posts were axed – an odd way of securing the global influence promised by Brexit, said the ex-permanent secretary Sir Simon Fraser.

Austerity was at once haphazard and focused on what voters would least notice. Older people tended to vote for right-wing parties, so pensions were safe. Benefits for the disabled and those out of work were fair game. Investment, largely out of public view and easy to postpone, was heavily cut. Auditors said the sale of both the Green Investment Bank and a large portion of the student loan portfolio were not thought through: the immediate aim of cutting the debt jeopardised long-term value. Similarly, the enforced sale by Network Rail of valuable railway arches. Defence was mostly out of sight; so were prisons, legal aid and offender management – the Ministry of Justice's budget fell by 40 per cent. The communities budget fell by 45 per cent, and transport by 70 per cent. If health and social care rose by 18 per cent, so did the population it was meant to support. One result was that health bulked larger in the overall scheme of things. By 2023 it will be 38 per cent of spending, despite suffering the harshest squeeze since the inception of the NHS in 1948.

The chop fell randomly. The Forensic Science Service investigated serious criminal cases, such as homicide and sexual assault, using DNA analysis; it was abolished in 2012, and police and prosecutors had to fend for themselves. What happened next was entirely predictable: private forensic laboratories struggled to meet acceptable standards. The government covered its back, claiming a regulator was keeping things honest. But Dr Gillian Tully, the forensic science regulator from 2014 onwards, bravely said justice was being endangered; financial pressures had compromised quality, and she needed the power to ban substandard providers.

During our visit to Eggleston Steel in Derby, we were struck by a remark made by the boss, Richard Hewitt: 'There are not enough health-and-safety inspectors. This is a very high-risk business, and we are sticklers, very careful. But when I do deliveries, I see the state of other companies, and I don't know how they get away with it.' The chances of being inspected now had shrunk to almost nothing.

Councils Bear the Brunt and Take the Blame

In early January 2016 Kate Vanloo, a keen amateur athlete, was cycling home from training with the Rugby Triathlon Club to the Warwickshire village of Napton. According to evidence presented at the coroner's court, she hit a pothole that was obscured by a puddle and was thrown from her bike into the path of a car. She died at the scene. The hole had been identified in an inspection a year earlier but had not been repaired for 'financial reasons'. By 2019 English councils' road repair backlog was £10 billion.

Potholes were hot local issues, and councils tried to put them at the top of their agendas, diverting grants intended for health and social care. The public tended to focus on what was on their doorstep or under their wheels, and would lay the blame locally. Before the Conservatives came to power, a Tory shadow minister boasted they would 'devolve the axe'. And so they did. Abiding ignorance of local government finance meant they could claim to have supplied the money, but councils were inefficient (or Labour-controlled). In England, spending cuts were concentrated on councils, allowing ministers to point complainants to the town hall and local councils, who would shoulder the blame for unfilled potholes (7.8 million of them, the Local Government Association said) and deferred bin collections. The grant received by English councils from the government fell by 60 per cent to 2020, and was due to be entirely abolished by 2022. To twist the knife, the government posed as the taxpayers' friend by castigating municipal extravagance and barring local authorities from raising council tax beyond a puny 1.9 per cent a year unless they held a referendum. In England, the spending power of local authorities – money received from both grants and council tax – fell by nearly a third after 2010. At the same time, councils' employment costs rose, with extra pension contributions and a new apprenticeship levy.

They stopped doing things. Spending on ensuring the food served in restaurants and cafés was hygienic fell by a fifth and on food standards staff by a half. 'Local authorities are failing to meet their legal responsibilities to ensure food businesses comply with the law,' the NAO said. Levels of food-borne illness remained broadly stable, but the risk had risen. When we visited Huntingdonshire District Council, we found fewer trainees being taken on and fewer visits being made to premises; environmental health was under increasing strain.

At the same time, demand and need were growing. No councils could escape ageing: those responsible for adults' social care had already overspent their budgets by £1 billion in 2016–17. They cut buses, youth services, planning, housing, libraries, highways and roads maintenance by a third. All this diminished the social purpose of councils, with over half of their funds spent on one function alone: adults' and children's social care, which went unseen by most voters. Government

added to their financial woes with a 2015 pre-election sweet-
ener: they imposed a cut in council house rents costing
£2.6 billion, which was uncompensated for. Councils lost
another £3 billion when Osborne exempted developers from
having to make a social contribution when they won permission for building schemes.

Children in the care of councils rose from 64,400 in 2010 to
75,420 in 2017. Child protection and support services fell into
financial crisis, with the heaviest losses in the north of England
and in the most deprived areas. Councils lost 29 per cent of the
grants they received for children's departments – equivalent to
£3 billion – despite spiralling demand. Here was evidence of the
short-term mentality. The Early Intervention Foundation estimated that failure to prevent domestic violence, abuse, unemployment and youth crime would eventually cost £17 billion
a year in England and Wales by creating knock-on problems
for the police, councils, the NHS and claims on the welfare
budget. 'Turning the Tide', a report by Action for Children,
the Children's Society and the National Children's Bureau,
showed that spending on early intervention had fallen by 40
per cent by 2016.

Yet if councils took the hardest hits, they were often complicit. Tory authorities that had boasted of keeping their council tax impossibly low were caught out. Northamptonshire
went bust; East Sussex very nearly. Conservative-led councils
were obedient, and their leaders were regularly rewarded with
knighthoods and honours. David Hodge, the leader of Surrey
County Council, appeared to be an exception. Come 2016 he

was bristling with indignation: 'We cut £450 million already, we squeezed every efficiency and we can do no more.' Schools in Surrey were in trouble: the county's growing population needed 11,000 more places by 2020. Social care costs were rising by £24 million a year. The number of over-eighty-fives was large; they live long in Surrey. In 2017 Hodge finally rebelled and declared that he would present the dire circumstances to Surrey's citizens and hold a local referendum proposing to raise council tax by 15 per cent.

It didn't happen. A deal was cooked up. In exchange for calling off the referendum, Surrey was given a bung disguised as a pilot scheme, allowing the county council to retain business rates revenue. Hodge backed down and fell silent. The Local Government Association, permanently Tory-run, followed suit. The government tried to ensure authorities in the south and east of England – coincidentally Tory-run – were given more. Spending per person on adult social care fell by 17 per cent in deprived areas, but by only 3 per cent in comparable affluent places. The pain was spread unevenly everywhere because poorer families rely more on public services. A Centre for Cities study showed the poorest areas bore the brunt.

Deficit

The cuts had never been anything but the product of electoral calculation, of what they could get away with, though it wasn't clear ministers knew what effects their spending plans were having – for example, in England's schools or on defence.

There was no single point within government that monitored the effects of funding reductions across all services, the NAO said critically. This was deliberate. Why would they want that inconvenient information?

4

Dislike, Disrespect, Distrust

Theresa May praised those who dream and strive, proclaiming herself champion of the 'just about managing', who worked hard for little reward. Emma Percy might have been exactly in her sights. A generation ago, she, husband Rob and their three children would have had the choice of renting a council house or, like their parents, buying a home of their own. Instead, like so many young families of their generation, they were subject to the whims of private landlords, constantly moving children from their schools, leaving neighbourhoods populated by family and friends in search of an affordable roof.

We visited when the family was living in a 1950s three-bedroom house in a quiet Folkstone street, the sort of place they yearned to own. But, priced at over £250,000, they didn't stand a chance. Later, the landlord cashed in and sold, and yet again these model tenants, who never fell behind with the rent, had to move on.

The story of their married life was now common among millions. They were never quite homeless, destitute or reliant on benefits, but never had a secure roof over their children's heads. They started out living above the pub where Rob worked as a chef, but had to leave job and home when their first baby was born as children were forbidden. The council put them in a Salvation Army hostel, where the toilet in the flat above leaked. For that, they paid

£800 a month. They found a cheaper flat for £700, and Emma went to work part-time in Sainsbury's. After six months the landlord raised the rent by £50, warning he'd raise it again by £50 in six months, as demand for lettings rose. 'The next place was a nightmare,' said Emma. 'Filthy, and the boiler was broken for five months in the winter, so no hot water, and still costing £750.' They sometimes stayed with family, but they were too many to squeeze into a spare room. Good and bad landlords, they had almost lost count of the times they moved.

In the crash, Rob was made redundant, but now he earned £24,500 a year as site manager at a school. Half his post-tax earnings went on their rent. They tried the council and housing associations, only to be told there was no chance, the waiting list a lifetime long. Emma was exceptionally thrifty, counting every penny, knowing that as Universal Credit rolled out in their area, she would lose heavily.

Now she was training to be a teacher on a one-year course based in a Canterbury college, which she had to drive to as trains were too expensive and buses too unpredictable. The extra cost was a burden. 'We get by, but only because all our clothes are secondhand.' They could never afford holidays. 'What does hurt is not being able to buy the birthday and Christmas presents they see other children getting.' When we met her this time round, she was proud her eldest had just passed all her GCSEs and was moving to a sixth-form college, but as ever, she was anxious that their lease could end at any time and they would be moving on again.

After she started earning as a teacher, the plan was to save every spare penny, enough for a deposit. Perhaps. Eventually. She

watched house prices rise. 'It all depends on interest rates not ris-
ing too high or food prices or everything else. But I think we can. I
think we must, however long it takes.'

It was a decade of 'dis-'. We distrusted and disliked each other
more, and 'disrespect' became a term of abuse. The country was more unequal, said the Equality and Human Rights
Commission in a statutory report. The commission, dating
from the Labour era, had escaped the carnage of the quangos,
surviving to tell embarrassing truths about worsening prospects for disabled people, increasing child poverty and declining access to justice.

The country grew apart in a physical sense: there was a
continuing increase in the number of electoral wards with a
non-white majority, suggesting communities became more
concentrated by ethnicity. The Right condemned those who
were different; the Left promoted diversity at the expense of
mutuality and shared values. In the middle were commonality
and fellow feeling, which polls showed had retreated. Thank
you, David Cameron: this was the Small Society.

Yet, until Brexit, the proportion of people feeling close to
those in their neighbourhood rose: up several points to 62 per
cent. The UK was not so different from other countries: after
social security benefits were taken into account, the proportion living in poverty was 15.9 per cent, worse than France
(13.6 per cent), better than Germany (16.5 per cent). But we
ranked below France, Germany, Sweden and Japan on sense
of responsibility to fellow citizens. Nonetheless, 60 per cent

went on saying it was the government's duty to reduce differences between people with high and low incomes, the same as in Sweden and Germany, and substantially higher than in the US. Levels of mutual trust were similar to in Germany and higher than in France, as measured before the *gilets jaunes* started rampaging.

'We're all in it together,' George Osborne mocked, as he tugged policy in the opposite direction. Unfairness was in your face as crony capitalism was displayed in the form of vast and undeserved salary packages and bonuses. Greedy company directors proved immune to public shaming: a day's embarrassment once a year from a few bolshie shareholders at the general meeting was well worth the millions. For their staff, low pay became endemic.

Shame presupposed at least some degree of social solidarity, but it was lacking. We decreasingly knew either who we were in a collective sense or what we owed in terms of obligations of care and concern for 'others', whether they were the poor, minorities, the frail – or, indeed, elites, southerners, Londoners, leavers or any other non-members of our tribe. That's a generalisation, of course; people did give and they did volunteer – we will look at the food bank phenomenon later – but did less than before. (Even the lifeboats, usually top of the giving charts, saw donations fall: they had to fight against a Tory and tabloid attack in 2019 on their tiny efforts to prevent drowning in Third World countries.) Pundits said identity politics was on the rise, with a heightened sense of nationality or of belonging to sexual or ethnic minorities or communities of belief. 'Leave' and 'remain' took on new meanings as diametrically opposed tribes. But to identify and belong was also to exclude others. Leavers tried to forget remainers, who were nearly as many in number as them, plus the quarter of the adult population who didn't vote. In Scotland, who 'we' were was relatively settled, but Brexit reopened the divide on how separate 'we' wanted to be from the rest of the UK; similarly in Wales. As for England, identity shifted shape like a 1960s lava lamp. The UK's central bank, and therefore also Scotland's, Northern Ireland's and Wales's, continued to be called the Bank of England, albeit run by a Canadian because no British citizen good enough could be found.

Mark Carney, the international national banker, belonged, like Manchester City's Pep Guardiola, to the footloose superstar migrant elite. Less distinguished incomers were a public concern. Day after day the *Daily Mail* showed swarthy men climbing off the backs of lorries; in Nigel Farage's infamous 'breaking point' poster they were threatening, anonymous hordes. Yet migrants were also attentive NHS doctors, deft baristas, bus drivers and IT specialists. When asked by nice people with clipboards, most included Poles, Muslims, black people, even asylum-seekers in 'us'. But put the question differently, and pollsters soon uncovered conflict and uncertainty. Politics resounded with dog whistles, coded references and increasingly explicit encouragement to label *them*, be they bearded, burqa'd or Bulgarian.

The Small Society

'Us' and 'them' overlaps with the divide between public and private, and the latter kept winning. Public space was appropriated for cafés selling costly cappuccinos, pricey private gyms, seminars, festivals and events for those able to afford tickets. Offices and shopping plazas belonged to property companies, policed by guards. The disreputable, youths, children and hangers-about were moved on. Metal studs sprouted on balustrades where the indigent and homeless might lay their unsightly heads. The 2,300 square metres of private landscaped gardens for private owners in Hornsey's Smithfield Square were three times the size of the courtyard for housing association tenants on the same site; the private flats housed eighteen children, the social dwellings 123.

Public spiritedness evaporated. Volunteering dropped by 15 per cent, as measured by hours offered. People simply had less cash and less time to contribute. Cameron's rhetoric about voluntary action was just hot air, an attempt to divert attention from austerity. Its only legacy was the absurdly expensive National Citizen Service, launched at the same time as councils were taking the axe to established youth clubs and cutting grants to charities. Yet, confronted with escalating need, some still stepped up to do good. Food banks had been virtually unknown previously: the Trussell Trust had just two before the crash. By 2020 there were well over 2,000: in Witney, in the plush Cotswolds; in Bath; even in deep-blue Surrey – hunger in Tory backyards. Trussell said that in the year to March 2019,

1.5 million emergency food parcels were distributed. In 2010 there were no food banks in Merseyside; the first opened in 2011. In Knowsley, the district centred on the town of Huyton, the Big Help Project now ran ten banks, handing out food to 10,000 people a year.

Knowsley was no longer the unemployment blackspot it had been, blighted by industrial decline and the misfortunes of geography. But wages, mainly from logistics and warehousing, were £40 a week under the national average, and joblessness among young people was still twice the average. A local head teacher told us all his high-achieving pupils left the area in search of better prospects elsewhere. The local authority had lost 57 per cent of its funds from government. Public health reports showed rates of smoking, drinking, obesity and gambling that were all above average.

The Big Help Project did far more than hand out food. It offered debt advice and ran a credit union, a help-to-work service and projects for ex-offenders and asylum-seekers. Here was a hub for the community, the place to turn to for help. Peter Mitchell, the dynamo powering it, had managed to pull in funds from multiple sources, and Big Help had thirty-five full-time staff and 126 volunteers every week. 'People do say to me we're letting the government off, we're filling the big holes they've made in the welfare state. And that's true, but what can you do?'

The government had dismissed food banks, in 2013 blocking a £22 million grant from the EU's Aid to the Most Deprived Fund to help finance them. Would-be intellectual toughs from right-wing think tanks sneered that nobody would starve in modern Britain. Lord Freud, a DWP minister (who had been brought in by Gordon Brown), scoffed, 'Food from a food bank – the supply – is a free good and by definition there is an almost infinite demand for a free good.' But what galled Mitchell most was the moment when the government, faced with growing public sympathy for the hungry, abruptly changed tack and started to extol food banks. Iain Duncan Smith, the minister personally responsible for so much suffering, invited the cameras to film him as he helped Christmas collections at a supermarket, telling reporters, 'I welcome decent people in society trying to help others who have fallen into difficulty.' Later, Conservative Central Office even urged its MPs to tweet pictures of their food bank efforts. But the party line also stipulated that hunger had nothing to do with benefit changes, even though the DWP itself issued vouchers for use at food banks, as certificates of claimants' neediness. Trussell reported food banks were four times busier in those areas where Duncan Smith's Universal Credit was being rolled out.

Going Hungry

'I was so hungry, all of a sudden it was like I got hit in my belly, like I got stabbed with a knife and it's still there,' fourteen-year-old Emmanuel told the Thomas Coram Research Unit. His brother Gideon went hungry at school lunchtime: 'You have no money on your card and then you just watch them eat.' The threshold for free school meals was lowered so that only families with an annual income of under £7,400 quali-fied, which meant many very poor children had to pay. Bryony, aged thirteen, said, 'If there isn't enough food at home, we'll get it' – Mum would go hungry. Other children told of the effort their parents made to hide their hunger, claiming they had eaten earlier. Children themselves made excuses to avoid joining friends in a café they couldn't afford, never asking them round to homes with no food to offer.

In 2017 one in seven said they were struggling to make ends meet, below the EU average of one in five. Scrimping and half starving is so far beyond the experience of most fam-ilies that the daily reality of life for many fell below the social radar: people did not believe the reports nor followed the hate-mongers of the *Daily Mail* in blaming parental inadequacy and 'bad money management'. Poor families are, in fact, often the best of managers, especially mothers, rationing out the rice and pasta with great care.

Disbelief had been the old self-defence of the comfortable, who wrote letters to the press commending porridge and len-tils. Teachers, social workers and volunteers could attest from first-hand experience that growing numbers of parents were fre-quently unable to feed themselves or their children, with the fridge empty towards the end of the week, the cupboards bare of cereal or baked beans. This was absolute want, Beveridge's giant evil resurrected. Study after study showed how poverty in child-hood and the early teens permanently damaged life chances. Children forced to find themselves excluded from ordinary life-styles were scarred, their faces pressed up against the life that school friends, neighbours and people on television took for granted, with no birthday parties, no holidays and often actual hunger. International convention defined a household in poverty as living on 60 per cent of the median income or less. Ministers, MPs and the *Daily Mail* stuck their fingers in their ears, so it had to be repeated time and again that poverty is *relative*. As the economy grew and GDP rose, so did general standards, along with the pain and deprivation of those unable to match them. The right-wing press could not bear the thought of poor families having mobile phones – though without one the low-paid could not apply for Universal Credit top-ups. Without internet access how can children do their homework?

Outright abolition of child poverty by 2020 had been Tony Blair's target as he brought in the first minimum wage. Labour missed it, but by 2010 a million children had been lifted out of poverty. After that progress halted and was then reversed. The proportion of children living in households where no adult had paid work fell, a reflection of the number of jobs around. 'Look at us,' said successive Tory chancellors, 'we do care, which is why we are raising the minimum wage.' Osborne had appropriated the name National Living Wage from campaigners, without setting it at the level they estimated was needed to keep a family. Increasing the minimum did make a difference, and raised wages cost the Treasury nothing – in fact, it gained as the bill for tax credits fell when people earned more, even though the individual worker might be no better off. The minimum wage was supposed to rise fast, to reach 60 per cent of median income by 2021. By 2019 it was £8.21 an hour for adults, paid to one in eight employees – which showed how widespread low pay had become, covering a quarter of all staff working in hospitality. The parties competed in the 2019 election over who would increase it faster, but enforcement was weak and a fifth of those entitled to it were not getting it. We wanted to find out why and kept asking HMRC to let us see what their minimum wage inspectors were doing; there was no official refusal but we received no access and obtained no interviews, suggesting they were embarrassed at the disparity between their efforts and burgeoning low-paid work. In 2018 the total number of cases closed was 2,402, in only half of which were arrears paid to workers cheated out of the legal minimum.

The effect of raising the minimum wage on household income was fiendishly complex, and many families found their benefits withdrawn when pay rose, losing up to 65p for every extra pound. Imagine the consternation if top earners faced a marginal tax rate of 65 per cent. The National Living Wage did not prevent more children from being brought up in poverty, the number of whom rose continuously after 2011. After the freeze on benefits was repeated for another year in April 2019, the Resolution Foundation projected that an extra million children would be in poverty by 2023 – 37 per cent of all children. Their parents weren't skivers, slackers or any of those adjectives wielded so freely by Duncan Smith and his ilk.

One cut was totemic: the abolition of child benefit ended the post-war principle that the state should give a helping hand to every family bringing up children. Now it was means-tested and withdrawn from the better-off, so it became just another benefit for those on lower incomes. Yet this further redrawing of the public/private boundary provoked remarkably little political fallout.

Not One of Us

The poor had long been the butt of social contempt and moral disapproval, as Jeremy Seabrook recounted in his fine 2013 book *Pauperland*. New were the deliberate name-calling, the stigma and the importation of American tropes, such as 'welfare queens'. Beveridge envisaged a social-security system based on reciprocity, which provided a platform for all citizens; now, the poor were to blame for their condition, including the sick and disabled. The theme was taken up by makers of tendentious documentaries such as *Benefits Street*, caricaturing claimants as exemplars of folly, fraud, addiction, criminality and idleness. Official efforts were made to deny the existence of poverty by manipulating or even abandoning the collection of data. When a United Nations inspector, Philip Alston, toured the UK and reported his dismaying findings of deepening poverty, he was personally attacked and ridiculed by ministers and their claque.

The austerians correctly calculated that benefit withdrawal would hit council estates and renters, far away from the political centre. The brief outbreaks in 2011 aside, there were no riots, no significant protests. The poll tax brought Margaret Thatcher down because it affected so many and everyone understood its fundamental injustice. Benefits were for the weakest and poorest – the 'others'. Attitudes did mellow, somewhat. The British

Social Attitudes Survey (BSA) reported that in 2010, 55 per cent said they thought benefits created dependence, but by 2017 this was down to 43 per cent.

The poor suffered the additional affliction of being ministered to by Duncan Smith. The Roman Catholic standard-bearer and failed Tory leader had set up a think tank, which said that poverty was not a lack of money but the result of inadequate morality and the absence of aspiration, work ethic and even marriage (of the heterosexual kind). Personal responsibility mattered more than state intervention. This led to one of the Cameron coalition's oddest moves: giving married couples a tax cut that was denied to mere cohabiters. The amount of cash involved was tiny, £4 a week; evidently, couples living in sin would not need much incentive to legalise their status and stay together happily ever after. The rate at which people got married continued to drop; most of the payments, which cost £700 million a year, ended up being given to long-married older folk.

The policy illustrated the deployment of new, evidence-free sociology by policy-makers. Or rather, the evidence consisted of freakish, idiosyncratic cases. In 2013 Michael Philpott was jailed for killing six children by burning down the house where they were sleeping in order to make an insurance claim. Philpott had fathered seventeen children by five different women. 'Vile product of welfare UK,' sneered the *Daily Mail*, as Duncan Smith claimed the country was full of idlers whose families had been out of work for three generations. Research from his own department showed only 130 families with ten children claiming an out-of-work benefit; only one in twelve benefit-claiming households had three or more children.

Welfare Fared Ill

Adults of working age had it hard. Those in work suffered as tax credits were cut. Those out of work were victimised. The attack on welfare was announced in 2010 but not fully realised until later. It's worth recollecting how deliberately Cameron and his crew singled out the neediest to bear the brunt of austerity – a policy unchanged by May and one almost entirely unmentioned in the 2019 Tory leadership scramble, certainly not by Boris Johnson. Other than pensions, benefits were frozen from 2016 to 2020, despite inflation rising. The result, the House of Commons Library said, was that between 2010 and 2021 the incomes of families with children would fall by £3,000 a year. For lone parents the drop would be £5,000, almost a fifth of their income. Families with disabled members or three or more children would lose even more. These were life-altering sums.

Labour had tightened eligibility but also upped payments to disabled people. Now it was if people with disabilities were guilty of an offence, and both eligibility and payments were reduced. Demonisation worked at first, and wheelchair users reported being taunted as frauds – a new phenomenon. Claimants were put through gruelling work-capability tests administered by non-medically qualified assessors, who had been instructed to drive down the number of claims, even those by people with incurable wasting diseases. Disability Living Allowance (DLA) was replaced in 2013 by Personal Independence Payments (PIP), which were intended to cover the additional costs of having a long-term health problem and were worth £87.65 a week, plus a conditional mobility supplement. More than half of people with epilepsy already getting the DLA were turned down for PIP. The fact that three-quarters of those who challenged the decision won on appeal showed how vindictively the new, tougher conditions had been applied.

Other countries, such as France and Poland, had 'natalist' policies – they tried to encourage mothers to have babies to boost the population. The UK adopted an anti-natalist policy for the poor of which the Reverend Malthus would have approved. After April 2017 a third or subsequent child born to a family on working-age benefits would be excluded from the calculation of the benefits and tax credits due. Professor Jonathan Bradshaw of the University of York said, 'The two-child policy breaks the fundamental link between need and the provision of minimum support and implies that some children, by virtue of their birth order, are less deserving of support. It is a very large direct cut to the living standards of the poorest.'

The amount payable in housing benefit was capped, which penalised those living in higher-rent areas. The London Councils association found that as a result, none of the rooms available for private rent in the south-west of the capital was affordable by those claiming housing benefit. One of the most controversial measures was the bedroom tax: it was actually a claw-back, benefit being reduced if households were deemed to have surplus accommodation. The housing stock was mal-distributed and some 7.6 million households had two or more 'spare' bedrooms; unsurprisingly, most of this excess belonged to owner-occupiers. But it was social tenants who were targeted. The assumption that the number of rooms minus people in a household equated with 'spare' ignored social facts: disabled children needing a room of their own or a room kept for a son or daughter returning from service with the armed forces (that one embarrassed even the Tory tabloids). An early victim was the Hartlepool family of a ten-year-old child who had recently died: they were told they must pay up for her now-spare room or move out.

Vindictive in its application, the bedroom tax proved to be remarkably ineffective. Tiny numbers of poorer tenants actually moved out. The rest (mostly middle-aged) preferred to see their benefits cut and go without food and heat in order not to move away from where they had brought up their children, where their family and friends lived. Food banks reported bedroom-tax victims turning up as soon as it was imposed. Even more telling, there were no smaller local social homes to move to.

Ever since the end of the poll tax, the government had paid a grant to councils so they could subsidise poor households that were unable to afford their council-tax payments. The grant was abolished in 2013, leaving councils to find any subsidy themselves. Many said no. In the first half of 2018 over 320,000 people in England contacted an advice line for help with their council-tax debts. Councils started sending in bailiffs to dispossess their own tenants. Arrears were up to £3 billion, with 2.2 million households behind in their payments, said Citizens Advice.

As their spending overshot income, people borrowed more. Some 8 million were thought to be struggling with debt. They tended to live in rented accommodation, often with young children, and to rely on benefits; many had fallen into the clutches of short-term lenders. Charities such as PayPlan, StepChange and Citizens Advice did their best, but an estimated 600,000 people a year who needed debt advice could not get it. The interest paid on unsecured loans through credit cards and overdrafts rose in 2019 to its highest level since the crash in 2009. A sign of the times was the rise of loans companies, lending small sums at extortionate interest rates to tide families over. QuickQuid charged a typical rate of 1,294.1 per cent APR. Borrowers were found to have been seriously misled about loan conditions by the Wonga company, and it went bust in August 2018, claiming it could not cope with the thousands of claims against it registered with the Financial Ombudsman Service. Against stereotype, the places where payday lending was most heavily concentrated were not in the north but Croydon and Romford, though Birmingham was not far behind.

Labour had tightened the screw, but the extreme duress now put on working-age claimants was Dickensian. Like latter-day workhouse overseers, job-centre managers set targets for throwing people off social security. A deep-throat informant described to us how they assessed staff monthly on their refusal rate and how many claimants they removed from the roll. Look out for the weak and feeble, and if they are a minute late for an appointment, strike them out; trip them up with hard-to-understand instructions and lengthy obligations to apply for scores of jobs a week. If they erred, they were sanctioned for weeks, months. This key word – 'sanctioning' – was brought to wider attention in Ken Loach's angry films. The brutal procedure left many with nothing to live on for long periods. That tipped many into homelessness.

Universal Credit

Ministers were recklessly ambitious, time and again ordering top–down reorganisation of systems they did not fully understand, with no evidence their shiny new schemes would work. The height of ambition was Universal Credit (UC), a monumental experiment in reshaping working-age benefits, which arose from the same economistic mindset that powered the assault on the NHS and the privatisation of probation. It, too, was dreamt up in right-wing think tanks, and it became dogma, an article of faith. These think tanks assumed that people were ultra-rational, cash incentives ruled and the state should withdraw into a residual role. (By 2019 they started to admit defeat and said it was time to return to 'security' as the goal of government, glossing over what had gone before.)

UC was launched in the teeth of austerity, and the result was hardship, debt and hunger for hundreds of thousands. The basic idea was far from new and had been abandoned several times as impracticable. Ideally, the tax employees pay and the benefits they and their dependents receive should be melded, and it should flex as people move in and out of jobs, change the number of hours they work, have children, move homes, take in elderly relatives, and so on. Keeping household income stable as conditions changed was a laudable goal, provided you understood and cared about how poor people lived, worked and got by. Families and work and housing and children and the ways they interact are complex; social security will always have to shape itself around untidy lives. No system can be simple unless it is brutally unfair.

Duncan Smith chose the latter, petulantly waving away objections. Even if we accept that his intentions were sincere, he exemplified a prevalent shortcoming in ministers. Once, you could have assumed secretaries of state possessed some minimum level of technical competence, knowing which buttons to push to make a policy work. Now, politicians combined self-regard with deep ignorance and even indifference as to how complex delivery systems operated and, crucially, how 'ordinary people' lived their lives. Lacking technical competence, ministers were taken in by promises that IT would sort it. Systems need software, access protocols and administrative mechanisms, and from the start UC lacked them. It was supposed to be done and dusted by 2013; by 2018 only 1 million of the expected 7 million households had been transferred to it, and full implementation was far off. Auditors found that by 2018, the promised administrative cost of £173 per claim had risen to £699 and was still going up.

Forcing claimants to cope with a fifty-page form ignored the fact that many were on benefits precisely because they found long forms hard to follow; forcing claims to be made online penalised those lacking access to, and experience of, computers and the internet. No one would be worse off, Duncan Smith had declared. But sticking to that promise would not deliver the austerity savings demanded by the Treasury. Insoluble were the tapers – the rate at which benefits were withdrawn as income from work rose. Under the old system, payouts had been weekly, those on housing benefit having their rent paid directly to landlords. This was morally wrong in Duncan Smith's eyes: claimants should be like salaried employees, paid just once a month. They were to get no cash for five weeks from the date of their claim, with the result that UC pushed them straight into debt and rent arrears, from which many could never escape, even after their benefits kicked in. Landlords started to refuse to let property to UC claimants.

UC did bring some families more money, but the gains were outweighed by the obstacles and errors it threw up. The Resolution Foundation estimated that while 2.2 million working families would eventually be better off, thanks to an average increase of £41 a week, 3.2 million would be worse off, with an average loss of £48 a week. The NAO's conclusion was damning: 'The project is not value for money now and its future value for money is unproven.' Duncan Smith's successors tried to keep the show on the road, but in February 2019 Amber Rudd was forced to admit that its introduction had impoverished families, to the point where many had no choice but to resort to food banks. Amid the confetti of promises in the 2019 election, however, Tory commitments to ameliorate, let alone rescind, UC were noticeably absent.

After a long wait and many requests, in 2019 we were allowed into a job centre in Middlesbrough. It was eerie, like visiting Seahaven in *The Truman Show*, where all the staff were happy, workloads easy, sanctions 'very, very rare' and claimant queries were answered within an hour. Staff denied that there had ever been targets for throwing people off benefit. A test question: what did they think of the wider situation in Middlesbrough, where the council has been hit hard? 'I've not noticed we've got a lack of anything round here.'

We checked back with our uncensored informant. In his job centre, it was 'panic', with caseloads of over 400, everyone flat-out on backlogs of payments that had left people stranded. The Middlesbrough office was fabricated to please the Whitehall minder we had in tow. Experts had warned loudly about the UC disaster, but there was not a word from the senior civil servants. Why, time and again, did permanent secretaries never say 'No, minister' to impossible demands and preposterous reorganisations? Why were they so willing to conflate the short-term, partisan interests of their ministers and their party with the wider, long-term interests of the public and the state – to which they surely had some obligation? Senior civil servants connived with ministers to mislead the public and bypass parliament. The Rolls-Royce mandarins of the Great British System had either been suborned or, in the culmination of a process started with Thatcher, lost sight of the vocation they once had: to serve the state, something much bigger than here-today-gone-tomorrow politicians. They took their knighthoods and left chaos and social inequity behind.

Unequal Shares

Income inequality did not change much, which may be surprising given both austerity and boardroom excess. But while most incomes fell or flatlined, in an odd balancing act those at the top took a hit from the lingering effects of the crash, while benefit freezes and restraints only took their full effect later, preserving the incomes of the poorest for a while. The Gini coefficient measuring income inequality may pick this up later. But already, within the top category of income earners, a gap had opened between the super-rich and the affluent also-rans, and it grew. Inequality in wealth – as far as can be accurately gauged – increased.

Nearly two-thirds of the UK's highest-paid people were in the capital or the nearby south-east, where some 205,000 people were paid more than £150,000 a year – two-thirds of all those earning this much in the whole of the UK. Together Westminster and the borough of Kensington and Chelsea were home to 12,000 people in this income category, amounting to one in twelve residents of the latter borough, who, of course, included those in Grenfell Tower. Some 9,370 people were worth at least £23 million each, which in 2019 was 9 per cent up on the previous year.

Nigel Green, the founder and owner of the deVere Group, is 'high net worth', the euphemism for being exceedingly rich. His wealth-management firm looks after the investments of 100,000 clients, mostly British expats, advising them on the tax-efficient zones in which to park their money. His firm has 1,500 employees in fifty countries, from Switzerland to Botswana, China and Luxembourg to South Africa. His base is in Dubai, which is where he was when we spoke to him, but he lived, he said, mainly on planes.

'It's been very good for the markets: low interest rates, low inflation and, yes, quantitative easing as well.' QE had dramatic redistributive effects, as we saw, and inflated the value of assets. 'Clients' accounts have done very well.' Green had few worries about protectionism or nationalisation or clamping down on tax havens: 'You can't fight globalism. It won't stop.' Brexit was an error, but Johnson at the helm meant less tax: 'People need encouragement. Entrepreneurs need to be motivated.'

At sixty, his own peripatetic life offered few chances to spend the £500,000 he took out of the business each year. 'I have a nice house in Dubai, but I'm not often there.' His daughter dealt in property in London, but his son had joined the business. 'But I'm not giving up for another thirty years!' Pleasures? He sometimes flew to top football matches and Formula 1 races, otherwise he had no hobbies. Was he a philanthropist, doing good works, which has often been a justification for high earners? 'Not really. I have run marathons for charity in the past.'

His clients were avoiding paying the taxes their countries surely needed. 'As long as you stay within the law, it's up to governments to set the rules. If they allow you to make tax-efficient plans, it's for them to change the rules, if they want. Most would say income tax and inheritance tax [in the UK] are far too high. We can see *there is still huge waste – look at the NHS. People's tax money does not get well spent. Where does it all go?' Austerity? 'It hasn't gone far enough.'*

Social Immobility

You didn't hear such bloodthirsty language from government ministers, not in public anyway. Instead, there was Theresa May on the steps of Number 10 (and neither Cameron nor Johnson would say any different): 'When it comes to opportunity we won't entrench the advantages of the fortunate few. We will do everything we can to help anybody, whatever your background, to go as far as your talents will take you.' Did that imply, against the odds, the Tories were worried about *inequality*, a word that enjoyed a puzzling frequency of use in the vocabulary of the 2010s?

'Social mobility' was the preferred euphemism. Cameron rebranded a Labour quango the Social Mobility and Child Poverty Commission, before in 2016 abandoning all official mention of child poverty. A year later, its chair, ex-Labour minister Alan Milburn, resigned – along with the other commissioners, including former Tory education secretary Gillian Shephard – saying the government was sending social mobility into reverse. Milburn's resignation letter savaged austerity and failed economic policy, saying they were leading to 'more anger, more resentment and [creating] a breeding ground for populism'. Owning wealth had become more influential: the child of a homeowner was three times more likely to own their own home than the child of a non-property owner when they grew up. In the 1990s that had been only twice as likely.

The public conversation was surreal. At the moment members of the Bullingdon Club cemented their hold on Downing Street, reports highlighted how few people from working-class backgrounds there were in the arts, theatre, music, law, journalism or finance. Children from professional backgrounds were 80 per cent more likely to go into professional jobs. Older artists and performers from working-class backgrounds who had sailed through arts and drama courses for free a generation back warned that future Hamlets would all be Harrovians. The OECD reported that in the UK, the floor was less 'sticky' than in other countries, meaning children from poorer backgrounds could advance. But only so far: the ceiling was particularly sticky, meaning incumbents wouldn't give up without a fight. The number of partnerships in top law firms, entry-level jobs in investment banking, openings at Opera North were inherently limited. Only 4 per cent of the undergraduate intake at Cambridge came from the poorest backgrounds, and 60 per cent of Oxford's came from private schools.

When Tory ministers talked about mobility, they always meant up, though without downwards mobility slots would not open up. Two in five UK bankers had parents who also worked in the sector. In insurance, more than half the staff followed their parents. Only if the privately (and grammar-school) educated made way would working-class children become mobile. That was not what MPs, ministers or the *Daily Telegraph* had in mind. No, the rhetoric was only about rising, which conveniently elided with the attack on welfare, pitting aspirers against the static skivers.

The evidence showed that more equal countries had more mobility, and moving people up the scales of income and occupation necessarily involved redistributing money and opportunity from haves to have-nots. Umpteen reports found an eleven-month gap in attainment at the age of five between children growing up in poverty and their peers (which grew as children advanced through school). 'More was to be done' to close the gap, said education secretary Damian Hinds in 2018. But it suited him – and many commentators – to load the obligation on schools. The principal cause of the difference in life outcomes was poverty at home. By the age of four or five it may already be too late to change most children's life chances. Lee Elliot Major and Stephen Machin's book *Social Mobility and Its Enemies* described an education arms race, as platoons of private tutors, paid for by sharp-elbowed parents, helped some state-educated children secure the best exam results and get the grammar-school places.

In response to this criticism, the May government devised 'opportunity areas'. Being charitable, you could say the initiative was well intentioned. For example, eight poorer wards in Derby received a share of a £845,000 project to 'encourage parents to talk to their children', including training and support for childminders, children's centres and nurseries. This was Elastoplast on a suppurating wound: the principal budget streams for schools and children's centres had been cut and nothing was being done to restore them. The opportunity areas were marked out exactly where councils had most damaged young people's life chances.

Generation Games

Possessors and the privileged fight tooth and nail to protect their own. One battlefield is age. To be older was now (on average) to be better off. Once, to be old was usually to be poor; now, only one in six older people fell below the poverty line – those with no private pensions or property. The division was apparent in voting, and in the 2017 election, the gap between old and young voters was fifty points bigger than the post-war average. Differences were growing, with just 14 per cent of under-twenty-fours voting Tory and 62 per cent choosing Labour. On the material front, policies adopted since 2010 had helped older homeowners, including quantitative easing (as Nigel Green of deVere pointed out), as well as restrictions on building and benefits, though many hated their benefits being called the same as those going to people of working age.

In 2011 the state pension payable at sixty-five (rising to sixty-six in 2020) was triple-locked: it would rise by 2.5 per cent a year, by the current inflation rate or by the annual increase in average earnings, whichever was the highest. Within five years, that delivered an increase in value of 22.2 per cent. The UK now spent 6.2 per cent of GDP on state pensions, but only 4 per cent of GDP on benefits for people of working age. The old tended to be homeowners: three-quarters of them. Only a quarter of those aged under thirty-five owned their homes.

House prices rose fast, at least until Brexit: the average price of a home was £155,000 in 2009 and £230,000 by 2019, far beyond the reach of many young families, who were destined to rent like Emma and Rob Percy in Kent. During a background war of words about the fair treatment of different generations, the Tory ex-minister David Willetts led the charge with his book *The Pinch*. Baby-boomers appeared to have had it all – free public services, free universities, a flourishing public realm. Now the young saw all this taken away, university fees leaving them in debt, jobs plentiful but low-paid, no chance of buying a home, public services dwindling before their eyes. If the young are, perennially, the hope for the future, why in austere times did public policy so favour the retired?

Capitalising on perceived affluence among the elderly, the coalition announced their liberation. From 2015 pension pots were set free; they no longer had to be used to buy annuities that guaranteed a stream of income. Retirees could draw money out of their pensions to spend on anything they liked, even – chortled the Liberal Democrat pensions minister, Steve Webb – a Lamborghini. Webb, who once worked at the IFS, had been regarded as an expert. Now he was gripped by the spirit of the age and its model of economic ultra-rationality, and he failed to see that many pensioners would, underestimating their own longevity, abandon safe company schemes to get hold of a lump sum, ruining their future prospects. Pension schemes saw huge withdrawals, and only later did the Financial Conduct Authority, a typically weakened regulator, try to catch up with the financial finaglers using high-pressure tactics to sell bad investments. The consequences will take some time to become apparent.

So it was not all plain sailing for the old. John Major's government had equalised the state pension age for men and women in the 1995 Pensions Act, to be phased in. Labour raised the retirement age. Cameron speeded things up, leaving many women in their fifties and sixties hard done by, some having to work much longer than they had planned or felt able to. A major pensions reform enacted under Labour came in during 2012, auto-enrolling all employees for the first time into pension schemes. People were free to opt out, but few did, and as a result 10 million people earning over £10,000 now had the prospect of a pension for the first time. Since earnings were still low, only a fifth of them were estimated to be saving enough to pay for a decent level of income in retirement, but take-up of the scheme, branded NEST, was impressive.

Betrayal of Childhood

A pervading sense of social bonds fraying was fed by what happened at the other end of the age range. Children were receiving less; they were paying the price of austerity. By 2020 total spending, including education and benefits, was £10,000 per child, over 10 per cent lower than the £11,300 spent in 2010. On the ground, those figures meant, for example, play parks shutting. 'We have the least physically active generation of children ever and our focus should be encouraging children to play out, not play less,' said the children's commissioner, Anne Longfield, looking more and more forlorn. Play that was once free might now cost £18 a child – the charge levied by the company Go Ape, which took over the open access adventure playground in Battersea Park at the instigation of the Tory Wandsworth Council. 'We're seeing a lot of parks looking at introducing facilities that generate income,' said Drew Bennellick of the Heritage Lottery Fund. 'Whether it's crazy golf sites, multi-use football facilities that are floodlit, or cafés – they're all exploring ways to potentially generate income to offset the cost of running the sites.'

Some social indicators showed stability. Referrals of children deemed to need protection by the state rose only in line with population growth, by 7 per cent, but the number being looked after rose to 75,400, a rate that was triple the growth in the number of children in the population. This followed growing holes in the safety nets supporting families on the edge, fewer social workers, school nurses and health visitors, all overburdened with enormous caseloads. Child protection assessments rose dramatically, by 77 per cent – perhaps because social workers under pressure were more cautious. More children aged over sixteen were taken into care, and because they were often the hardest to place in foster homes, the use of costly residential care rose. Reasons included domestic abuse, addictions and mental health problems among parents. The cost of residential care rose by nearly a quarter, and two-thirds of councils had insufficient places; Ofsted rated more than half the councils as inadequate or needing improvement.

We saw before that under austerity, local authorities focused on their minimum, statutory duties, and so they cut prevention,

Sure Start and children's centres disproportionately. The official data could be deceptive, and councils covered their backs. Cumbria County Council was keen to say that by 2019 it still had the same number of Sure Start centres as in 2010, but their opening hours had been reduced. They were swung away from a family to a welfare service, targeted on the neediest. The story from Norfolk – Tory-controlled, like Cumbria – was that closing thirty-eight of its fifty-three children's centres would allow it to 'target' families.

Children and young people faded from public view. In 2017 the Royal College of Paediatrics and Child Health complained about lack of progress on smoking in pregnancy, infant mortality, breastfeeding and childhood obesity. Paediatrician Al Aynsley-Green, a former children's commissioner, wrote *The British Betrayal of Childhood* in response to the neglect of children's interests in policy-making. In it, he cited exam stress – the product of Tory schools policy – and less cash support for families with children.

Young people's mental health had long been a blind spot in the NHS, where children were offered far less help than adults, with shamefully long queues for treatment. Acutely mentally ill children were sent to beds hundreds of miles from home. Theresa May called this a 'burning injustice', promising school support and reduced NHS waiting times in her 2017 Green Paper. Mental health services could only deal with an estimated 25 per cent of those needing help; the modest goal was 33 per cent by 2021. But even that ambition was submerged in the overall gap between need and NHS spending. It wasn't just health money either: better family services were needed, along with action on domestic abuse. The 'narrow focus misses the opportunity', said the King's Fund.

With childcare, critical to the well-being and productive potential of so many mothers and families, the line was contradictory. Ministers simultaneously cut councils' capacity to provide care and nursery education (and regulate what was provided), while increasing subsidies to parents to pay for (mostly private) care. An initial promise was a voucher to meet the cost of thirty hours a week of nursery care for three- and four-year-olds, plus disadvantaged two-year-olds. Until then, the entitlement inherited from Labour had been fifteen hours. But vouchers were withheld from jobless parents, even though many who wanted to return to work or take up training needed first to arrange (and afford) childcare.

This was social policy on the cheap. No money accompanied the pledge to support the nurseries themselves, which were mostly privately run; the voucher money per hour did not meet rising costs, so nurseries tried to duck the obligation to provide free hours, added extra charges or closed. Parents, especially in the poorest areas, couldn't find places. The Early Intervention Foundation reported that disadvantaged children remained well behind the better-off in their age cohorts, and MPs concluded the childcare offer failed to benefit those who needed it most.

Homelessness Returns

Social difference, division and distinction are most visible in our homes – if we have them. The proportion of under-thirty-fours who had failed to flee the nest and were now living in their parents' homes rose from a quarter to a third. Younger people were starting their families later. The old escalator that was to sweep everyone into property ownership had broken down. Private renters could see just how badly their prospects of owning their own homes had been blighted.

Even the extreme austerians were embarrassed at the physical manifestation of housing need, in the shape of the homeless people tumbling back onto the streets. Bundles of humanity sleeping on the Strand had been an inconvenient emblem of Thatcher's Britain: one of her ministers complained about having to step over them coming out of the Royal Opera. Now here they were again, not just in central London, but under pedestrian passageways in Aylesbury and Milton Keynes, as well as the big cities.

The government prevaricated, denying that the growth of homelessness had been caused by its welfare policies, then telling councils to sort it out while both restricting housebuilding and denying any extra support. 'We will abolish rough sleeping,' the government promised – but not till 2027. Council spending on single homeless people fell by £1 billion, or more than half, leaving signs of brute need everywhere. The death toll among the homeless – 597 in England and Wales in 2017 – was up 24 per cent in four years. Manchester had nearly 1,500 families in temporary accommodation in 2019, up from 150 at the start of the decade. Councils responded with imaginative schemes. But Oxford City Council was now spending 10 per cent of its entire budget on the homeless. One set of ministers in the communities department enjoined councils to cut homelessness, while at the same time those in the Treasury and the DWP helped push it up. None of this laid a single brick, pointed out Simon Bowkett of the charity CoLab Exeter, ruefully.

The stock of affordable dwellings was falling. Homes available for social renting dropped by 166,000 from 2012 to 2016, the Chartered Institute of Housing reported, as dwellings were sold under the right to buy and not replaced; a further 370,000 dwellings were predicted to go by 2020. Social renting from councils and non-profit housing groups had fallen from 30 per cent of tenures to 17 per cent. The government gave up on anything resembling coherent policy. Entire town centres were given over to students in places such as Durham, affecting locals, their children and the commercial ecology. Bristol mayor Marvin Rees deplored the exemption universities enjoyed from paying local business rates and the boom in council tax-exempt student flats that cut his income. Asylum-seekers were dispersed to the cheapest places by private companies on Home Office contracts. The result was migrants and ethnic minorities clustered together, the councils disempowered and not even informed when large numbers moved into the area, too weak to prevent over-concentration and ghettos.

The old Tory dream died as home ownership fell as a proportion of all tenures, down to 64 per cent in England. For homeowners *in situ*, low interest rates were good news. For households with a mortgage, the proportion spending at least a quarter of their disposable income on housing costs halved. But rising property values pushed up rents for those who couldn't get on the fabled stairway. In London, private rents increased 32 per cent in the ten years to 2016, when average earnings rose by only 16 per cent.

In a council house at an affordable rent, Emma and Rob Percy would have lived well. Their experience exposed the fiction of a ladder open to all. Children of well-off parents could always be given a leg up. The others, unable to afford deposits, had to make do with private renting, which rose to 20 per cent of all tenures. The number of families with young children renting privately tripled in the ten years to 2016. One in five newborns lived in a privately rented home; that used to be a rarity – only one in fourteen in 1996. The proportion of those aged thirty-five to forty-four in private rental accommodation was 13 per cent when the financial crash began; by 2018 it was 41 per cent.

In the face of this historic shift, housing initiatives arrived thick, fast, panicky and skewed towards the housing haves. Overall supply had fallen way short. From 1990 the population had grown by 17 per cent, but the number of households by 32 per cent. From 2010, 227,000 new households were being formed each year in England, which established the baseline. Only 144,000 new dwellings had been completed each year between 2000 and 2010; the average figure for the 2010s was higher, at around 190,000. Better, but still an annual deficit of 37,000.

Bribing Builders

The government craved banner headlines. Overlapping initiatives tried to bribe developers and encourage would-be owners. The Home Building Fund (£3 billion) and the Shared Ownership and Affordable Homes Programme (£9 billion) were meant to encourage the supply of slightly lower-cost dwellings. Confidence was recovering by 2015, and building expanded. Adding in conversions – there was a mini-boom in turning office space into flats – by 2018 the annual housebuilding totals were back to where they had been on the eve of the crash, and from 2007 the stock of homes increased by 8.5 per cent.

Much of this commercial construction would have taken place anyway – housebuilding was a profitable business – so the cash handouts went straight into the developers' pockets. Subsidy was crack cocaine, someone said, because the instant effect of sweeteners to buy homes was to push up prices, which fuelled an orgy. Help to Buy (£10 billion) gave loans of up to 20 per cent of a property's value (40 per cent in London), with sufficiently loose conditions to ensure that applicants often had incomes well above the median. They were allowed to buy homes valued up to £600,000, and many were not even first-time buyers but upgraders. It was an 'impressive example of economic illiteracy', as Neil Collins put it in the *Financial Times*. The good times lasted until Brexit fears and uncertainty hit developers' share prices in 2018 and 2019.

The benefit restrictions described earlier hit housing association balance sheets and stopped them raising capital in order to build on the security of their rental income, thwarting the government's own declared aim. The Local Government Association pointed out something obvious: had councils been allowed to build, fewer people would have ended up in high-cost rental accommodation, thus reducing the housing benefit bill. Labour had similarly discouraged council building, favouring housing associations. Encouraging both local authorities and non-profit landlords to build would have been cost-effective, their borrowing costs in an era of low interest rates dwarfed by the high cost of the state subsidising private rents. That's the perpetual trade-off: subsidise the building of social housing or end up subsidising private landlords at higher cost, with nothing to show for it. Tory ministers chose the latter.

For the purposes of grants and permissions from the government for housing associations and councils, 'affordable' used to mean rents that low-income families could pay; now it meant as much as 80 per cent of market rents, unaffordable for the likes of Emma and Rob. The government's focus shifted up the income scale (towards their own voters and their children). To identify land for private developers to exploit, a New Homes Bonus was dangled over town halls. It had marginal effect. The government fixated on supply, not daring to confront the demand-side fact that prices were too high. It ordered public land to be released; the NAO found that little usable land was.

To secure more genuinely affordable dwellings for rent would have meant abandoning the flagship Thatcher policy of selling off council homes at a high discount. Instead, right to buy was strengthened. In 2012 discounts were increased, and in 2016 powers were taken to force housing associations to sell cheaply to their tenants. Once council tenants bought their homes, many resold for a high profit; the new buyers filled them with students or transients at higher rents, upsetting previously stable communities of long-term residents. In London, 40 per cent of dwellings sold under right to buy had found their way back into the rental market, under private landlords this time, so councils were paying far higher rents to house homeless people. Leicester's stock of 38,000 council dwellings had fallen to 21,000 through the enforced sales; now there were 6,000 people on the city's waiting list for a council tenancy. The only homes the council could afford to build were for private sale. Sir Peter Soulsby, the city's Labour leader, said, 'At the very least right to buy ought to be suspended in cities like Leicester until we have dealt with the housing crisis.'

Councils showed enterprise by creating arm's-length companies that were able to borrow outside the usual restrictions. Eventually, the meagre numbers – only 1,900 new council dwellings completed in 2015–16 – proved unacceptable even to ministers. Their next move wasn't so much a U-turn as a grudging acceptance that councils were irreplaceable as builders; sotto voce, ministers told councils they could borrow more, and the pace of construction quickened. But what they were building were – that word again – ghettos. Once, housing estates were places for people in work; now, in London, 68 per cent of those in social renting had no jobs, because only the most disadvantaged qualified for the diminishing number of properties – the old, disabled or out of work.

We have followed the fate of the Clapham Park estate, once designated the worst in Lambeth, since it was first chosen in 2000 under the Labour New Deal for Communities (NDC), which granted residents £56 million to try to improve the quality of their lives. We went back to see what was left of the great endeavour.

The news was mixed. Donna Charmayne Henry was still there, chairing the legacy charity that struggles on as the last remnant of the NDC. Born in St Kitts, brought up in Oldham, and working as an optometrist's administrator, she has lived on the estate since 1975, bringing up her son there. At first, she was amazed to find herself pulled into community organisation; now, she is the stalwart. At the NDC's height, as well as drawing up a mighty masterplan and holding votes to get it agreed, volunteers were given training in reading spreadsheets and in organisational skills. 'Those skills have stayed on the estate with people who were involved back then,' Donna says. With the projects gone, most are no longer involved. 'But it left them different people, better able to know how things work. It changed a lot of lives.' The masterplan was abandoned and the estate handed to a housing association. Since then, managers have come and gone, and the origins of the programme are almost obliterated. An estate like this has a high churn rate, and around 40 per cent of residents have moved away. Those moving in are often in the direst need: the disabled, the sick, non-English-speaking new refugees and the very poorest – new residents who know nothing of the scheme that was.

New, good-looking blocks have been built, but the worst of the 1930s blocks, which had been scheduled for demolition in the noughties, still stand. A parade of shops with a popular pub was closed and left derelict. Redevelopment is due to increase the 2,000 homes to 3,780, but all the new ones will be private or under shared ownership. The developer's hoardings promise 'a global village green', which makes Donna smile wryly.

The charity has kept going against the odds, teaching young people mechanical skills, the police giving them unclaimed stolen bikes to strip down, renovate and keep. It runs coffee mornings for the lonely, a lunch club for the elderly, support for community enterprises, support for volunteer gardeners in the small park and an advice centre, funds scraped up from any grant-maker they can find.

As for the outcome of the NDC's original aims – a healthier, better-educated, safer community – no one now collects data. Donna's impression was the best evidence, as she walked us around the place. Before the NDC, there were crack houses, drug dealers at every bus stop and prostitutes all down one street, and people were afraid to go out at night. All that was cleaned up when the NDC hired neighbourhood wardens to patrol the estate. Though the wardens are long gone, it's still orderly. 'I think people feel safe,' says Donna. 'It's one of the safer estates now.' Clapham Park is not the place dreamt of in the masterplan, but it is a better place. What was learnt was that regeneration demands unrelenting effort, stop–go is wasteful and volunteering depends on funds and council services, and they disappeared. After 2010 the government showed scant interest in improving such estates, beyond selling off their precious housing.

No Solidarity for Minorities

One event crystallised the way housing expressed social difference. After seventy-two people were killed in the fire at Grenfell Tower, the charred stump stood for months as a reminder of what had happened to social housing, before it was wrapped in plastic and reconfiguration began. The Royal Borough of Kensington and Chelsea, Tory since its birth, had turned its back on the poorer areas, consigning management of the block to an arm's-length organisation, its physical state neglected; tenancies had become a lottery. While Grenfell showed the importance of local factors – including the resourcefulness and spirit of tenants and community groups – it also pointed to systemic deficits, including the physical state and safety of the rented housing stock.

Grenfell provoked awareness of how social differentiation by tenure overlapped with class and race. Consciousness of racism sharpened, both main parties embarrassed by allegations (and evidence) of discrimination in their own ranks. The former Tory chair Baroness Warsi delivered a stinging attack on her own party for failing to evict activists and councillors who had made racist comments or online postings. Labour's turmoil over anti-Semitism damaged a party that had always claimed moral superiority. The Community Security Trust, recording attacks on the Jewish community, reported 1,652 anti-Semitic incidents in 2018, a 16 per cent rise on the year before and the highest total since it began collecting data in 1984, with attacks on synagogues and desecrations of Jewish cemeteries.

Striving for a positive symbol in the midst of Brexit, Johnson proclaimed the ethnic diversity of his Cabinet. But the year before, the UN's special rapporteur, Tendayi Achiume, alleged that austerity and immigration policies had made the UK more racist. She cited the 'hostile environment' policy against immigrants adopted by Theresa May when she was home secretary, saying, 'The structural socioeconomic exclusion of racial and ethnic minority communities in the United Kingdom is striking.'

Reports of child abuse and the involvement of Asian men in grooming young girls caused widespread consternation, becoming a weapon in the battles around migration. The Home Office's own log of hate crime in England and Wales showed an upward trend, driven partly by better police recording of incidents. Brexit was a clear cause: an Opinium survey in 2019 found the proportion of people from ethnic minority backgrounds saying they had been targeted by a stranger was increasing, from 64 per cent in 2016 to 76 per cent. A study by Daniel Devine of Southampton University found a 'sudden increase in hate crime coming soon after the referendum and lasting for some time before declining back to pre-referendum levels . . . Hate crimes increased again following a spate of terror attacks within two months of each other: Finsbury Park mosque, London Bridge, Westminster and Manchester. Again, even following this, hate crimes decline soon after.' Media coverage – including social media – amplified incidents and alerted copycats.

Commissioned by the government to review social cohesion, Louise Casey confirmed that socioeconomic inequality cross-hatched but remained a driver separate from racial discrimination. Black boys were still not getting jobs, but white children from low-income homes were still doing badly in education; Muslim girls were getting better grades but lacked decent employment opportunities. She found England marked by the absence of solidarity, with groups, sometimes entire places isolated. She criticised not just government inaction, but also cultural and religious practices in some communities 'that are not only holding some of our citizens back but run contrary to British values and sometimes our laws. Time and time again I found it was women and children who were the targets of these regressive practices.'

While segregation had reduced over the population as a whole, ethnic concentration had grown in certain towns. There, residential areas, schools and workplaces were more seg-regated. Figures from 2015 showed 511 schools across forty-three local authority areas where at least half the pupils came from Pakistani and Bangladeshi ethnic backgrounds. 'That is driving more prejudice, intolerance, mistrust in communities,' Casey said. Culture clashes over schooling in mainly Muslim areas erupted from time to time, parents objecting to sex and relationship syllabuses that had been approved by inspectors and were widely used in other schools.

A year after her report, Casey attacked the government's fail-ure to carry forward the simple recommendation of free, easy access to English-language teaching, especially for ethnically isolated women. Worse, the government moved in the oppo-site direction by encouraging an increase in religious schools, for the first time allowing them to select 100 per cent of pupils by their religion. The suspicion was that this was a political manoeuvre to try to win over ethnic voters who traditionally leaned heavily towards Labour.

Casey also recommended that the government assert, propagate and teach 'British values', echoing recommendations going back to Gordon Brown and beyond. The trouble was, anything 'British' rested implicitly on solving the great problem of who we are. What if we can define ourselves only against others – Muslims, gays, Europeans? Councillor Peter Mitchell, of the Big Help Project in Knowsley, told us a depressing tale about collecting donations at supermarkets. Things had changed. 'I get people asking, "Is this food for British people?"' This was new. He sighed heavily. 'Brexit did this. It gives permission. I say to them, "This food is for hungry people."'

5

Not Feeling Very Well, Doctor

Nick Hulme, chief executive of Ipswich Hospital, had no idea why the ward sister had asked for the meeting. Jenny was one of his best, brightest, liveliest and most dedicated senior nurses. Promoted to run the difficult chemotherapy ward, she had turned it around within a few months. The ward cared for seriously ill people who were feeling at their worst; the deaths of patients whom staff had grown to know well exacted a heavy emotional toll.

She sat down, took a deep breath and told him, 'I've handed in my notice. I just can't keep going.' Hulme looked aghast. 'I can't switch off, and it's affecting my children. I love my job, every minute of it, and I know it's my fault, but Sunday night was the last straw. I was called three times in the night, and when I woke up in the morning I had so many missed calls.'

'But they shouldn't be calling you at night,' he said. She agreed, 'but they panic and I'm their security blanket. I've tried weaning them off calling me, but we're so short of staff, and there's not enough of them with the right experience.' He begged, beseeched, cajoled and promised to move her elsewhere, even to create a special role for her to oversee the improvement of other wards. He reminded her how she had taken over a chaotic ward and how it had sprung to life under her care, but she wouldn't budge: the strain of doing the job well and getting home to her young children

was overwhelming, with a husband who worked long hours, too. She would join the nursing bank to work occasional shifts – but her leaving would add to the estimated 41,000 nurse vacancies (one in eight of all posts) officially acknowledged by NHS leaders in 2018. Her team cried when she told them she was going.

Jenny's is the story of the NHS: one of dedication and enthusiasm crushed by the pressure of demand, patients, stress from targets and inspections, too few recruits and too many exits. Something went drastically awry with planning, training and recruitment, because all the numbers were foreseeable, including the spike in GPs reaching retirement age. The same ministers who talked social mobility abolished the student nurse bursary and jeopardised a tried and trusted upwards route, particularly for young women from poorer backgrounds.

Jenny had been one such woman, leaving school with few qualifications. 'I come from a very rough area. No one in my family did well. That's what made me so proud to reach where I am.' She took a humble job as a healthcare assistant. 'And I loved it straight away. It was for me. I was just so proud of my uniform, of my silver buckle. I was seventeen, and I've loved everything about this hospital from the start, and I worked hard to get my qualifications. Look at me now, a ward sister, but I'm thirty-two and I can't handle it any more. I'm heartbroken to be going.'

Hulme himself had also risen up the ranks. He, too, exemplified the depths of commitment that kept the NHS going despite the machinations of ministers, baffling bureaucracy and straitened finance. (Not long before, Hulme had fulfilled a pledge to his late wife by doing a coast-to-coast walk across England to raise funds for a hospice and specialist unit.) He had started out pushing gurneys along hospital corridors, before working his way up the management ladder, studying for an MBA in the evenings, and now ran not just Ipswich, but Colchester Hospital as well, only recently out of the 'special measures' into which it had plunged.

We might have gone anywhere and found the same pluses and minuses. The NHS's assets are its people, caring and compassionate, with a cool command of permanently constrained resources. Perhaps, in 2020, the great thing was that despite austerity, despite ideology, despite catastrophic reorganisation imposed by dilettantes in Downing Street, the NHS was still there, still saving lives, offering us the subliminal security of knowing that its free care and treatment covered our backs because they were allocated according to need. This chapter could just as well be called 'Solidarity' or 'Security'; people only had to glance across the Atlantic to see the bankruptcies and anguish caused by privatised medicine, which the Obama reforms – under fierce attack by Donald Trump – had yet to mitigate.

The NHS defeated the Tories – and not just because the first thing opportunists such as Boris Johnson felt they had to do was offer more money (deceitfully). It survived as a concept and social promise, having more or less successfully defended itself against the assault foretold in countless think-tank papers, private seminars and conference fringe meetings. In 2012 the same year as David Cameron's explosive Health and Social Care Act, millions roared approval at Danny Boyle's emotional evocation of the NHS at the London Olympics. An embarrassed Number 10 had to slap down the backbench MP who inveighed against 'the most leftie opening ceremony'. Gut Tory instincts crashed against a rock of public resistance.

The Cost of Care

The NHS had been boosted mightily between 2000 and 2010, when annual spending, adjusted for inflation, increased each year by nearly 6 per cent. Apparently anxious to keep up, Cameron said, 'I will cut the deficit, not the NHS.' But amid claims that his government was increasing spending, funding fell back sharply, to a historically low increase of less than 1 per cent a year. The NHS got *cash* increases, but they amounted to a cut, because the population grew and the number of over-seventy-fives increased by half a million. Not all the elderly get sick, but in 2016 there were over 1.6 million emergency admissions for people in the last year of their life, costing £2.5 billion and amounting to around 11 million days in hospital. Leave aside the extra that would have been needed to keep pace with technology, higher pharmaceutical prices or the diversion of public NHS money to banks and financiers through PFI; each year's increment had to be big enough to match the extra babies, children, adults and older people needing GP appointments, care plans and beds.

The NHS got progressively more stretched and strained. GP appointments became scarce; waiting lists ballooned; definitions of 'non-urgent' became more elastic. In July 2019 one in seven attending A&E had to wait more than four hours after arrival before they were admitted or discharged, and that month there were 2.2 million attendances, the highest ever recorded. Under acute pressure, the NHS again started making the nightly news, with hair-raising footage of ambulances queuing, emergency departments failing to cope, staff run off their feet, trolleys in corridors and, sometimes, people dying as they waited for admission. 'We concluded that financial problems in the NHS were endemic and that extra in-year cash injections to trusts had been spent on coping with current pressures rather than the transformation required to put the health system on a sustainable footing,' said the NAO.

Worried, the Tories had started making extravagant promises, which continued when Johnson succeeded Theresa May. In 2018 she had tried to exploit the seventieth anniversary of the NHS's foundation to shore up her parlous position, trying to link an upwards adjustment to the budget with the notorious Brexiter claim of a 'bonus' for the NHS. The NHS was to get £20 billion over four years, starting in 2020, but this was only 'extra' in relation to inadequate prior spending plans and was calculated to garner supportive headlines. The settlement offered a 3.4 per cent increase per year, inflation-proofed. But that and Johnson's subsequent promised increase still came in below the long-term minimum of 4 per cent the NHS needed, and did nothing to meet accruing debt. Nor did it cover the rescue of dilapidated buildings and out-of-date equipment, or of public health; nor securing the doctors, nurses and other staff to fill 2019's total of 100,000 vacancies. The NAO's admonitory verdict was that without addressing the backlog of maintenance and capital spending, the NHS would not be able to fulfil the long-term plan. The auditors added that raiding capital budgets had stored up trouble for the 2020s, as hospitals fell into disrepair and the new clinics and wards needed in areas where the population was growing were deferred or cancelled. The NHS remained the unproud owner of more fax machines than any other organisation in the world. No one else had such antiquated systems.

Public Health

The NHS isn't all of *health*. Could the UK have got better, whatever was happening to a service concerned with disease and accidents? You can't simply compare 2020 with 2010 and subtract. Our sense of what makes us both well and ill was changing. Latent problems waded into focus, among them air pollution from vehicle emissions; a new problem, for which certain newspapers and US-financed campaigners bore heavy responsibility, was more parents refusing to have their children vaccinated. The World Health Organization scrubbed the UK's measles-free status following several hundred confirmed cases in the first quarter of 2019. Ministers wrung their hands, hiding behind the health professionals. They might have noted that spending in England on measures to prevent ill health was £49 per head, compared to £1,742 on the NHS after they were ill. They might also have owned up to the consequences of transferring responsibility for public health in England to councils, with the result that it suffered disproportionately as they cut back. The British Medical Association found public health budgets diminished by nearly 10 per cent.

Good health depends on policies and attitudes spread across many Cabinet portfolios, the common element a predisposition to intervene, challenge individual behaviour and deploy collective resources – not one usually shared by marketeers, ideologues and sneerers at the 'nanny state'. Pulled one way by their public responsibilities and the other by their instincts, Tory ministers dithered. A grudging acceptance of the need to tax sugar was followed by Johnson's nods and winks to the industry that he would abolish the levy. Their response to new problems was generally half-hearted: for example, on pollution, the cause of 40,000 premature deaths a year in the UK. 'This is a health crisis,' said Sarah MacFadyen of the British Lung Foundation, after the NAO discovered that the UK was not going to meet EU air-quality targets before 2021 and a *Lancet* study found that one in five new childhood asthma cases each year were attributable to nitrogen dioxide pollution, a figure that was higher in cities such as Manchester. In February 2017 a coalition of charities and medical organisations called for a new clean-air act, arguing that air pollution cost the UK economy £20 billion a year. As environment secretary, Michael Gove said the UK had failed to live up to its obligations to improve air quality. He did not mention who had been in power for the previous eight years. Action was piecemeal.

Awareness of mental health was growing; people – including the royals – were readier to acknowledge both their own and their loved ones' depression, anxiety and other such conditions. The need was out there: prescriptions for anti-depressants doubled after 2008. Surveyed in 2019, nine out of ten mental health trusts in England said demand had risen, linking it to benefit changes, loneliness, homelessness and fewer council services. Labour had launched a scheme called Improving Access to Psychological Therapies, and the number given counselling for depression and anxiety under its auspices grew to 1.4 million by 2017, but waiting times were also rising. The plight of young people provoked anxiety. A fifth of seventeen- to nineteen-year-old girls were found to have self-harmed or attempted suicide. From 2016 a commitment to speedier treatment of those experiencing psychosis was introduced, and it was broadly met for a year, before performance started slipping – the promised funding having failed to materialise in many trusts. One study showed average mental health trust investment in community teams decreased by 20 per cent from 2012–13 to 2016–17. Whatever extra had been allocated out of constrained totals by central government, it rarely arrived in the promised amounts locally, often being siphoned off to keep sinking hospitals afloat.

In their 2010 manifesto, the Tories had promised extra health visitors. Numbers did rise, but a national target was not renewed after the 2015 election, and they fell back. Workloads rose, with some health visitors having to look after between 500 and 1,000 children. Little wonder that one in four babies were not getting the stipulated checks by the age of two. The UK's breastfeeding rates, already relatively low, dropped. Eight out of ten new mothers began by breastfeeding, but by the time babies were six weeks old, only two out of ten had kept it up. But what was the point of ad hoc health measures when the government undermined poorer children's welfare and cast many more into poverty?

Fat of the Land

Interest in healthy eating was avid, and not just among those taking their goopy cues from Gwyneth Paltrow. Perhaps the effects will show through in a while, but over the decade Britain got fatter: by 2017, 64 per cent of England's adults were over-weight or obese; 65 per cent of Scotland's were overweight, with 29 per cent obese. Along with adults, an alarming one-fifth of primary school children were obese. Being overweight leads to diabetes, which now affected 3.7 million people; the NHS in England recorded more than 700,000 obesity-related hospital admissions in 2017–18. With diabetes epidemic, 169 people a week (a record) were having limbs amputated as a result. Only 34 per cent of men and 42 per cent of women did the recommended 150 minutes of physical activity each week. The WHO named the UK the third most obese European country, better than only Turkey and Malta. Claudia Stein, its director for Europe, said the fact that Britons were among the biggest consumers of alcohol helped explain it. She might have added that the tax on alcohol had been cut by 6 per cent, and the government (Scotland apart) chose not to develop a coherent policy on drink. That point is worth emphasis-ing. Sometimes it is inaction that defines policy-makers, their unwillingness to recognise and do anything about a manifest problem.

Public Health England estimated that only one in eight of those believed to have a serious drink problem were being treated, leaving more than 500,000 getting no help. There were positive trends, though. The UK showed Europe's biggest fall in teenage drinking, with regular alcohol use among this group down by four-fifths, according to the WHO. Girls were still among the worst in Europe for binge drinking, and they were more likely than boys of the same age to have got drunk. Excited claims were made for the consumption of low-alcohol and alcohol-free drinks – up ten-fold since 2009, according to the Wine and Spirit Trade Association – but relative to the wider market volumes remained small. The pursuit of pleasurable release probably didn't change in aggregate. In 2016–17 one in twelve adults in England and Wales reported having taken an illicit drug – mostly cannabis – in the previous year, lower than previously. Total drug use dropped slightly, but the ingestion of cocaine grew, with nearly one in thirty taking it in powder form each year, raising consumption levels higher than elsewhere in Europe. The arrival of laboratory drugs – 'spice' among them – created havoc in prisons and on the streets.

The dramatic decline in smoking was a good story, following Labour's ban on lighting up in public places in 2007. Fewer people smoked tobacco, leaving only 15 per cent of the population smoking by 2020. Vaping and e-cigarettes were new; shops selling the nicotine-infused products in multiple aromas and flavours filled some of those vacant high-street slots. But tobacco smoking still led to 96,000 premature deaths a year in the UK and remained not just the leading cause of preventable deaths, but the strongest marker of the difference in death rates between rich and poor. Despite that, councils under pressure axed their stop-smoking programmes. The London Borough of Ealing (Labour) said it had 'no option' but to end its service, despite its clinics and classes recording a 47 per cent quit rate. Here was another example of austerity's enforced short-termism: Ealing council might save £400,000, but less effort going into preventing smoking would cost the NHS more in treating lung cancer and bronchial problems further down the line.

Some conditions improved. The UK hit international HIV targets, and new diagnoses continued to decline, partly due to the availability of pre-exposure prophylaxis. Yet spending on sexual health advice fell by a third; public authorities and charities, lacking money, organised fewer pop-up stalls in colleges, shopping centres and nightclubs to encourage condom use or offer free contraceptives and STI testing kits. Eighty-eight per cent of councils cut their sexual health budgets. Across town from the Ipswich Hospital is the Suffolk Young People's Health Project, or 4YP. Teens used to be able to walk in without anyone knowing; it offered swift and compassionate treatment. The council made cuts and recommissioned an all-age sexual health service, leaving 4YP in business, but able to offer young people much less. A recurring theme in sexual health, MPs said at the end of an investigation, 'was the complexity caused by fragmentation of both commissioning and provision as well as the variation in the level of services available to patients. We also heard of the time, energy and money wasted through repeated procurement and tendering processes.' That was the fallout from the calamity of an act introduced in 2012.

The Tories and the NHS

Readers will have long forgotten the man appointed health secretary in 2010, who was allowed to perpetrate a disaster before being sacked, given a peerage and becoming a private-health lobbyist. But the story of Andrew Lansley has to be recited, because it is symptomatic.

The Tories had always been uncomfortable with the NHS, embodying as it did principles and practices they found suspiciously socialist; just before 2010 a prominent Tory called the NHS 'a sixty-year-old mistake'. Since the 1980s Thatcherites had been keen to show that a health service free at the point of use was 'unsustainable'. Their progeny avoided frontal assault, seeing it as politically dangerous; we even found Lansley and Johnson (then London mayor) on a picket line, demanding that a north London hospital be kept open.

Behind the screens, Lansley and his think-tankers were hatching revolution. It's not entirely clear, in retrospect, to what extent he himself knew what he was doing, though his direction of travel was always towards creating NHS markets and competition. Under Margaret Thatcher and John Major, GPs had been made 'fundholders', being given blocks of money with which to buy or commission services on behalf of their patients. Now, under Lansley's 2012 Health and Social Care Act, the NHS was to formally split into 'commissioning groups' led by GPs, letting contracts for acute hospital care, mental health and ambulances go to 'providers', including companies. This entailed a destructive and needless reorganisation, consuming huge amounts of scarce time, depleting energy that should have gone on care. Sarah Wollaston, chair of the health select committee – and a Tory until she defected first to the Change UK rebels, then the Liberal Democrats – compared it to 'throwing a hand grenade' at the NHS.

It could indeed have blown up a comprehensive health system. All comers private or NHS – 'any willing provider' – could tender to provide services. Crude market theory said that NHS trusts, turning into analogues of commercial companies, would compete, driving down costs and (deep breath for some magic) driving up quality. To speed things along, the clinical commissioning groups were to function through 'support units' staffed by McKinsey and other management consultants, who were paid handsomely out of public funds. In Lansley's vision, hospital, mental health and community trusts would be challenged and, where necessary, replaced by Virgin and Serco.

The gory details are not worth recounting because what emerged from the legislation's protracted passage through parliament was only a part realisation of the original grand plan. Nick Hulme told us he had to spend 'hours in committees with GPs telling me how to run hospitals they had once worked in while training twenty years ago', but it soon became evident that GPs could not and would not run the NHS. Their perspectives and skills were usually too narrow, it wasn't financially worth their while, and they had neither the time nor the managerial inclination. The NHS, including many GPs, was both mystified by the complexity of the proposals and demoralised by yet another costly top–down exercise. The public did not have much of a clue, but Cameron's political instincts soon made him realise it had been a huge mistake, even if he did not have the courage to pull the plug. Within months of being enacted, key elements of the plan were junked, without explanation or apology.

But it was too late to stop nonsense and waste pulsing through the system. 'We soon learned [in the hospital] you got paid if you scored by treating a patient for "dehydration", but not if you wrote, "I put up a drip,"' said Hulme. 'We hired thirty clinical coders, whose job it was to code every item of treatment correctly to make sure we got the cash paid by the commissioning group. Then the commissioners employed armies of accountants to challenge our invoices. Outside companies were employed to do it. Millions and millions were spent on coding treatments and on challenging every one of them.' Cameron and crew, so critical of bureaucracy, ended up creating a massive paper-pushing, transactional industry: by 2019 the NHS was spending 14 per cent of its revenue on the cost of the extra lawyers, management, advertising tenders, billing and duplication. In Ipswich, they found perversity inbuilt: 'In the early days, we got £1,500 if we admitted someone from A&E, but only £800 for a day treatment, so the finance director wanted those beds filled overnight.'

But though multimillions were wasted and vast amounts of energy that could have gone into patient care were dissipated, the dismemberment of the NHS was thwarted. Part of the reason was inertia: the NHS is a tanker, impossible to turn around in a hurry. Another element was the revolutionaries' incompetence and confusion. In Lansley's imagination, services would be removed from the day-to-day control of ministers and civil servants, and the market would run itself. But the public and MPs demanded accountability; as Nye Bevan had presciently noted, a bedpan dropped in a district general hospital would always reverberate up to Whitehall. The biggest reason for failure was austerity. Companies would have piled in and demanded the government stick with it, if there were money to be made. During Brexit we saw that they had not given up on their hopes: witness how avid American healthcare companies were to get access to the NHS and how Trump's appointees pressed their interests.

Labour had invited private companies in to cut waiting lists for hip replacements, scanning, specialist mental health and community services. Back then, the money flowed; now, pickings were slim. Care UK, UnitedHealth, Circle and Capita did notch up gains around the edges, and by 2019 Virgin Care had garnered over £2 billion from more than 400 NHS contracts. Details were shrouded under a blanket of 'commercial confidentiality', but companies often won by bidding low, with consequences for the quality of care. The Churchill Hospital in Oxford tried to outsource PET-CT scans for cancer patients to the InHealth company, until protests stopped it, as it would have meant patients being ferried from the hospital by ambulance to InHealth's scanners four miles away in Littlemore. Attempts by the Hull commissioners to rationalise GP practices were thwarted by Virgin, whose lawyers claimed the plan would affect competitiveness. This was in a city that was severely 'under-doctored', with the equivalent of fifty-three full-time GPs per 100,000 people in the city, compared with an average across England of sixty. Circle burned itself badly when it took over Hinchinbrooke Hospital in Huntingdon. Boasts of miraculous future financial returns gave way to screams of investor anguish, and less than a year later the company walked away, leaving the NHS to pick up the pieces. In Cornwall, Serco's attempt to break into primary care ended ignominiously. Claims of superior private sector efficiency proved hard to validate.

All in all, private involvement was not boosted significantly by the 2012 Act. Reliable figures were scarce, but by 2019 NHS commissioners were estimated to be spending 7.3 per cent of their budget – £8.7 billion – on non-NHS clinical suppliers, including non-profits and charities. Some £5.9 billion worth of NHS work was being tendered annually, including lab services, research, training and pharmacies. That figure excluded NHS spending on private suppliers of cleaning, buildings maintenance and IT services – or GPs. The NHS remained predominantly a publicly provided service.

However, management consultants coined their profits, having first been brought in to dismantle the NHS, and then again to help rebuild and create a unified structure. American insurance and analytics outfits sniffed around the fringes. PFI schemes bequeathed by Labour continued to drain huge sums into private firms' balance sheets. Tory ministers went on believing in the miracles of private medicine. A former minister, George Freeman, spoke for many in his party by calling for an end to the 'apartheid' between the public and private sectors – meaning more opportunities for outsourcers and profit. He wanted 'a debate about how we fund healthcare' – code for making people pay more in a market. Johnson, wittering about 'reform of the NHS', may yet give the opponents of the NHS their head.

As the health secretary charged with mopping up the wards, Jeremy Hunt became hyperactive, intervening everywhere in complete contradiction to his predecessor's scheme. Simon Stevens, chief executive of NHS England since 2014 and a former close adviser to Tony Blair, proved something of a saviour. He set about making strenuous efforts to subvert the 2012 Act and reintegrate the NHS into a single organisation, demolishing as much of the commissioner/provider model as possible without substantive legislation.

So while half the decade was spent wrecking the NHS, the other half saw a concerted effort to reintegrate it – but without adequate funding. Stevens promulgated a 'five-year forward view', which we saw being implemented by Nick Hulme. His day job was running Ipswich Hospital, but as head of the area 'integrated care system', much of his energy went into attempting to align the hospital better with GPs, community services and mental health, so that patients received a more joined-up service overall. In early 2019 Stevens proposed replacing the

2012 procurement law with a 'best value' test that, in practice, would mean avoiding tendering. Stevens's stratagem appeared to be one of creating noise and throwing dust in the Treasury's eyes, gaining cover for recreating regional planning and stronger central control.

During the passage of the 2012 Act, the Liberal Democrats had squeaked objections, so to please them, Healthwatch committees were created (doomed never to be noticed by the public), along with Health and Wellbeing boards, convened by councils to look across both social care for adults and disabled people and the NHS. Whatever bureaucratic structure finally beds down, the public – patients, service users and those who care for them – are better served if the NHS and councils work in tandem, but in 2019–20, it was the union of a starveling and a skeleton.

Doctor Won't See You Now

A 'ten-year forward view' was published in January 2019, stating as priorities heart disease, maternity, mental health, stroke, diabetes and lung disease, plus a new focus on out-of-hospital care by GPs and community services. Medical optimists said they welcomed the focus; pessimists asked where the doctors and nurses needed would come from. Already, to visit your GP was to invite a diatribe or sad plaint about the inadequacy of consultation times and pressure of paperwork. Services needed staff, and they had gone missing. The Nursing and Midwifery Council reported that the number registered to work in the

UK had reached an all-time high. But in 2019 over 40,000 nursing posts were going unfilled in the NHS in England alone – this was after the number of nursing posts had been cut by 11 per cent. Only 4,031 full-time equivalent district nurses were working in England, down from 7,055 (a 43 per cent drop). Since 2010 there were 11 per cent fewer nurses in community services, 19 per cent fewer district nurses and 10 per cent fewer in mental health – despite repeated promises to boost resources and numbers.

Something had gone wrong with the pipeline: someone had blocked it. Abolishing bursaries for trainee nurses forced them to take out loans: one in twenty places to study nursing went unfilled, and the reason was often expense. Older healthcare assistants were willing and able to upgrade, but once they had families they could not afford the new fees. For staff in post, the problem was austerity, clamping down on salaries and pensions and making wards and clinics more stressful as demand built and supply was cut. In Ipswich, we heard Jenny's account of the unbearable strain of working in a high-pressure ward with too few nurses. An NHS surviving day by day had no capacity to plan for the predictable greying of GPs or the higher proportion of women clinicians, GPs, consultants and nurses who had childcare responsibilities and needed flexible hours. A rash promise had been made in 2015 to increase GPs by 5,000 within five years; instead, their numbers shrank.

It is hard to pass summary judgement on the Tory steward-ship of England's socialised health system – yet. Survival can be gauged only by looking backwards. A common proxy for the performance of hospitals is cancer: the emerging data seems to say that survival rates plateaued, falling for colon cancer, worse for bladder cancer. Generally, survival rates remained below comparable countries, which mostly spend more, though in 2019 death rates from breast cancer dropped to below the EU average, perhaps because of better NHS screening and despite controversy over the use of hormone replacement therapy. The layers of staffing and investment put in before 2010 took time to be peeled back. But by 2015 trusts were running deficits and started (with clandestine official encouragement) to sell off buildings to pay for day-to-day services. Performance standards declined from 2012–13 onwards. After waiting lists had fallen to their lowest-ever level – there were virtually no patients waiting by 2010 – by 2019, 4.1 million were languishing in the queue for non-urgent treatment. Delays in referrals for consultations and tests grew – and the public noticed.

The most graphic test of overall health is mortality. Suddenly, our expected lifespan was in freefall: by 2019 longevity was down by thirteen months for men and fourteen for women, compared with 2015's estimates. Actuaries scratched their heads at a phenomenon that was also being seen in other countries. Were efforts to prevent deaths from heart disease showing diminishing returns? Was it higher rates of winter flu? Mortality was up among working-age adults, which pointed to the potential effects of welfare policies. They undoubtedly helped explain another great shock: an increase in the number of babies dying at birth or soon after. Infant mortality had been on a long downward trend, which went into reverse in 2015.

British Social Attitudes found that only 53 per cent were satisfied with the NHS overall in 2018, 16 percentage points lower than in 2010. Fewer than two-thirds were happy with GPs, thanks to lengthening waits for appointments. Still, for a service attacked by the right for its lack of productivity, by 2018 the NHS in England was treating 1.5 million more non-urgent patients than in 2010. When people did get hospital care, they professed themselves happy: satisfaction ratings for outpatient services were still high, at 70 per cent.

Getting Old, Needing Care

The Isabel Blackman Centre's final days were full of sadness. The day centre, a haven for the frail, was joining the seven that had already closed in Hastings since 2010. As packing cases were being filled with pictures from the walls, we talked to Rose, Mary and Sal, old friends sitting together as they always did, but now for the last time. The sixty people here, most with dementia, or suffering from strokes or other severe infirmities, would be separated and might not see each other again: the centre's bus that used to collect them each day had been decommissioned. No more art, music, singing, visits from animals, yoga, quizzes or games, nor visits from a chiropodist to keep them mobile, nor a hairdresser to sustain their well-being.

At home alone, without the stimulus and friendships a day centre offered, older people would be more likely to be admitted to hospital emergency departments, malnourished or dehydrated. The centres helped recuperation after a hospital stay. Carleton Astley, manager of the Isabel Blackman Centre, said, 'I can show you who will have to be going into residential care very soon after we shut, and that costs around £1,500 a week.' Here, again, was the perversity of austerity: scrimp a bit now, cost a lot later. The small capital gain made by the council would produce a far higher cost to the NHS in the longer run.

The centre had been run by a charity, but the building was owned by East Sussex County Council, which was selling to developers. Sue, administrator for a quarter of a century, said that as a child, her mother had used the public bathhouse that once stood on the site. 'This area was a slum where the fishermen lived. Look at it now – it's gentrified here on the seafront.' That, she says, is why the council wanted to sell.

Across England, the number of day centres for the elderly was cut by 41 per cent between 2010 and 2018. By 2019, 7.7 million people lived alone, most elderly. An estimated 200,000 older people never talked to a friend or relative in a month, with rising bus and train fares trapping people on their own. A Tory MP, Tracey Crouch, was appointed 'minister for loneliness', saying nobody should feel alone or be left without anyone to turn to, but as a minister without money or clout, she brought no sign the Treasury had any intention of reversing the cuts to council budgets and lasted only a few months in the post.

Care was needed for adults with disabilities, as well as older people, and circumstances differed hugely between families. Most care was given at home by unpaid relatives – an estimated

5.4 million people, usually women – and was said to save the state more than £132 billion annually. But they needed help, and some people don't have families, with the result that social care was now consuming over a third of all council spending and was set to rise to a half in the early 2020s – and that was at present levels of eligibility, which were universally judged as inadequate.

Need was rising fast. Some 850,000 lived with dementia, and prescriptions for drugs for Alzheimer's had risen six-fold since 2010. In a grey area in terms of responsibility, an older person might fall and break a bone, needing medical care (free from the NHS). Once the bone was set, the council would in theory take over their rehabilitation and care, but charge on the basis of a means test. Relatives couldn't or wouldn't take granny in, so increasing numbers were stuck in hospital despite being 'well'. If there weren't enough district nurses to tend to a wound, and no day centre to keep an eye on them, they would sooner or later end up back in hospital, and often get stuck there.

Labour had planned that everyone with funds or property on retirement would be required to pay a lump sum into a fund that would pool the risk between those who would need expensive long-term care and those lucky enough to drop dead without it. The Tories scored a direct hit, dubbing the plan a 'death tax'. But they had no substitute, promising but failing to write their own Green Paper for fear of frightening the voters. Johnson added his own airy promises. Andrew Dilnot, the esteemed economist, had devised a scheme to address the unfairness of some people qualifying and others not. Even though his remit had ducked the question of extra money, Cameron shelved his report.

Public satisfaction with the state of care fell to 26 per cent. But it never quite jangled political nerves in the way the NHS did. Or pensions. Older citizens used their muscle to secure their pensions, but grey power was not mobilised over care, except to proscribe financial solutions that might hit their property. Procrastination and underfunding had little or no electoral consequences for the Tories, either in local government or at Westminster. Perhaps too few were afflicted; perhaps people were clueless about the complex interactions between welfare and disability benefits, the NHS and councils. Ian Hudspeth, Tory leader of Oxfordshire County Council, said social care was invisible: 'Only about 2 per cent of our population have anything to do with it, yet 55 per cent of our budget is spent on it.' Perhaps things were not yet bad enough: after all, the Care Quality Commission (CQC) rated 71 per cent of care homes as good, and two-thirds of state-funded residents said they were very satisfied. Against that, the charity Independent Age found over 2.6 million over-sixty-fives living in areas where an increasing number of care homes were rated 'inadequate' or 'requires improvement' by the CQC. Manchester scored worst, with four out of ten care homes rated inadequate or requiring improvement.

Councils in Wales allowed people to have assets worth £50,000 before they started to charge for residential care; in Scotland, the limit was £28,000; in England and Northern

Ireland, it was £23,250. For residential care the value of a person's home was included, but not for domiciliary care. The government talked about uniform, countrywide eligibility criteria, but nothing was said about how to pay. Most practical solutions involved risk sharing and pooling money raised from the older people who had accumulated untaxed wealth through the housing booms. In Theresa May's snap 2017 election, she proposed raising the cap on assets for residential care to £100,000, but those receiving care at home would for the first time have their property taken into account as an asset. This immediately became a 'dementia tax', and May panicked, famously claiming that her own published manifesto was untrue. Care was inextricably bound up with housing, property wealth and family fears that legacies (the houses in which elderly relatives were living) might be eaten up. In surveys, half of all homeowners did not think they would have enough money to fund their own care, even if they sold their home.

So provision deteriorated. By 2019 Public Health England said that there were just 10.1 care beds for every hundred people over the age of seventy-five, down from 11.3 in 2012. Spending on adult social care fell between 2010–11 and 2016–17, despite an increase of more than 14 per cent in the number of people aged over sixty-five in need of it. The result was predictable: nearly 2 million old people who would have qualified for care at home in 2010 were no longer receiving it by 2019, according to Age UK. Worse, over 54,000 died in 2018 waiting for care packages they were due, but which hard-pressed councils never provided. The minimum annual increase in social care budgets was calculated at 3.9 per cent, given rates of ageing and the growth in the number of younger adults with disabilities – and the think tanks calculated that figure on the basis of existing, tightened eligibility. Anything more generous would mean funding would have to grow at a faster rate. Free older-age care for all would cost £15 billion a year, and £8 billion just to return to 2010's ungenerous levels.

Private equity companies had earlier moved into care homes, thinking demography was a sure route to profit. The private sector now provided accommodation for 410,000 residents in England. Among the providers was Barchester, with 200 care homes and 11,000 residents, a company owned by the billionaire Irish racehorse owners Dermot Desmond, J. P. McManus and John Magnier. Racehorses, care homes – not much different. Companies were squeezed as councils screwed down fees, paying 10 per cent less than the actual cost of places. In 2018 more than a hundred care home operators collapsed. Terra Firma borrowed £825 million to finance its purchase of home operator Four Seasons, which was then saddled with the debt. Such leverage required high margins from the old folk. Private owners in turn squeezed hard, paying the minimum wage – or less – to staff, while rewarding their directors, meeting high interest rates and returning profits. According to a think-tank study, those profits amounted in 2019 to £1.5 billion a year, or 10 per cent of private care home operators' revenues.

Care staff were in short supply, and no wonder: not only were wages low, but the Brexit vote drove away care assistants who hailed from the EU. Tracing the flow of money was far from easy: companies such as HC-One, which took over from the collapsed Southern Cross, with 22,000 beds in 340 care homes could rely on the state's fear of another bankruptcy tipping people into the street. 'This company is ramping up its debt while leaving the risk with residents, employees and the state,' said analyst Nick Hood; dividends were 'completely inappropriate for a business dependent on taxpayers'.

6

Flatlining

Magnomatics was founded in 2000 to exploit the invention of an entirely magnetic gearbox by the University of Sheffield's engineering department. With no contact between its moving parts, it saved 35 per cent in fuel, yet cost the same as conventional gearboxes used in making cars and turbines. Chief executive David Latimer showed us round their headquarters in a smartly renovated old railway building near Sheffield's station. He had long experience of navigating across the chasm separating lab bench and factory, which some called 'the valley of death'. Patience and funding had often been in short supply in the UK.

Before, Magnomatics had proudly aimed to get the first of the new gearboxes into vehicles and on the road by 2022. Now, we learnt that money from the EU's Horizon 2020 fund had not been forthcoming in a recent round – because, Latimer suspected, the UK was seen to be on its way out. But the start-up was still poised to sign its first major contract. The trouble was, though Magnomatics had wanted to maintain its identity – perhaps even manufacturing in Sheffield itself – the contenders for the deal were not British. Two companies were vying for the rights: one a £28 billion Chinese firm; the other a £25 billion concern from another Asian country. 'We wanted to manufacture here,' said Latimer. 'But that's not going to happen now.' He tried to talk to the Department for Business, Energy and Industrial Strategy in order to negotiate a grant. 'We got no response at all. Eventually they said they were too busy, up to their neck in Brexit work. So we'll build the gearboxes abroad. China is very keen.'

Magnomatics will keep the technical design work in the UK, but the innovation will enhance Chinese cars and wind turbines. Here was an invention catapulted out of an excellent UK university, but just as it reached fruition after nearly twenty years of development, it was being snatched away abroad, along with possibly thousands of manufacturing jobs, for lack of domestic backing.

Those jobs would have been high-productivity employment, of which the UK had much less than other advanced countries at the start of the decade. After 2010 the gap grew. A few miles south of Sheffield, at Sports Direct's notorious distribution shed in Shirebrook, the truth about output from work was more likely to be found. Here's the headline: up to 2018 output per hour worked in the UK grew by only 0.5 per cent a year, compared with 2.2 per cent in the period before 2008. Total output grew thanks to the extra numbers of employees and the number of hours they worked, not their technical capacity. As David Latimer had experienced, blame lay partly with a lack of long-term finance – pretty ironic for a version of capitalism that in the UK had become so 'financialised'. Plenty of other reasons also suggested themselves: underspending on infrastructure, taxation, restrictions on development and research funding and low-quality education. Conversely, too much high-quality education was also a contributing factor: the ONS reported that a third of all graduates had 'more education' than was required for the work they were doing, and the trend towards over-qualification had accelerated. Threading through all of that was unfairness: uneven development between individuals, groups and areas of the country.

Productivity

Growth and rising incomes depended on improving output per person, which in turn demanded high skills, business investment and innovation. But the UK's exit route from the financial crash lay in expanding low-skill, low-wage work. Of every four employees one was low-skilled and less likely to be trained. Less skilled workers were more likely to be found outside the south-east. The UK's productivity problem did not begin in 2010; it just got worse. A link between low pay and low productivity was seen in France and Germany as well, but in the UK jobs growth was concentrated in low-productivity sectors. France had 80 per cent more industrial robots than the UK, in a manufacturing sector approximately the same size, which was part of the reason why on a comparison of weekly output with the UK, the average French worker produced more by the end of Thursday than the average British worker in a full week. Brexit hit productivity: in 2018–19, annual growth fell to a negligible 0.2 per cent. And the prevalent Cameron–Johnson ideology played a part: to improve productivity required generous, state-backed skills training and investment in education and transport, as well as pointed interventions in boardrooms and markets to reshape the culture and competence of companies.

Up to 2008 productivity grew in computing, finance and professional services. After the crash, productive companies lost momentum and zombie firms stalked the land, said Bank of England economist Andy Haldane. Once a nation of shopkeepers, in Napoleon's words, England was now the land of small businesses, which employed 16 million people – 60 per cent of private employment – but not productively. The UK wasn't getting results from investment in IT, either. It had the thirty-fifth-fastest broadband in the world, with average speeds that put it behind almost all the other EU member states and Madagascar.

Peeing in a Bottle

Despite stalling productivity, work became harder. The 2018 Skills and Employment Survey found a workforce under increased strain: a third worked at high speeds all, or almost all, of the time and were exhausted after work, subjected to technology that was harder to switch off. Workers in an Amazon shed had to pee in a bottle to avoid being disciplined for taking a toilet break. Ambulance call-outs to high-paced (and low-paid) distribution centres increased. People who had generally found it hard to get work before, such as ethnic minorities and those with disabilities, were now employed – but in jobs offering no upward opportunities nor paying enough to lift families out of poverty. If this was a 'jobs miracle', the economists said, the flip side was a productivity disaster.

Study after study confirmed that restoring decent pay required a better balance of power in the workplace between workers and employers. But union membership fell to a quarter of the workforce, mainly in the public or ex-public sectors, compared with half when Margaret Thatcher became prime minister. In the unions' absence, employers exploited the opportunity. *Financial Times* reporter Sarah O'Connor discovered people in Leicester's garment district who were being paid as little as £3.50 an hour, less than half the minimum wage. She found clothes for brands such as Boohoo and Missguided being produced in UK sweatshops, where staff reported receiving no sick pay. Many of the jobs were taken by migrants from within the EU and Asia. In this twilight world, taxes and NI weren't paid, safety standards ignored. HMRC's policing of the minimum wage was extraordinarily weak. Professor David Metcalf examined the work of the Health and Safety Executive and the Labour-era Gangmasters and Labour Abuse Authority and the Employment Agency Standards Inspectorate and found their coverage flimsy and the number of prosecutions few. Metcalf complained that they had yet to tackle low pay in agriculture, nail bars, car washes, social care and hospitality – the 'help wanted' hot spots.

Industrial Strategy

Tory ministers were once expected to have business backgrounds and cherish UK plc, but this lot were curiously unconcerned about the shape or condition of the economy as experienced by staff, business owners and investors. States and markets have always been mutually dependent, but ministers' willingness to intervene to improve market outcomes was half-hearted. Their strategies for transport, telecoms and infrastructure turned out to be wish lists, with little sense of how they fitted together and how they were to be paid for. George Osborne had promised 'the march of the makers'; by 2020 the march had not prevented the closure of Honda in Swindon, British Steel in Scunthorpe or Ford at Bridgend, and the shutdowns continue. The GMB union calculated a drop of 600,000 in manufacturing employment, but manufacturing as a proportion of GDP nonetheless stabilised. Some thought conventional definitions failed to capture the new boundary between making things and making software and systems for making things.

Theresa May promised a reinvigorated industrial strategy. What she meant was unclear; her weak government could not muster the effort to drive a coherent policy through different departments. It was all bits and pieces, not a strategy at all. Only the state could regulate nuclear energy, transport, the electro-magnetic spectrum – the range of frequencies used for radio communication – and so could have been a major player in securing productivity improvement, but a lack of political will or coherent objectives meant its involvement was piecemeal.

Life sciences were another bright example, future-orientated, highly dependent on public spending on universities and R&D. But they were bang in the path of hurricane Brexit, which hit investment, confidence and staffing. The withdrawal of the European Medicines Agency from London signalled shrinkage ahead.

Great science was being done: in quantum technologies, in the UK's contribution to CERN and the Large Hadron Collider (which was, of course, a large European collaboration in which scientific sovereignty was pooled, just like the EU). But where was the joining together with company investment plans, equity markets or other public policies? As we have noted elsewhere, it was as if the government acknowledged the question, but its answer was sketchy, underpowered, marginal. So, by 2019 an Office for Artificial Intelligence had been set up, which sounded like positive anticipation of technological change – but, said the IfG, everyone was distracted by Brexit, and no pound signs were attached to plans.

Any UK government in this era could and should have had a strategy for data and connectivity. For better or worse, they were the future. David Cameron had bleated about the poor quality of mobile-phone signals in his Witney constituency. Boris Johnson, in turn, expostulated about fibre and 5G. Neither grasped that this, in some measure, was a national emergency and a huge opportunity for state and business to combine in future-proofing the UK and enhancing national productivity. Signal strength is not a phenomenon of nature, but rather the result of commercial decisions. Hands off, they left it to the telecommunications companies, which haphazardly put up masts or commandeered church towers for booster units with random coverage. BT was supposed to supply a high-capacity fibre network through its peculiar offshoot Openreach. Industrial policy was essentially made by the regulator Ofcom, which worked to its own script. Where did BT's vaunted target of supplying full fibre coverage to 15 million homes by 2025 come from? In 2019 only one in fourteen UK properties was connected to a full fibre line, and BT's growth rate (5 million connections over ten years) was perilously slow. But, of course, it was a private company, with profits to cosset (£7.4 billion in 2018–19). Labour took its cue, making broadband coverage a theme in the 2019 election.

For a decade the government hesitated and stood back, unwilling to think afresh about privatisation or its regulation. It refused to require train operators to speed up wi-fi provision or to link household smart meters with a data network. 'Talks beset by infighting,' reported the *Financial Times*, as O2, Vodafone, EE and Three tried to escape an Ofcom injunction to ensure 95 per cent of the UK's landmass was covered. In a confused tangle of rebates on licences and opaque bargaining with the regulator, the companies' disunity and the government's unwillingness to push were exposed.

To get from research to improved productivity takes time and may involve circumambulation, but a path connects the two. Its existence was eventually grasped, and in 2019, as the May government fell apart, it promised higher spending on R&D – reaching 2.4 per cent of GDP at some point in the

2020s. (Finland spent seven times more than the UK, and the international target was already 3 per cent, while the government figure made heroic assumptions about the willingness of business to invest.) But what was missing, still, was a large-scale relief map showing the joins between knowledge and research and the economy, consumer preferences and public policies.

Take transport. Again, that phrase 'national emergency' is apposite, to capture the seriousness of combating climate change at a time when consumer preferences were on the move. What was the plan for moving people around our small islands? Where was any vision for the future of UK motor manufacturing, even before Brexit threatened supply chains or trade wars were launched by the Trump administration? Here was a global business, with no opt-out. Jaguar Land Rover, Ford and the others – and their workforces in the West Midlands, Oxford, Derby and the north-east – were going to find it hard to cope, and closures and cutbacks started before Brexit was resolved. (Jaguar Land Rover was going to build electric cars at Castle Bromwich, safeguarding 2,500 jobs, it said, though sales had fallen in 2018 and a threat still hung over the plant's future.) Profit margins on electric vehicles were smaller – as was the tax take, which extracted revenue from petrol and diesel. Government was going to have to be involved in order for the comprehensive supply of electricity to be organised. Already the industry was saying that it would be inhibited by a failure to plan ahead and install enough charging points.

Industrial *strategy* entailed foresight, planning and compulsion. When Jim Ratcliffe, the prince of frackers, complained about a 'non-existent energy strategy', he was right – though the absence stemmed in part from their sharing his own selfish worldview. Ministers who were once keen on fracking backed away when it affected Tory-held constituencies in the Sussex Downs, leaving in place highly restrictive seismic thresholds which the Johnson government wanted to lift, until buildings started shaking and the Fylde coast started fracturing. Wind power was a similar story. The not-in-my-backyarders objected to turbines and ministers caved in, endangering at a stroke the UK's leadership in a sphere where the country had abundant natural resources and some technical prowess. Turbines were erected, more expensively, offshore and (mainly foreign-owned) companies massed to take advantage – in the Channel, off Humberside. Danish Ørsted's Hornsea One scheme would cover 407 square kilometres, with 1.2GW capacity, enough to power a million homes.

A strategy for the UK's energy had to match climate-change imperatives, with an end to financial manipulation by energy companies and a radical revision of regulation, if not nationalisation of supply and transmission. Wind and sustainable energy were hard to distribute through the existing grid, which had been designed for one-way, large-scale, predictable input from coal and nuclear generators (less predictable now, as the August 2019 blackout proved). Re-planning required a central authority, but the logic of privatisation specified competition, and that is what the regulator, Ofgem, sought to apply, turning the National Grid company into a mess of separate entities – including a gas distribution arm owned by the Australian Macquarie

Group. Here was the emblematic company. It picked the carcass left by the 2017 sell-off of the Green Investment Bank, which had been set up by the Cameron coalition to push sustainability. But Macquarie's money-spinner was its part ownership of Thames Water. The Treasury, ostensibly the guardian of the public interest, signed off on a 'super-sewer', which would drain London north of the Thames. But engineers contested its necessity: smaller projects could take care of storm drainage. The scheme's attraction was financial. The Macquarie consortium was to be financed by loans, many of which were written off against tax; it would get its money back, and more, long before completion. Thames Water customers, who had no choice, would start paying before the sewer was built and go on paying long after it was finished. Just to cut the financial risk further, the government also offered a guarantee against cost overruns. Austerity, it turned out, was not for everyone.

Water, like energy, was regulated under the old Thatcher rules, which sought to minimise public control (and knowledge) of what privatised companies were up to. Ofwat (chaired by the former boss of Anglian Water, who took away a £9 million bonus when he left in 2013) said it was applying the screws and announced in 2019 that 'we are close to peak intrusion'. In fact, water companies were coining it, manipulating their balance sheets and borrowings, which were mostly tax-deductible. Directors' Croesus-like remuneration had 'yet to change', the *Financial Times* reported, in a largely risk-free industry where investment returns were generous and suppliers of water and sewerage in Yorkshire and elsewhere had been allowed to pile up massive debts in order to fund the payout to investors. Scandalised, Labour pledged to take England's water back into state ownership.

Productivity was linked to competition, but in complex ways, and you did not find much clarity or consistency from the Competition and Markets Authority. Doing battle against Sainsbury's move to acquire Asda sounded like an attempt to keep capitalism honest. But where was any parallel effort to police the monopolistic internet giants from which consumers could not escape? Where, indeed, was the industrial policy for retail, the modern equivalent to coal and steel? No 'industrial strategy' encompassed the effect on jobs and the growth of financial engineering and market manipulation by private equity firms. Greybull Capital was outed as the malign owner behind the demise of British Steel at Scunthorpe, but that was only one example of what the *Financial Times*' Jonathan Ford called 'systems set up to guarantee fat fees and payments regardless of performance, channelled through tax suppressing structures . . . Private equity looks like an exploitative racket.'

Infrastructure

'All infrastructure has a form of government guarantee,' writes Simon Taylor in *The Fall and Rise of Nuclear Power in Britain*, 'in that if it fails the state must pick it up and make it work.' Long-term consistent funding was required to back the investment on which productivity improvement depended, in private as in public sectors. The Tories seemed to grasp the principle but failed miserably to supply the wherewithal. The Labour-era Infrastructure Commission was resurrected in 2015, having been abolished in the macho early days of the coalition. Its bipartisanship was supposed to be guaranteed by the appointment of Labour peer Andrew Adonis as chair, but he lasted only as long as the Tory commissioner, Michael Heseltine: a matter of months. Both were apparently too keen on spending, regional development and active government. The commission sank into the oblivion of planlessness: what was the point of building roads or railways without simultaneously projecting housing, public services and land use?

Without plans, growth was formless. Policy decisions, including HS2, were almost whimsical. Everyone could see that as online shopping grew, so did deliveries: over the five years to 2017, light goods vehicles' mileage increased from 41.4 billion to 49.1 billion. That in turn added to congestion, but deprived of funds, councils did not spend on road maintenance, further increasing delays. Most people continued to spend most of their time on the move in their cars, driving 78 per cent of the total distance travelled and making 62 per cent of all trips by car. Many had no choice but to drive, even though 9 per cent of UK households had fallen into debt as a direct result of owning and running a car. More buses might have helped. They were key to reducing emissions, cutting urban pollution and making towns liveable. But the number of journeys by bus in England fell, pushed downwards by infrequent and disjointed services, reduced council subsidies, higher fares – and a reduction in the number of routes of 3,000. Outside London, bus services were 'fragmented, incomplete, overpriced, fragile', according to Andy Burnham, the mayor of Greater Manchester. From 2017 he and the other big-city mayors acquired some stronger powers, including running their own buses, but they were severely limited. A *Guardian* investigation (data weren't collected by the Department for Transport) found short-distance single bus tickets costing over £5. The problem wasn't private provision in itself since franchising worked in London; it was empowering councils to plan, organise and link travel options and increase subsidies, which were now running at about 40 per cent of bus income. Even in London, individualism – using Uber, for instance – started to eat into passenger numbers, as Transport for London struggled with its finances. We will look later at the growth in the importance of place: how opportunities to move – or a lack of them – became a stronger determinant of life chances.

Though only a small proportion of journeys were made on trains, they bulked large in the imagination of business and policy-makers as the key to intercity and inter-regional mobility. The story here was a growth in numbers, followed by a tail-off, as passengers were turned away by cost, unreliable service and mismanagement. As with energy and water, the regulatory model adopted by the privatisers in the 1980s and 1990s no longer worked, if it ever did. The government intervened ad hoc; no one was clear where the remit of the publicly owned Network Rail stopped and that of the profit-making railway companies started. What travellers experienced were dire services on certain franchises and fares that were complicated and high. Overall, the cost of train travel rose by 46 per cent, hugely in excess of both inflation and average wages. Behind the scenes (then out in the open, around Johnson's Cabinet table), the privatisers had not given up, despite the failures: plots were afoot to sell stations, break up Network Rail and hand over trackside telecoms networks and cabling to private firms.

Why was performance on Northern Rail so bad compared to Chiltern, when both franchises were held by Arriva, which was owned by the German state railway? Nobody knew. Big capacity constraints inhibited movement in the corridor between Liverpool and Hull via Manchester and Leeds, and Northern travellers experienced what Manchester mayor Andy Burnham called 'appalling levels of delay and cancellations', especially after the introduction of a new timetable in 2018. Arriva's promised new trains did not arrive. Meanwhile, ministers and civil servants connived with Southern over driver-only operation, helping provoke strikes. This franchise was crazy: Southern did not get the revenue from fares; instead, it received payments from the government, giving it no incentive to maintain, let alone improve, services. Stagecoach and Virgin, as franchisees of Virgin Trains East Coast, had been allowed to walk away from the losses they were making on the London–York–Edinburgh contract because they had miscalculated. When it came to the bidding process for the west coast route, the DoT excluded them, provoking Richard Branson's ire. The franchise was won by FirstGroup, whose biggest shareholder (a predatory private equity group) promptly threatened to sue the board for their success. It wasn't the consequent disappearance of the Virgin brand from the railways that was regrettable but the government's waywardness, its profligacy with accumulated knowledge and expertise in operating rail, and the way staff were shunted around from employer to employer like the expendable factors of production that market theory considered them to be.

Of course, many journeys were completed on time and, with clever advance booking, at reasonable cost. Improvements were made: Paddington's Grade I-listed roof and Brunel's wrought-iron arches were renovated; Reading and Birmingham New Street stations rebuilt. But the electrification of the Great Western route was halted: the NAO found that the operator and infrastructure were uncoordinated and costs were escalating; inexplicably, Network Rail had even underestimated how many bridges it would need to rebuild or modify. Crossrail – linking Reading in the west with Abbey Wood in south-east London and Shenfield in Essex – involved massive tunnelling and station-building in the heart of the capital. A Labour-era project, it ran into difficulties with signalling after the major works were completed, embarrassing both London's Labour mayor, Sadiq Khan, and May's unembarrassable transport secretary, Chris Grayling (though his successor, Grant Shapps, may yet give him a run for his money). Due to be opened in 2018, the inauguration of the £14 billion (rising to £17 billion-plus) project was deferred *sine die*. Was this an example of some distinctly British failure in completing infrastructure? Or was it a more mundane instance of the sheer difficulty of bringing big projects to fruition, as paralleled by problems with Berlin's additional airport or refurbishing the New York subway?

HS2 was one of the era's great anomalies, a great wodge of spending in the midst of austerity and capital starvation. The line acquired talismanic properties and should perhaps remind us that policy decisions can take on a ritualistic, symbolic quality. This one, so Tory ministers believed, showed they cared about the north – even though evidence, such as the impact of the high-speed links between Lyon and Paris, suggested London would end up benefiting more. Labour leaders of northern cities were persuaded, and in Liverpool and Manchester they talked the project up: We've been left behind, that's why we are so passionate about it, said Adrian Smith of Nottinghamshire County Council, extolling the jobs and homes to be created alongside the line. But he seemed not to have noticed that the government said nothing about who would pay for the homes and supporting infrastructure that would crystallise any benefits from the new railway. Big and disputed claims were made about additional capacity, and the route of the new line was controversial (it missed major centres and did not link up with the existing network, even at the London terminus). As its projected costs mounted, HS2 appeared more like a vanity project than an integral part of England's infrastructure, with a possible extension of the fast link to Scotland too far ahead to be meaningful, given the possibility of another independence referendum. Johnson, with a keen eye on Tory constituencies and mainly negative party sentiment, ordered a review, creating further uncertainty.

The expansion of Heathrow Airport showed the same pattern: no serious appraisal of the consequences for carbon emissions, deference to private operators, no comprehensive plan. First, the Cameron coalition deferred a decision, despite the enthusiasm of its business backers. In September 2012 the banker Sir Howard Davies was given orders to maintain Heathrow 'as Europe's most important aviation hub', and recommended one additional runway by 2030, to be paid for by the airport's private owners. But 'where a surface transport scheme is not solely required to deliver airport capacity and has a wider range of beneficiaries, the government will consider the need for public funding', the government said, opening a treasure chest of potential subsidy; it did not specify whether 'international connectivity' was a public or a private interest. No plan integrated jobs and growth in the south-east – or elsewhere in the UK – with Heathrow, which would not be on either Crossrail or HS2. A government that did not believe in intervention was prepared to hand massive subsidies to the foreign owners of Heathrow. Expansion was approved in June 2018, with a planned completion date of 2026; legal challenges citing lack of consideration of environmental factors were lost. Heathrow's users objected bitterly to the cost implications for them. 'Heathrow's on a massive gravy train . . . the total bill for expansion is already running at £32 billion, yet they are trying to deceive everyone that it can be done for £14 billion': that was Willie Walsh, chief executive of the International Airlines Group, the no longer British owner of British Airways.

The Academic Path

You can judge a society and an era by how schools, colleges and their students fare. Young people are all our futures; on them depend tomorrow's productivity and the system's ability to pay pensions to the elderly. 'Education, education, education,' the Blairites chanted in unison; now, the cries were discordant – free schools, grammar schools, academisation . . . Neither camp solved the UK's pressing need for technical skills and an articulated system of vocational training. In 2015 Neville Beischer, head of Wright Robinson College in Manchester's Gorton district, summed up his criticism of the UK's system. It wasn't the intense, narrowing pressure on standards; it was the rigidity, the insistence that every child, regardless of background and ability, had to take the academic path. As a result, Beischer's school had been forced to drop vocational qualifications in hospitality, health and social care, despite increasing employment opportunities in those fields.

Of course, education is about much more than knowledge or skills, but it must in part be about equipping young people for jobs. And these were changing. The internet was now arriving with a vengeance in retailing and logistics. Finance fell from its giddy height, while health and social care expanded, along with that amorphous bunch of jobs called 'professional services'. And hospitality. How many teachers ever said to a class, 'You'll find your vocation waiting on tables'?

Children were told by schools minister Nick Gibb that exam stress was good for them because it prepared them for the 'real world'. Two years later, Theresa May tried to make her swan-song a programme of mental health for schools, made necessary at least in part by exam stress. Action for Children found children to be struggling, anxious, and their parents, grand-parents and carers increasingly worried about them. Teachers despaired. Robin Bevan, head of Southend High School for Boys, talked of a lack of a 'narrative of hope', compounded by Brexit and poor housing prospects.

Schools were caught in a maelstrom of unnecessary reorganisation and confusion about what education could and could not do, loaded with a new responsibility for securing social mobility that schools alone could never realise. Many got on with their vocation, ignoring as best they could the policy mayhem. In 2010 Oakthorpe Primary in Palmers Green sported a new electronic board out front; in 2020 it maintains a Twitter account, and inspectors still rate it as outstanding, in an area with a dense ethnic mix and significant numbers of children on free meals. What had not changed was the weight of expectation. Under Tony Blair's and Gordon Brown's stewardship, schools would right social wrongs; under Cameron and May, they would magic away impediments to opportunity and economic achievement and promote social mobility. Parents continued to believe in exam grades and a link between schooling and earnings; some, lacking confidence in what schools could do, paid tutors and crammers, whose numbers grew. Above the parents and heads and the ministers and their academy promoters floated an uncomfortable truth: schools couldn't turn the social and economic tides. Study after study confirmed that most pupil attainment is not accounted for by schools – they were only responsible for between a tenth and a fifth of the variation. How well a child did (let alone their enjoyment of school) depended on home income, the parents' jobs, their educational level and what they owned – in other words, on class. Here was a scary conclusion, which will define Britain in the 2020s: inequality, not education, was a principal part of the explanation for a lack of productivity.

Of course, school and college made a difference. That was shown by the association between education spend and GDP growth. International and historical comparisons suggested the UK should be spending more than 5 per cent of its GDP on education; the figure was only 4.3 per cent in 2018. Worse, core education spending was falling; schools were poorer. The government, typically, tried to massage the figures, but the impeccably honest IFS calculated that per school pupil spending in England fell by 8 per cent between 2010 and 2018. Growth under Labour gave way to decline, though not uniformly. Spending on nurseries in England rose to £3,200 per child, but what sense did that make when Sure Start and childcare subsidies were simultaneously slashed? Universities enjoyed a bonanza, but not further education colleges: in 2018 £8 billion supported 1.2 million undergraduates in higher education, compared with just £2 billion for the 2.2 million students in further education. For young people in sixth forms and post-sixteen colleges spending per student fell by a fifth.

Perhaps we should welcome penitence. Realising just how much schools and teachers and their pupils had suffered, Tory wannabe prime ministers vied to promise some restoration of funds, Johnson winning with a figure of £4.6 billion. However, like his £1.8 billion for hospital investment, this was flaky. When and for how long, and did it cover teachers' pay and pensions? The most that could be said was that at last they were acknowledging the damage they had done.

Gove's Legacy

In 2010 a government concerned about future prosperity could have built on sound foundations, while paying attention to vocational preparation. Instead, schools in England got Michael Gove and Dominic Cummings. They attacked careers education, with inspectors finding four out of five schools were failing to provide it (though Eton maintains a large, well-staffed careers advisory department). Tory think tanks were heard to ponder whether teachers even need a professional qualification to teach. Gove abolished the General Teaching Council established under Labour. In its place he concocted a £370,000 plan to send all schools a copy of the King James Bible, under his personal signature; it was all they needed as a source of good English. He set out his own prescriptions for GCSEs, taking an unashamedly traditional view (Shakespeare, the Romantic poets and, in history, no Mary Seacole, the black Crimean War heroine). GCSE resits were banned, written testing increased. Gove's monuments outlived him, as in 2020 pupils will for the first time sit the entire range of GCSEs in the 'more demanding' format he pushed, with grading in numbers rather than letters. The change is not going to make any difference to the class profile of the results: in Lancashire, where a quarter of secondary-school students were eligible for free school meals, by the time they took their GCSEs the poorer students were one year and eight months behind the rest.

In retrospect, the Cameron coalition's fixation on reorganising England's schools was extraordinary – or maybe not, in the light of what was happening in health. There were philosophical similarities in approach. Academisation, an ugly polysyllable for an unattractive policy, had been mooted in the 1990s. Labour had singled out 200 of the lowest-performing schools in poor areas to link with business sponsors and be 'freed' from council control. With concentrated and additional resources, they were to have new focus. Now, despite a lack of good evidence that administrative status mattered much, it was decreed that all schools were to be transformed – but without extra money for the system, meaning that if one school got more, another would lose out. Gove first centralised school funding, then smashed the capacity of councils to plan for numbers or pupils with special needs, while pushing 5,000 schools into academy status. Schools would be administered by shadowy, 'multi-academy' trusts, with 1,000 of them in existence by 2017, which proved a ripe feeding ground for heads who fancied themselves as chief executives and were attracted by the salaries and perks that went with the title, plus trustees with an eye on lucrative side contracts for themselves or their brothers-in-law. Not all trusts were commercial opportunities. In 2010 we saw the progress made at Lea Valley High in Enfield, despite the incubus of Private Finance Initiative payments for its building. Its development continued, with Ofsted rating the school as good in 2019. But what had that to do with its emancipation from the borough council and absorption into the Cedars Learning Trust, with its apparatus of chief executive and chief operating officer, both drawing salaries that might have been spent in classrooms?

The Moulsecoomb estate on the edge of Brighton is as 'left behind' as any northern satellite town. Only a couple of miles away from the gaudy glitz of the promenade, its people barely connect to that other, more affluent Brighton. Tucked up against the Downs, it's tight-knit, with a strong sense of community, shaped by adversity.

Moulsecoomb Primary had problems. When Adam Sutton arrived as headteacher in 2016, before he had a chance to get his feet under his desk the inspectors descended and declared the school 'inadequate'. That automatically triggered 'academisation': the school was to be removed from the control of Brighton and Hove City Council, to be administered by a 'multi-academy trust'. Opposition was fierce, with all the councillors against, including Tories, parents, teachers and Moulsecoomb itself. The council had a good educational record, with most schools rated good or outstanding, but it was struggling with lower spending.

Sutton's inheritance was dire. 'A constant budget in cash terms has had to cope with teachers' pay rises, pensions and inflation,' he said. 'A staff of fifty fell to thirty-three. When I started, six classes had no permanent teacher. Teaching assistants have gone. There used to be specialist teams to help with pupils facing difficulties;

now, it's just occasional visits, if we're lucky, and no attendance officer, no safeguarding support. We face terrible delays in help for children with special needs, and Moulsecoomb has many.'

What would academisation bring? 'Not new money, which is what we most need. The council provided services. The chain will charge more for them, top-slicing 3–5 per cent off.' Just as Ofsted judgements can't be appealed, there's no remedy for compulsory academisation. 'The inspector was sympathetic. He said, "I wish I could delay and come back in a year, because I can see how fast you are improving," but to no avail.'

'Parent power' had been the original cry in 2010. Local groups were encouraged to set up 'free schools', subsidised by diverting mainstream education funds. But the policy co-existed uneasily with autonomisation, pursued since Thatcher, by which schools would turn into quasi-companies, competing for parents and pupils, and then – hey presto – improved quality and exam results would leap out of the hat. It was indeed a kind of magical realism. In Moulsecoomb, and in many other places, there was no practicable competition, and the main issues were money for the school and the privation and solidarity of a poor community.

A curiosity of the times was to hear academics and think tanks saying that evidence should be amassed before decisions were taken, while, simultaneously, ministers operated randomly, ideologically and often with blithe disregard for facts or analysis. Academy schools were the example. At Lea Valley High in Enfield, what mattered, and would always matter, were catchment, ethnic diversity, home income, aspiration, the local economy and job opportunities, and teacher morale and capacity. Being an academy, part of a chain, would make no difference to any of those factors, even if it might, theoretically, help improve school leadership, though that, too, was principally about budgets and money.

Propagandists picked on individual academies and extolled their results, ignoring the context, even when the Sutton Trust, a disinterested think tank, said the key to a school's standing in the league tables was the proportion of disadvantaged pupils. Free schools and academies tried to exclude them, along with difficult pupils, hence the practice of 'off-rolling', whereby pupils are removed from an academy's register before exam season. Eight out of ten of those excluded had special needs or were poor or otherwise in need.

About 40 per cent of trusts that operated more than one academy showed progress that was below the national average, while 29 per cent were average. Some chain schools failed altogether and had to be taken over. Others misused public money by paying excessive salaries and giving jobs to members of trust boards. At the Durand Academy Trust and Bright Tribe Trust, operating in south London, auditors found serious failures. Parents had to fight even for basic information, despite notional supervision by Department for Education regional commissioners; the schools' accounts were misleading; some of them weren't dealing with asbestos; and school inspectors and civil servants were not monitoring their performance. The Public Accounts Committee knocked on Ofsted's door and found no one at home: 'We were disappointed that HM Chief Inspector seemed reluctant to offer her views about wider issues affecting the school system.'

Getting Rid of Councils

Despite widespread Tory control of county councils, the government determined to get rid of the local democratic element in schooling. Parents and councillors protested in vain against edicts removing schools from local control. Bizarrely, councils were instructed to ensure enough local places were provided for the growing numbers of children but barred from actually providing those places themselves. Schools now had disincentives to collaborate. Local efforts to pool knowledge and practice in, for example, Manchester were commendable, but councils and schools had to fight against the tide. Incoherence grew when ministers said schools were supposed to cement a common identity, while at the same time encouraging growing numbers of religious schools, which had stronger powers to exclude children outside their own faith, many using religion as a covert means of social selection.

One of Gove's signature decisions had been to end overnight Labour's giant Building Schools for the Future programme of capital works. Which left a lingering stink at Gillotts School, a comprehensive for eleven- to sixteen-year-olds in Henley. It had been chosen for a full rebuild under the Labour scheme, but now its capital budget was barely £18,000 a year – not enough to cope with the smell in classroom X2 when a forty-year-old heating pipe burst. The capital budget for schools was then skewed: large sums were paid to secure sites and buildings for the favoured free schools and academies. An NHS trust in London, thinking of selling a redundant clinic, was approached by a shadowy Whitehall intermediary acting on behalf of the academies who effectively said, 'Name your price.' The Treasury, so fierce and unforgiving in austerity, was underwriting the extravagant purchase.

It was hard to make sense of education policy, beyond that perennial sense with Tory governments that what was being done to the schools was being done to benefit *their*, not *our*, children, who would, like Cameron, May and Johnson, be selectively, if not privately, educated. No effort was made to spare state schools from austerity, and the main government grant to schools was frozen in cash terms right away. The Liberal Democrats claimed to have made a difference when Nick Clegg insisted on a 'pupil premium' – extra funds for schools with disadvantaged pupils – and it ensured average school budgets rose until 2015, increasing by approximately 3 per cent, or 0.6 per cent per pupil. The boost didn't outlast the coalition. By 2019 more than a thousand schools were turning to crowdfunding websites to raise funds, with many appealing for basic supplies such as pencils, glue and textbooks.

Theresa May's interest in education was confined to her party's long-cherished ambition of giving some parents grammar-school places for their children, a policy gaudily dressed up in the rags of social mobility. Her lack of a parliamentary majority prevented the widespread creation of new grammar schools that she had planned, but a few existing ones were allowed to open annexes, which amounted to the equivalent of eleven new schools. Though only partially accomplished, here was another example of policy flying in the face of evidence. If the extra grammar-school children were, as the theory said, being given the impetus to get to university and secure better jobs, how would their individual benefits outweigh the detriment to the rest, who were consigned to what were effectively secondary moderns? The few council areas still with grammar schools, such as Buckinghamshire, revealed worse results overall. Grammar schools showed a marked high-class social profile: the average proportion of secondary pupils on free meals stood at 14 per cent, but in grammar schools it was below 3 per cent. Fee-paying primary schools (in Kent, the *Messenger* reported) 'actively promoted their track record in getting children into selective schools through coaching'. They would, wouldn't they?

Standards

Governments in Scotland, Wales and Northern Ireland eschewed the standard assessment tests (SATs) administered in English primary schools but still measured both pupil and school success in similar ways. Gove's reforms to the SATs taken by ten- and eleven-year-olds made them more rigorous, it was claimed, though the National Education Union found that nearly all primary teachers wanted to end them because they were damaging children and narrowing the curriculum.

After their introduction, the proportion of children reaching the expected standard for eleven-year-olds in maths and literacy rose slightly. That conforms with the broader picture of schools hunkering down, maintaining standards, but in a narrower range. Though Ofsted judged eight out of ten English schools to be good or outstanding, claiming teachers were better supported and had improved promotion prospects, it's hard to dispel a sense that many schools were not happy places. The inspectors' survey of teachers' well-being found Ofsted itself a cause of stress. Teachers in England worked more hours per week (forty-eight) than in other countries (forty), reducing their time for thinking, training and development, with many of those extra hours spent collecting data and preparing for inspectors' visits.

School reports became cut-and-paste efforts, not always individually detailed, though teachers were required to keep weekly technical records of every student's progress. Teaching assistants became a rarity, though class sizes grew. How to take children out of school on trips and visits when support staff disappeared? School leadership was probably improving, but filling vacancies for heads became harder. Later on, one of the transient education secretaries, Damian Hinds, responded to the flight of teachers by making noises about lightening their burden, job-sharing and making it easier to work part-time. 'Exam results will no longer be used to define "failing" schools,' the headlines said. It was on a par with the police minister and others suddenly realising (without owning up to it) that austerity had damaged people, professions and public services.

Teachers' pay had been held down. The NAO found that overall teacher numbers kept pace with pupil numbers, and though the retention rate for newly qualified teachers was stable, nearly a third of those joining the profession in 2010 quit within five years. Teacher shortages developed in disadvantaged schools and in maths and science. The proportion of physics classes being taught by a teacher without a physics degree was rising. The mooted sharing of teachers between private and state schools – like the sharing of gyms and sports fields – came to nothing.

Higher Gets Higher

Parents paid for exclusive secondary schools to help their offspring get on, which for most meant going to university. Here was an institution that, financially speaking, was treated very well, but which was ignored and marginalised in other respects. Money-wise, schools suffered and further education colleges were strained and neglected, while universities had rich pickings. As we saw in 2010, on every campus – the former polytechnics and smaller colleges, as well as Oxbridge, the London elite, Manchester, Leeds or other Russell Group universities – cranes were swinging, plush student flats were going up and some very highly paid professors and academic managers were to be found. Universities spread across entire small cities, such as Durham, and the centres of big ones, among them Glasgow, Manchester and Liverpool. This may have fended off urban decline, but only accidentally, since no one was keeping the score, and definitely not the government. Confusion grew about what universities were for – surely not all should be doing expensive research or teaching students along Oxbridge lines – amid deep unease on the part of the academic workforce. Professors and lecturers were liberal and often left of centre. They lost out not only on Brexit, which threatened the universities' international identity, but also saw all their research evidence about inequality, austerity and so on being ignored.

Labour had opened the door on student fees, establishing the principle that students should pay, helped by loans and grants for those from poor families. Cameron abolished the latter and tripled fees, to be paid for by expanding loans and debt. He found it surprisingly easy to get Clegg to renege on the pledges every Liberal Democrat candidate had made in 2010 (student fees would sink Clegg's party). The policy turned out to be a massive failure, on two counts. It was based on the same Thatcherite idea that was being applied to schools and hospitals: they would be forced to compete. Universities were supposed to charge different prices for courses, based on costs, students' earning prospects and so on. Instead, from 2012 they all charged the same – the maximum £9,000 (later £9,250) – behaving like a cartel.

Fees policy was based on fiscal deceit, though it is not clear, in retrospect, whether ministers – even those as bright as David Willetts – quite understood what they were doing. The ruse was that loans issued to students appeared in the public sector accounts as an asset; hey presto, the universities got billions, without a penny of public spending being recorded. The austerity imposed on the rest of education and other public services was miraculously absent. Only when the Office for Budget Responsibility looked into the numbers did the Treasury shamefacedly acknowledge that up to two-thirds of students were never going to repay their loans. Far from being assets, these were liabilities that could eventually total £300 billion.

Universities were flush with money. They got £28,200 on average for putting on a three-year undergraduate degree, which was 60 per cent higher than their unit income in 1997. From 2015 they were free to admit as many students as they cared to, especially lucrative foreign payers of higher fees. 'Come here to study,' said both prime minister and chancellor. Osborne had been wooing China, and it accounted for a quarter of all non-EU applicants. But 'Don't stay,' said May, as she cut the length of time post-study that foreign students could stay and work. She was adamant in refusing to remove the numbers of foreign students from the total migration figures, even when a vast majority were shown to return home after a brief spell of post-graduation work. Although Brexit hit sterling's value, making higher education in the UK attractively cheaper, the emotional impact of the vote hit the number of EU students applying for a place in a hostile country.

Universities escaped scrutiny. What explained the continuous increase in the number of higher grades being awarded? The proportion of first-class degrees rose from 16 per cent to 27 per cent by 2017. At Surrey University, it doubled to 50 per cent, while at the University of Bradford it tripled to more than 30 per cent. Oxford University historians were 178 per cent more likely to score a first than their predecessors in 1990, and chemists had a 127 per cent higher chance of earning a first. A new regulator called the Office for Students (OfS) was created, to which the Tories tried to appoint Toby Young, a loutish right-wing journalist. The Department for Education claimed he had held teaching posts at Cambridge and Harvard, which was untrue. Young's boorishness proved too big a barrier, and he withdrew. The universities didn't like the creation of OfS, but some regulation was clearly necessary. The new regulator found five university heads who received more than £500,000 in 2017–18, including pay-offs. 'It's good to see signs of pay restraint at some universities,' it said. Some took large risks and plunged into technical insolvency (the University of Reading, for example). Grand overseas ventures folded and expansion at home curtailed. The higher education sector reported a collective deficit of £1 billion in 2017, despite the fees bonanza.

Evidence on the disincentive effect of higher fees was mixed. Students, including many from lower-income backgrounds, expected to get jobs paying less than the loan repayment threshold; only 30 per cent of the cohort of full-time students starting courses in England in 2017 were likely to repay in full. Debt incurred by a typical undergraduate now amounted to £50,000, and that overhang made fees a touchstone issue at the 2017 general election. Promising to abolish them secured applause for Jeremy Corbyn and prompted May to say that 'fees charged do not relate to the cost or quality of the course. We now have one of the most expensive systems of university tuition in the world.' This was disingenuous. It was Tory ministers who had reckoned they could avoid the choice of either cutting admissions or direct subsidy to universities by magicking up higher fees. Shortly before May stepped down as prime minister, the inquiry she had appointed, led by Philip Augar, recommended a cut in fees, to be compensated for by larger direct grants to higher education – in other words, resurrecting the problem she, David Willetts and Cameron thought they had solved.

Augar also said something radical, if far from novel. Students and universities were treated fabulously in comparison with those aged eighteen-plus who were doing courses in the residual sector called 'further education'. Productivity improvement depends on skill and dexterity: to program computers, make things work, organise operations and so on through a long list of practical skills. That pointed to the further education colleges and vocational training. But the Social Mobility Commission discovered a 'vicious cycle', in which those in routine and manual jobs got little or no in-work training and precious little help if they tried to upgrade on their own: the UK spent just two-thirds of the European average on improving adults' skills. Suddenly, in 2019, like Rip Van Winkle awakening at last, the education secretary began making anxious speeches about middle-class children not studying for technical qualifications and how the Germans did vocational education better. Then he was sacked.

Before exiting, he might have admitted that further education funding had fallen by 13 per cent per student since 2010, compared with a university student increase of 22 per cent. The total number of adult learners was falling precipitously, mostly because fewer were taking low-level qualifications (below GCSE). Total funding for adult education and apprenticeships fell by 45 per cent between 2009–10 and 2017–18. The Department for Education's own assessment was damning: the aggregate value of the skills supplied by further education each year dropped from a baseline score of 100 in 2012–13 to just seventy-three in 2019. The City and Guilds exam group complained of competing policies that lacked clear success measures and often ignored evidence. After years of prevarication, a new set of technical exams to run alongside A-levels is due to be introduced in 2020 in a few places, but it has received remarkably little publicity. The Tories' main effort had been to avoid public spending and to pay for apprenticeships by a levy on larger firms. This was worse than half-baked; it was incompetently delivered and open to fraud. Big talk of 3 million apprentices starting by 2020 became in reality a mass refusal by employers even to draw on the funds available, except for those clever enough to rebadge their existing training. Some even tried to claim that highly paid staff on MBA courses were 'apprentices'. The disastrous net effect of the levy was that the numbers starting apprenticeships fell by a quarter from 2016.

7

States of Mind

Bristol has long had a creative buzz, with the BBC's studios, high-prestige courses at its two universities, Aardman Animations, the Theatre Royal and the Tobacco Factory. In 2017 the city was given the UNESCO 'City of Film' designation, the city council and its partners working hard to support locally based productions and encourage the city's diverse population to consider jobs in the creative industry.

A recent addition to the mix is the Bottle Yard Studios, with its workshops, costume and production rooms and eight stages. Run by a not-for-profit company, when we visited the backlot was decked out as a Georgian townscape, the set for Andrew Davies's ITV adaptation of Sanditon, *Jane Austen's unfinished last novel.*

These thriving studios, booked to capacity for 2020, had just produced the revival of the 1970s TV show Poldark, *while a Tudor palace had been erected on another stage for the hit American television series* The Spanish Princess. *Channel Four's* Deal or No Deal *was also produced on site, as was the BBC's* Wolf Hall *miniseries. Harvey's Bristol Cream used to be made here; the site was then acquired by the local authority, which oversaw its transformation.*

In a decade when Netflix and Amazon grew hugely as producers of content, film and television nonetheless still depended heavily on the public sector, as illustrated by Bristol council's role in Bottle Yard Studios. And, whatever happened to its journalism, the BBC remained central to the musical life of the country – perhaps even more pivotal as council grants were withdrawn and companies such as the Birmingham Symphony Orchestra suffered.

Overall the 'national mind' appeared still to be in good shape. Despite, or because of, the higher student fees we discussed in the last chapter, universities went on performing impressively in the international league tables. The UK contributed disproportionately to the advance of science, receiving an average of more than one Nobel prize a year, including British winners no longer living in the UK and foreigners based here. Plays, shows and other writing abounded with treatments of the contemporary themes of identity, ethnicity and gender.

'Culture' can't be easily linked to the economy or public affairs. Time is important, and the cultural capital laid down under Labour in the noughties lasted throughout the subsequent decade. The relationship between austerity and art is not linear. You can plot the popularity of *Downton Abbey* or *Peaky Blinders* against economic and societal trends (or, in the latter case, against Birmingham's sense of identity), but the fit isn't neat. In sports, women's cricket, football and rugby rose in prominence over the decade, paralleling the response to #MeToo, but a gender pay gap persisted. This chapter tries to match political and economic circumstances to how we produced and consumed culture and what we told pollsters about our state of mind.

Courting Failure

Headline sporting achievement belied austerity. You won't get, for example, a Liverpool supporter saying otherwise. Thanks to the athletics infrastructure built up on public subsidy in the noughties, the UK's gold-medal tally at the 2012 and 2016 Olympic Games (respectively behind and ahead of China in the top three, with the US in first place at both) was impressive. But would it last when, since 2012, over a third of English secondary schools had cut timetabled PE, and fewer than one in five children were now meeting the chief medical officer's daily sport and physical activity guidelines? Austerity is having its effects on the pool of tennis talent: in summer 2019 Sport England found the number of public-access tennis courts had fallen by 5 per cent since 2010, there were 371 fewer courts with disabled access and 159 fewer school courts.

Sport, like art, lives in a bubble. When they watched football, leave voters apparently had no qualms about migrants pushing up standards as both players and managers. Under an Englishman, Gareth Southgate, the England football team reached the semi-finals of the 2018 World Cup. With Eddie Jones (Japanese–Australian) at the helm, England's rugby team won the 2016 Grand Slam and reached the final of the 2019 World Cup. Brendan Rodgers (Northern Irish, father Catholic, mother Protestant) left Celtic, who reigned supreme in Scottish football, to take over from a Frenchman, Claude Puel, at Leicester City. Rodgers's new club was under Thai ownership, in a city where people classed as white British had fallen to under 45 per cent of the population. Black footballers were abused by bigots empowered by the Brexit vote, but sheikhs, Chinese and American owners were tolerated. Sport may be a field of dreams, but it is also a tissue of emotional contradictions. Sky, owned by Rupert Murdoch until 2018, ceded its brilliantly successful cycling squad to Jim Ratcliffe, who shared the media mogul's hatred of Europe. Yet he coveted the ultimate prize in cycling, an essentially European sport, which was the yellow jersey of the winner of the Tour de France.

Rattle Returns

Austerity cut the budget of Arts Council England by 17 per cent. George Osborne worshipped Wagner at Bayreuth and proclaimed himself an arts lover, but that did not stop grants to arts organisations from all sources falling by 30 per cent. Arts money had been topped up by the National Lottery, but its revenues were falling. The Arts Council responded by backing selected organisations and painfully casting off others: the Arnolfini gallery in Bristol lost, while English National Opera at the Coliseum was restored to grace. Support for dance increased as a proportion of total funding. Audiences at Sadler's Wells have doubled since the early noughties, and a significant increase has also been seen in audiences watching live relays of ballet in the cinema.

In other words, austerity was far from uniformly negative in its immediate impact, but the seed corn is eaten and tomorrow's harvest will be meagre. However, much rejoicing accompanied the return of Sir Simon Rattle, steeped in the culture and musical institutions of Europe after sixteen years with the Berlin Philharmonic, who chose to become music director of the London Symphony Orchestra in 2017 and promptly began planning a new concert hall built to Hamburg standards. By the measure of bums on seats, theatre was in fine fettle, with foreign visitor numbers buoyed by sterling's depreciation after the Brexit vote. A huge new theatre complex opened at White City with 2,000 seats, together with openings in Walthamstow and Soho, helping total London theatre audiences to go up by a third since 2000. We saw at the Bottle Yard in Bristol the positive storyline for television content. Netflix, spending billions, sought a UK production base, while Disney made *Mary Poppins Returns* at Shepperton Studios, promising more UK productions to come.

Measly

A distinguished gallery director, Sir Nicholas Serota of the Tate, became chair of the Arts Council and suggested that as the rich were doing so well, social pressure should be applied to those of them who did not make philanthropic donations. Sir Lloyd Dorfman, the founder of Travelex and a large donor to the National Theatre, said, 'You would think that at a time of reduced public funding people should be applauding and encouraging others to come forward.' You would think, unless you knew how greedy and philistine today's rich have turned out to be. Established philanthropists went on contributing:

the Wolfson Foundation to the Victoria & Albert Museum, the Sainsbury family to the Royal Opera House, Len Blavatnik to Tate Modern (and the University of Oxford). But the new rich preferred their yachts. Only one in ten of the UK's highest-net-worth individuals were charitable donors, and the median annual gift of those worth more than £10 million was a measly £240 a year. Serota would find it very hard to generate a sense of shame, and the UK rich could not even be bribed: tax reliefs produced only marginal increases in giving.

Besides, some money was tainted. Among the most generous donors to the arts had been the Sackler family, their name adorning the Serpentine Gallery and other good causes. However, after much litigation relating to the role of the family's pharmaceutical companies in the US's opioid epidemic, the Sackler name became almost as toxic as their medicine. As the climate emergency regained its hold on public and political consciousness in 2018 and 2019, Oscar-winning actor Mark Rylance spearheaded the campaign against fossil-fuel use and greenwashing by resigning from the Royal Shakespeare Company in protest at BP's sponsorship. Another national treasure, Miriam Margolyes, followed suit. The RSC divested.

Cultural Vandalism

The (physical) book market started growing again, one in the eye for those who said printed pages would go the way of CDs, DVDs or vinyl – so said Philip Jones, editor of *The Bookseller*. Actually, vinyl itself was being reborn, with 4.2 million albums sold in the format in 2018 (the top sellers being the Arctic Monkeys, who sang about neither the condition of England nor Brexit). The number of independent bookshops, previously in long-term decline, also grew, among them Category Is Books in Glasgow, dedicated to LGBTQ work, Storysmith in Bristol and Lost in Books in Lostwithiel, Cornwall. Book festivals flourished, with some of them even starting to pay authors. From Chipping Norton to Shetland, literature and arts festivals became sites of pilgrimage, attracting Britain's growing population of affluent older citizens.

But borrowing books from a public library became more difficult. People took to the streets in Hadleigh deploring closures that were 'cultural vandalism', in the words of Andy Abbott of Save Our Libraries Essex. Libraries, museums and the arts faced disproportionate cuts, with Councillor Philip Atkins, the Tory leader of Staffordshire County Council, saying 'unprecedented demand' for social care had forced councils to shift funding. In England, council funding for libraries and arts fell by almost £400 million, about a third. The Tory council in Hertfordshire flogged its art collection to 'balance its fiduciary duty to council taxpayers'.

Museums: 'Doing More Weddings'

They help define places; they guard local history and the artefacts of belonging. But after Lincolnshire County Council pulled its funding, Grantham Museum only stayed open thanks to volunteers. Lancashire County Council sold five museums.

Conservation work on local collections of art and artefacts was hit. Curatorial staff at Leicester's museum and gallery were sacked, raising doubts about the future of its Picasso ceramics and a geological collection that included the Rutland dinosaur. The council promised the curators would be replaced by an 'audience development and engagement team'. Labour-run Birmingham City Council's support for the city's museums dropped from £7 million to just over £2 million a year. Now run by the arm's-length Birmingham Museums Trust, the museums cut staff and opening hours but still won a prize at *Third Sector* magazine's 2019 awards, commended for their work with the city's diverse communities. Meanwhile, 'We're doing a lot more weddings and late-night events and we're exploring doing business with China,' said Ellen McAdam, director of the trust.

Rescue from the East or a new imperialism? Sheffield sold its palatial art deco library and art gallery to the Sichuan Guodong Construction Company to be turned into a five-star hotel. Eastbourne cut funding of the Towner Art Gallery by £200,000, halving its support from public funds. Borough leader David Tutt, a Liberal Democrat, said the decision was 'inevitable' given the fall in government grants. Local authorities did sometimes try to protect their heritage: a *Guardian* award went to Cheshire West and Chester Council for the conversion of Chester library into a multipurpose venue.

Funding for national galleries and museums fell to half its 2008 value, but the principle of free admission mostly went unchallenged. The National Museum of Scotland reopened after a refurbishment in 2011; like the big London museums, it moved to increase paid-for special exhibitions and revenue-raising add-ons. The privatisation of the Royal Mail was a give-away of public assets, but from the Mount Pleasant sorting office arose a new postal museum; the child's entry price of £9 included a ride on the underground postal railway. Still, record numbers visited not just Tate Modern in London, but the World Museum in Liverpool and attractions in Scotland, including Doune Castle. Bernard Donoghue, of the visitor attractions association, said it wasn't just numbers: 'Museums, galleries and attractions seem to be pushing the envelope, taking new risks, doing creative things.'

The Arts Tomorrow?

Austerity undercuts tomorrow's cultural life. One teacher said despairingly, 'There is little money in school for glue, paper and clay. I have to ration my resources extremely tightly, and it limits what I can offer. For years we've only had a dirty, broken and worn-out box of mismatched musical instruments.' Already some instruments (French horn, bassoon) are only being taught to pupils who attend private schools. The curriculum narrowed, at the same time as extracurricular provision of music by councils was also disappearing. Jess Gillam from Ulverston wrote a letter to the *Guardian* to say that music wasn't an add-on or 'soft' subject; it was 'part of the fabric of our society; it sits at the heart of human experience . . . learning an instrument can teach fundamental life skills, promoting discipline, empathy, determination and cooperation.' Only just over half of pupils took an arts subject at GCSE, many fewer than before. Ofsted chief inspector Amanda Spellman said arts subjects only mislead pupils into unrealistic expectations of their future career prospects. But what about tomorrow's audiences?

Michael Gove said he was freeing England's schools; he was also reducing their outdoor space and the time children spent exercising in it. To protect their income, academy schools and councils were under pressure to sell sports fields. Indirect evidence of the effects of downgrading school sport came from the rising levels of obesity. Tomorrow's artists and audiences, sportsmen and -women risk emerging only from families paying privately for luxuries that used to be a solid part of the curriculum.

In a disused Lambeth library, Omnibus arts centre tries to feed bodies as well as minds. This half-term, with no free school meals to see them through the day, children are hungry. Breakfast cereals, juice and brioche vanish quickly, before warm-up games in the big upstairs rehearsal room to ease their shyness, as they get to know each other and their drama teachers. By the end of the week they will have written a play with the help of a dramaturge and performed it in the theatre here. Acting in a play on stage in a theatre is an experience these children will treasure for life, helping them to understand what it means, how it feels and how to create.

Keesha says her grandmother, who cares for her, is too poorly to cook, so they have takeaways when there's enough money. She's bouncing with enthusiasm for this arts scheme, top of her class in primary school, but yes, sometimes she and her grandmother go hungry, she tells us quietly. Volunteers here cook lunch for the children – macaroni cheese today – or local restaurants bring in meals. One restaurant brings pizzas at the end of the week to celebrate the kids' finished play, which is full of jokes and tells the story of a king who needs to be taught a lesson in order to rule well, with a lot of references to Fortnite and sci-fi portals into other dimensions. The children long to come back for more. The aim for the summer holidays is to take in another twenty children each week, the food a motive for the parents to get them here, with the art, the imagination and the fun all extras. But Omnibus gets no public funding and only survives on uncertain donations and by hiring out its space. It has to raise £40,000 a year to pay the rent to the council.

Arts Council England and the Creative Industries Foundation warned that closing down arts education jeopardised an economically significant sector, while assorted stars told of their training in subsidised venues that were now disappearing. Ed Sheeran warned, 'You just won't have any home-grown talent at all. The music industry in England is one of the most powerful in the world and one of Britain's best and most lucrative exports. It just makes no sense not to support it.' The likes of Oscar-winner Olivia Colman and *Luther* star Idris Elba said they had been nurtured in their early days by grants and by subsidised arts organisations and venues.

Altered States

Excited talk about altering eating habits was much heard but turned out not to be a reliable statistical guide. Kebab shops were not going out of business. More than half of the UK's diet still consisted of ultra-processed food, high in sugar, salt and saturated fat. Across the Channel, about a seventh of the French diet was similarly constituted. Sustainable food consumption became fashionable, and might prove to be a precursor to a major change in habits. A survey by Waitrose (taking in all supermarkets) said one in eight people in the UK were now vegetarian or vegan and one in five flexitarian – and most of them had adopted the habit recently. Such figures were probably wishful thinking, as other surveys said only one in a hundred was vegan and one in thirty vegetarian. The lower figures matched meat consumption, which was fairly stable: more than 95 per cent of people still ate it once a week or more.

Some behaviour did change, and for the worse. There were now fifteen times as many gambling ads on television as in 2005, and in some towns one in every fourteen retail sites was a betting shop. Psychiatrists began opening the first specialised addiction clinics. The total lost by punters in 2007 was just over £10 billion; it rose to more than £15 billion over the next ten years. Fixed-odds terminals were now generating £1.7 billion a year in gross yield, and even the non-interventionists at Westminster felt they had no option but to cut the maximum stake from £100 to £2 to mitigate the harm the machines were doing to the finances and well-being of low-income households.

Some behaviour changed for the better. A cynic might say that anxiety about plastic did not go far in avoiding the main event, global heating, but consumers did accept charges for shopping bags with little protest. Pioneered in Wales, a 5p fee was first introduced in larger retailers in 2015, with smaller shops exempted; the charge is to double in 2020. Within just three years supermarkets were dispensing half as many single-use plastic bags. As environment secretary, Gove banned plastic straws in a feeble gesture, going with the grain of public sentiment. YouGov found 46 per cent 'felt guilty' about the amount of plastic they used.

With Brexit having sucked the breath out of public activism for so long, the sudden eruption of climate-change protests in spring 2019 was all the more surprising. People had seen hot summers, dry and mild winters and extraordinary weather events without previously joining the dots to global warming. But programmes such as David Attenborough's *Blue Planet II* seized the attention. Surveys said half of adults were 'more worried' now than before and that younger people were generally in favour of action. According to the government's own attitudes tracker, support for using renewable energy reached a record high of 85 per cent in spring 2019. The public had cause for concern: an analysis of data by the *Financial Times* and Greenpeace in November 2019 found the UK was 'on course to miss many of its looming environmental targets' on air and water pollution, biodiversity and recycling.

Old Habits Die Hard

Social media's ubiquity made it harder than ever to distinguish online noise and opinion from actual changes in behaviour and general attitudes. After Hollywood women spoke out against casting-couch rape, exploitation and unfairness, the #MeToo wave saw others from one profession after another stepping forward with similar tales.

Unite the Union found that nine out of ten women workers in the hospitality sector had suffered sexual harassment but most did not think reporting it worthwhile, complementing a TUC survey that found half of all women had been harassed at work. The fate of low-paid women workers in hotels was highlighted in January 2018, when undercover journalists from the *Financial Times* found the men attending a Presidents Club charity dinner exercising *droit de seigneur* over female staff, groping, harassing and propositioning them unchallenged. The charity folded, but follow-up reporting a year later showed a remarkable lack of contrition in the business circles that had supported it.

The long-term trend towards more women taking degrees (proportionately more than men) continued. But they did not necessarily get their just rewards. For the first time, in 2017 the government made all larger employers report the difference between what they paid women and what men received. The results showed an average gap of 9.6 per cent. Finance and insurance paid men 22 per cent more. Just 38 per cent of those in the top quartile of salaries were women, who congregated at the bottom of the wage distribution in catering, caring and retail. It was unclear whether publication of the data would force change. There were more people called David or Steve at the head of FTSE 100 companies than there were women or people from ethnic minorities.

The balance sheet on gender showed pluses and minuses. Theresa May, more conscious of female inequality than Margaret Thatcher, opened a consultation on protecting women from redundancy after pregnancy, with 54,000 mothers fired within six months of returning to work. But the police reported more domestic-abuse-related crime: two women a week were murdered by their partners. Pressure on household budgets and a lack of outside help were blamed – in other words, austerity. The number of places for women to escape to suffered heavily as councils truncated their grants. By 2019, 60 per cent of the women referred to refuges were being turned away, with Sunderland and Devon among the areas of England that were left with no provision at all. A domestic abuse bill was published in 2019, which campaigners said would be of little use when places of safety were available so randomly. The bill died when Boris Johnson rushed to prorogue parliament in order to damp down Brexit debate.

Cuts in social security and services harmed women far more than men: they were the ones most reliant on public transport, the ones juggling childcare, care of parents, family health, housework and – with women's employment expanding vastly – lower-paying jobs. Women still did 60 per cent more housework than men. Official statisticians began to measure this 'unpaid productive activity', estimating the value of care and housework at £1.24 trillion a year. Men did sixteen and women twenty-six hours a week, a third versus two-thirds. Women had certainly not won the war: to Johnson's foreign secretary, Dominic Raab, feminists were 'obnoxious bigots'.

The recognition and celebration of differences in sexual orientation kept moving into the mainstream. David Cameron and George Osborne paraded their metrosexual credentials by legislating equal marriage rights for people of the same sex. But the breakthrough had come earlier with civil partnerships: would the Tories have dared add marriage if Labour hadn't changed tax law and fundamental rights? No one was foolish enough to claim that law and policy in relation to sexual orientation were done and dusted, even when leading politicians could come out, marry their gay partners and have children (the Labour and Tory women leaders in Scotland did much to normalise the status of gay politicians). Johnson had talked of 'shirt-lifters' with homophobic glee, and more than 130 Tory MPs had voted against gay marriage.

Non-Binary

Formal politics was often irrelevant as far as views about gender and transgender identity were concerned. The Economic and Social Research Council reported that young people were moving away from traditional 'binary' identities and adopting a more nuanced understanding of gender. However, statisticians found no change in the tiny proportion of the population identifying as lesbian, gay or bisexual (2 per cent), or as 'other', which was 0.6 per cent in 2017. Some 4 per cent did not know or would not say. The UK remained an overwhelmingly heterosexual nation (93.4 per cent) where, still, 49 per cent of gay men and 32 per cent of lesbians professed a reluctance to hold hands with their partner in public.

Sensitivity sharpened around exploitation of the vulnerable, with an explosion of concern about child sexual abuse, past and present, real and imagined. The number of child sexual offences recorded by the police in England increased by 178 per cent, including a 355 per cent increase in rapes of boys under thirteen. Austerity endangered children but wasn't the entire explanation. Online abuse was reaching 'epidemic' proportions, the National Crime Agency said, estimating that 80,000 people in the UK presented some kind of threat to children online. The government response was to foist new responsibilities on schools. Personal, social, health and economic (PSHE) education was expected to carry a very heavy burden, not just in sex education but also over children's safety online, with new PSHE guidelines issued in 2019. But where were the youth workers councils used to employ, or the school nurses and social workers to support them? Female genital mutilation became a public focus for the first time, with schools and medics alerted to the risk, alongside other barbaric procedures practised within small sects of ethnic and religious minorities.

God kept on dying. The 2019 British Social Attitudes Survey showed a remarkably rapid decline in all religious belief: half now proclaimed themselves non-believers. Hymns no longer featured in the top ten musical choices for funerals, a list topped by 'My Way', followed by Ed Sheeran with the mawkish 'Supermarket Flowers'. The old saying about Scottish Calvinism was now completely inaccurate: 59 per cent of Scottish residents identified as non-religious, rising to 70 per cent among those aged under forty-four. Anglicans, like Theresa May, were at 12 per cent, Roman Catholics 7 per cent. Some 25 per cent now boldly stated, 'I do not believe in God.' Encouragingly, the BSA found the decline in faith was matched by a growing tolerance of other people's beliefs – presumably excluding what they thought about Brexit – though two-thirds agreed that 'Looking around the world, religions bring more conflict than peace.'

Well-Being

When the statisticians measured well-being using various proxies, as well as direct questions about happiness and satisfaction, they found average levels surprisingly high – well over seven out of ten – and buoyant in the midst of austerity. People had been glad to see the back of the financial crisis, and average life satisfaction improved from 2011; from 2015 the happiness and 'worthwhileness' measures levelled off, but given the parlous state of the UK, remained puzzlingly generous.

However, the picture was mixed. In 2017 Gallup's international index showed its highest recording of stress, anger and worry, which tallied with economic anxiety, political dislocation and the rise of angry, hate-filled parties. The Prince's

Trust reported that sixteen- to twenty-five-year-olds' sense of well-being was at its lowest level since its annual index was first compiled in 2009: one in four of the young felt 'hopeless', and many felt bad about job prospects and money. People took more drugs to combat anxiety: NHS figures showed that prescriptions for antidepressants doubled over the decade. The public conversation turned towards mental health. Admitting a problem became almost fashionable: ministers, the royal family, charities, professionals and others said they were breaking down the stigma that was attached to mental illness. Brexit played its part: the Mental Health Foundation extrapolated from polling evidence to say millions had been left feeling powerless, angry and anxious, the inhabitants of London especially.

Older people were some of the most satisfied according to the well-being scores – yet also the most dissatisfied, if their voting patterns said anything about their emotional state. In the UK, life satisfaction now reached its peak between the ages of seventy and seventy-four. The 'old' felt life was most worthwhile, as indeed it certainly was for most of them, economically. Odd, though, that the group most regretting lost Britishness were, on these measures, personally today's happiest.

Being employed had direct and strong effects on people's sense of worth, so a period when jobs were plentiful should have made them feel reasonably secure. The ONS found that in the UK, health, social security and housing were the most important concerns, while across the EU, the most frequently cited issue in 2018 was unemployment, followed by health and social security. Averages, of course, conveniently conceal extremes.

The proportion of people reporting a 'poor' sense of life satisfaction did decrease, while the proportion reporting 'very good' well-being rose – but the increase at the good end of the scale was significantly larger than the decrease at the poor end.

Zeitgeist

So sensibility and economic circumstance did not link straightforwardly, nor mood and overt behaviour. In April 2019 we saw Maggie Smith in *A German Life* at London's Bridge Theatre. Here was a British star in a German-originated piece which assumed a deep interest in continental history, produced without subsidy in a 900-seat space that opened only in 2017. Were all the audience remainers? Did that just point up the fissures – remain versus leave, London versus the provinces, artists versus the masses?

Mind, culture and politics connect, but timings are subject to leads and lags. Little England nativism has been around for a long time. You could read into the Rooster Byron character in Jez Butterworth's play *Jerusalem* (2009) anticipation of leave's themes: in Albion's dark heart festered resentment and a paradoxical sense of victimhood. Authors anticipated, they followed, they cried in the wilderness, in a shelf of works, fictional and factual, about climate change and the environment. Meg Wolitzer, author of the successful novel, then film, *The Wife*, said novels did not just track what was happening in the moment; they looked round the bend and backwards, 'at why we got to this point'. But some simply ignored it.

As for readers and viewers, when they borrowed, down-loaded or bought books, songs, programmes and films, their choices must have reflected contemporary themes, but only up to a point. From where in the collective psyche did enthusiasm for television shows about serial killers, bent coppers and ditsy thirty-somethings spring? Some cultural pathways did wind back to Brexit. A year before its residents backed leave, the provocateur artist Banksy chose Weston-super-Mare as the site of his Dismaland 'bemusement park' critique of decay. The snarling, politically charged electro-punk of the Sleaford Mods reached a global audience. Nostalgia was certainly vogueish: witness the outpouring of musical nostalgia at David Bowie's death and the cult of Freddie Mercury and Queen, which was boosted by the 2018 film *Bohemian Rhapsody*. But most song-writers and artists just wrote the songs and painted the pictures.

Certain books reflected the theme of identity (ethnic, national and gender), others the talking points of sexual abuse, climate change, automation, the invisibility of women in public spaces, the unsustainability of our eating habits, slavery, the meaning of home, social 'ascent', faith. Amanda Craig's *The Lie of the Land* crammed in Englishness, migrants, city versus country, along with ethnicity, murder and pies; not much new there. Lincolnshire, in Adam Thorpe's *Missing Fay*, was an uneasy place, ugly physically as well as morally, its denizens hopeless and demented, misogynistic, perverted and sexually frustrated – welcome to the land of leave. Austerity and Brexit make for ugly characters in an ugly Britain in *Broken Ghost* by Niall Griffiths. John Lanchester, in *The Wall*, created a Britain where climate change has destroyed the life we know and a giant structure keeps the rising sea and rising numbers of immigrants at bay; the future is bleak, divided and tribal. Walls and bleak tribalism got a lot of play, of course, in the plotlines of *Game of Thrones*. According to Amazon, customers who bought Jonathan Coe's *Middle England* went on to buy books bearing no obvious relation to his assembly of characters and events around Brexit, for several of whom there's a happy ending when they decamp to idyllic rural France, with nary a sign of the *gilets jaunes*, leaving the rump marooned across the Channel in an 'equivocal future'. Maybe Brexit was playing out in the background of other fiction querying Britain, gender, class, ethnicity and nationality – Sarah Moss's *Ghost Wall*, Max Porter's *Lanny*, Bernardine Evaristo's *Girl, Woman, Other*. In Ali Smith's *Autumn*, on Brexit day, 'All across the country there was misery and rejoicing,' and a house in a village is daubed with 'Go Home'.

Sifting through the mass of books published, plays promoted, songs recorded and programmes and films made for distribution on the internet or in cinemas, patterns can be distinguished, but any content analysis is bound to be rough and ready, running the risk of selection bias, overinterpretation and reductionism. Novels by Sunjeev Sahota, Guy Gunaratne and Kamila Shamsie wove narratives around migration, terrorism and the life and times of people from minority backgrounds; on the stage, *Nine Night* and *Barber Shop Chronicles* showed aspects of the migrant experience; *Small Island*, a new play based on Andrea Levy's novel, produced at the National Theatre, explored British West Indian relationships, the nature

of which had been exposed, again, by the scandalous treatment of the *Windrush* generation. The voice of the second-
generation Britons sounded out louder, as if seeking redress for
their parents' experiences.

Culture Wars

The phrase 'culture wars' was imported from the US to reflect
the political divides in art and consciousness. After leave's victory in the big Brexit battle, murmurings and expressions of
an anti-diversity, anti-egalitarian, sometimes overtly racist kind
were heard. Strife broke out unexpectedly, over apparently eso-
teric questions: for example, the Boer War and the death rate of
internees in Great British concentration camps. This formed part
of an intermittent effort to rehabilitate the empire, coincidental
with Brexit, and a concomitant push to attribute historical guilt
for the empire – for instance, in protests over memorials to historical figures such as Cecil Rhodes. Questioning the UK and
its past at home and abroad disturbs some but invigorates others. Cambridge University's inquiry into its own historical links
with slavery and Glasgow University's robust self-examination
are brave; from them may come a joint understanding of colo-
nialism and a fuller sense of common identity, or unbridgeable
dissent and fractiousness.

In the midst of it all were journalists, broadcasters and a
new cast of social media activists, mediators, arbiters, shock
troops and doughty defenders. Never before had the party
affiliation of newspaper writers been so clearly displayed. Not

just the owners and editors, but the reporters and headline writers outed themselves as ideologues first, deliverers of truth a distant second. The BBC and the other broadcasters had a hard time of it. Playwright David Hare compared the way he was treated on *Today* – respectfully – with the BBC radio programme's routinely hostile handling of politicians. Yet for many, *Today* exemplified the failure of the BBC to deal with untruth, and its failure to interpret and interrogate the claims and lies around Brexit.

Because it was the *British* Broadcasting Corporation, the BBC was cast into the thick of a culture conflict, in which playing 'Ode to Joy' or waving EU flags at the Last Night of the Proms was deemed an outrage. The Tories froze the licence fee, installed one of their kind as chair of the BBC, then ordered that the corporation take on the cost of the World Service and free licences for the over-seventy-fives, previously borne by the government. Services were curtailed, including BBC Three, while children's programming and BBC Radio 6 Music were saved, thanks to a vocal audience. A new royal charter settlement was negotiated, putting the BBC under the supervision of Ofcom. The licence fee, now £154.40, survived despite its increasingly anomalous nature: a growing proportion of the audience for programmes never watch traditional television channels on traditional television sets. BBC Radio was losing its audience, too, thanks in part to the promiscuous listening habits encouraged by Alexa and her ilk.

An optimist might say that for the BBC to have survived in fine fettle – queries about its journalism notwithstanding – was an immense positive, given the unremitting and politically influential hostility of Rupert Murdoch and his tabloid allies. But by the middle of the 2020s only half of all viewing will be on an 'old' television. Netflix and Amazon now account for 7 per cent of all viewing, against 80 per cent for traditional broadcasters, with young people spending more time on Netflix than on all of the BBC's services. But tuning into programmes on a television set remained the favoured way of watching across all age groups. *The Bodyguard* (written by Jed Mercurio and broadcast from August 2018) could still achieve mass, simultaneous viewing, garnering the highest figures for a BBC production since 2008. Indeed, the BBC continued producing a huge output of music, drama and popular entertainment, and appointed a new female Dr Who, although its treatment of women journalists came under scrutiny. Mark Rylance, mesmerising as Thomas Cromwell, said no broadcaster other than the BBC could have made *Wolf Hall*, the adaptation of the Hilary Mantel novel, which was broadcast in 2015.

Data

Wolf Hall is another example of the intractability of culture: whence the interest generated in early Tudor history, the biographies of Thomas Cromwell – who would have guessed donnish Diarmaid MacCulloch would become a star – and the Shardlake series of historical detective novels? Stories and histories are content; what no one could quite fathom was how the channels and changing forms of communication shaped and strained it. Some 81 per cent of the adult population now owned a smartphone, up a third over the decade; for eighteen- to twenty-four-year-olds the proportion was 96 per cent. Smartphones allowed 86 per cent of people to go online 'daily or almost daily', compared with 35 per cent in 2006. These figures help explain why the volume of letters handled by Royal Mail declined by 12 per cent after its privatisation – though that might also be related to its headlong pursuit of profit and increased stamp prices.

Men spent six hours and nine minutes a day on leisure pursuits, the ONS found, compared with five hours and twenty-nine minutes for women. The gender gap was greatest in the north-west, where men spent an average of 36.2 hours a week engaged in leisure activities, seven hours more than women. Everyone spent most of their leisure time watching TV, reading or listening to music.

After revelations about the manipulation of data collected by Facebook, the sheer irresponsibility of the tech giants became too much. The government vacillated over taxing them but felt obliged to promise to regulate and hold them responsible for what they published; their line had always been that they were merely vessels for what users generated. A White Paper published in spring 2019 promised a statutory duty of care by social media firms and an independent regulator, funded through a levy on them. Social media were established and had become a new source of insecurity.

8

Insecure?

The control room rippled with horror as details of the latest call appeared on screens. Nothing hardens you to the shock of suicide. A mother just home from work had found her twelve-year-old daughter hanging by a scarf, blue in the face, in cardiac arrest. An ambulance was arriving now, police on their way, nothing more to be done.

On a Friday night in the Bedfordshire Police control room, few of the 999 calls were to report crimes familiar from the cop shows. The majority were about mental health. Suicides (and attempts) ranked high, as did missing persons and families worried about self-harming. In real time the call handlers tracked a stepfather who was in breathless pursuit of a child across a dark park on his mobile, and who was warning that the boy might kill himself, as he'd tried before. Officers were on their way.

Callers were known to staff. Here was Ravinda, again, calling incoherently to say her boyfriend had gone missing, indignant when asked to slow down and explain. Every call is treated with the same calm efficiency, no matter how eccentric. No one can ever be sure which one will be a real emergency or when it will come.

Domestic violence reports were frequent, too, usually made by a neighbour: Mrs X can see the man banging on the window next door, his ex-partner telling him to go away, young children screaming. The crew that dashed to the scene later said that they found a young woman with a baby in her arms. She had a swollen eye but would make no allegation. These days, the police won't be fobbed off. Emerald Team specialises in domestics, and a man was arrested and later bailed on the condition that he stayed away.

Here, as in other public services, record-keeping was immaculate, the professionalism punctilious. Yes, they were watching their backs: the public was unreasonably risk averse. What media outlet would turn down a story about some slip-up? Bloggers and social media posters rarely take account of what austerity did to resources: people – and the media – expect the same service or better.

By 2019 things were far worse. Bedfordshire's Chief Constable Jon Boutcher had detailed the force's overstretch to a local MP, who read his letter out in the Commons. On a single night, stabbings put seven young men in hospital, five warders were assaulted in Bedford prison, four rapes were reported and there was a serious traffic accident involving young children, all of which needed attending. The force was 400 officers short. Demand had increased: they used to get 250 calls a day; now it was over 400.

'We need more intelligence, the kind we used to get from neighbourhood policing,' Boutcher said. 'We are sending officers back into schools, permanently, and they hear about gangs and extremism at first hand. I run out of officers regularly for 999 calls.'

The growing insecurity in Bedfordshire could be matched across England. But getting the measure of crime and logging its import for how we lived and voted are hard. Crime appeared to fall over the decade, but then (measured by public anxiety, if not actual offences) rise again dramatically. It spooked the Tories, such that by 2019 Boris Johnson struggled to offer assurances on crime, as if he and his party bore no responsibility for any growth in insecurity during preceding years.

Eras have their signature crimes, megaliths on the moral landscape, and among ours was the murder of Fusilier Lee Rigby in May 2013, near Woolwich barracks. More were killed in other atrocities – on Westminster Bridge, by London Bridge, at Manchester Arena – but the death of the serving soldier struck deep. His assassins were Britons of Nigerian descent, Christian-raised but recent Muslim converts. The police who responded first were unarmed, like PC Keith Palmer, stabbed by another terrorist as he patrolled Parliament in 2017. At some level of consciousness, Lee Rigby's murder focused fear and anxiety about race, Islam, migration, suburban street safety; it may have fed Brexit. In our midst were real and imagined extremists, but in the mix, too, was half-acknowledged guilt at the way soldiers and soldiering had been pushed to the margins of policy and society.

The centenary commemorations of the First World War were inordinate for the same reasons. The war was rewritten as a British event, the eastern and non-European fronts (Gallipoli, too) and French and German deaths ignored. During 2019's remembrance of the Normandy D-Day landings, the Italian campaign and the eastern front went forgotten. This was memory without history. Symbols such as the Tower of London's cascade of red poppies reflected English ambiguity about

Europe, as well as a nostalgia for sacrifice and a longing for national identification, however hollow. Were the poppies celebrating 1914's volunteer soldiers or expressing regret at the exhaustion of imperial power? What was entirely absent was any sense of pending threat, from abroad or at home; for the vast majority of the nation's inhabitants, terror bombings, Russian poisonings and the lingering presence of UK forces on foreign lands and seas barely ruffled the surface of life, transient items on the ten o'clock news.

You could not call *this* insecurity. Brexit proved the point, as did the elevation of Johnson himself. A precondition for both was a puffed-up sense of assurance that we could take a punt, indulge in expressing dislike of Muslims, Poles, the modern world, whatever, regardless of consequence. Ignored went NATO, European security, Russia (which turned out to be trying to manipulate the Brexit vote) and China. This was not a moment of geopolitical reflection. Voters didn't want migrants, but also didn't want to know about the besetting conditions for migration; they applauded calls for a global Britain, as long as it didn't involve commitments. The attention commanded by foreign affairs shrank – and it wasn't at a high level to begin with. 'Do less' had been a predominant reaction to the Iraq adventure; whatever the merits of UK participation, Blair had failed to convince the public. Now, defence – grappling with fewer personnel, ageing equipment, superfluous ships – preoccupied few, even on the Tory right and the jobs-conscious left. Any appetite for foreign adventures evaporated: to public approbation, MPs refused to back President Barack Obama's call to arms in Syria; the UK's Libyan intervention was brief and costless (to the RAF at least), and succeeded, like the invasion of Iraq, in creating yet another failed Middle Eastern state – and in this case, one from which migrants were attempting to cross into the European Union. As for the Houthi rebels in Yemen (or elections in Brazil), they were flashes on a screen, unintelligible and largely unobserved.

Security at Home: Policing

People, mostly, felt secure enough at home to permit a remarkable political volte-face. Keeping the peace and protecting citizens from danger always used to be the first duty of the state, even for those on the right who don't much like government. Now, however, the traditional party of law 'n' order subjected the police and criminal justice system to amputation, jeopardising the public peace – by the subsequent and vocal self-admission of Johnson and crew. For eight years or so, they got away with it. Theresa May was right in claiming the relationship between police numbers and crime was not linear or straightforward, but relationship there was, and steep falls in police numbers and capacity began to alarm the public (and the victims of knife crime), provoking a screeching U-turn from her successors.

Initially, a trump card was what looked like a falling crime rate. But later the number of homicides in which a knife was involved increased significantly, producing a moral panic. In London and other big cities, headlines daily recorded the anguish of parents of mostly young, male victims. May said there was 'no direct correlation' with the fall in police numbers: knife killings had previously peaked in 2007, when police numbers were rising. But it wasn't just the police: English council budgets for youth services shrank by £400 million. There had been a 51 per cent drop in council-supported youth centres since 2011, and a 40 per cent cut in youth service staff. Cambridgeshire's youth service budget fell from £3.5 million in 2011 to £700,000 in 2019; knife crimes rose from 201 to 430 between 2013 and 2018.

Public alarm at specific crimes coexisted with a general lack of concern – at least until 2018. Crime recorded by the police rose by 22 per cent, but the official measure, based on the public's experience, showed crime fell, then flatlined. Burglary rates had fallen to 1973's level, but towards the end of the decade, theft from the person, burglary and vehicle-related theft ticked up. Horror stories started to be told. Gangs were being organised with great sophistication, and their drugs networks arrived in small towns, among them Llanelli. Swansea Crown Court heard how the Welsh seaside town had become a thriving market for class A drugs, spilling over from London and Birmingham. Children were targeted as sellers and transporters of drugs; the link taken out by one arrest could be replaced 'in an afternoon', one chief constable noted.

If the total volume of sexual offences and domestic violence incidents did not change much – studies often linked the latter to economic stress – awareness of them grew, generating pressure on the police.

The stats did not pick up new crime, especially internet fraud. Besides, as we saw in the Bedfordshire control room, dealing with crime only ever occupies a fraction of police time; they are the public service of last resort, to which social services, A&E and mental health turn in emergency. And recall this oddity: many people had (according to the polls) willed austerity but still allowed their expectations of public services to grow.

Nonetheless, the overall crime figures – a Labour legacy – gave May her pretext and excuse. Police numbers were chopped by 15 per cent – 20,000 officers. There are now 40 per cent fewer community support officers, and other police staff went down 21 per cent. One study found forces had lost at least a fifth of their neighbourhood policing capacity. HM Inspectorate of Constabulary and Fire & Rescue Services reported that the cracks were widening. One in seven detective posts went unfilled; if thefts and assaults were investigated at all, it was by underqualified officers. If you were robbed or assaulted, your chances of justice diminished. Detection rates for homicides fell by 10 per cent. As for financial support to victims, awards by the Criminal Injuries Compensation Authority halved.

Budgets for crime prevention were cut in half. At the same time, government grants to pay for local policing fell by a third. Overall, police budgets fell by 19 per cent in real terms between 2010 and 2019. The NAO concluded that 'while no police force has failed financially, there are signs emerging that forces are finding it harder to deliver an effective service'.

Little wonder that officers fell ill. The Police Federation collected individual narratives. David Stubbs, of Staffordshire

Police, sought counselling after stress left him unable to sleep. He was going from one tough job, such as a car crash, to another, such as a stabbing, with no down time during his shift, and with rest days and time off cancelled as his force struggled to cope with the loss of a third of its officers. 'You start playing over jobs in your head and not sleeping,' he said. Ali Livingstone, a Suffolk sergeant, left the force, driven out by the stress of exposure to trouble and trauma every day.

Tory backing for the police had faltered before. Margaret Thatcher had depended on the police to shore up her government, especially during the miners' strike, but Tory ministers had afterwards taken on the chief constables, finding them guilty of restrictive practices. As the anti-state tide ran high, the Cameron government created elected commissioners to sort them out.

This was an odd episode: big promises made amid administrative upheaval but, at the end, precious little to show for it. Police commissioners were established in England, likewise in Wales, which despite devolution remained under the Home Office's thumb. In Northern Ireland, budgets and operations were supervised directly by ministers. What happened in Scotland went with the trend of putting policing more firmly under political control: a single force was created to cover the whole of the country, which made its chief constable and senior appointments subject to parliamentary debate and political machinations. In England, policing had always been political in a sense; deployments during civil disorder or strikes had shown that. But the new commissioners, they said, were going to make chief constables directly accountable to politicians.

The initiative was neither coherent nor consistent. Along with commissioners – ostensibly giving more local control – came centralisation, which was more suited to the instincts of the home secretary. In 2019 Priti Patel showed the Tories' own indifference towards their own creation by cutting the commissioners entirely out of the planned deployment of police to cope with the disorder their Brexit decisions could create. A College of Policing was created, along with a National Crime Agency, apparently beefing up the previous arrangements to improve policing. But MPs later reported that the stronger national agencies had not reduced the inconsistency in standards across England's regional forces; they did not prevent serious organised crime spreading into other counties; and their coordinating centres for human trafficking and slavery did not coordinate.

Commissioners were symptomatic of policy-making in these years: sketchily thought-out, purposes unclear, introduced half-heartedly, then largely ignored. Voters agreed: the turnout at police and crime commissioner elections was derisory. Outside London, where the post of police commissioner remained unelected, few had a clue who they were. They might have justified their existence by mitigating spending cuts, except that many commissioners were themselves Tory and toed the party line. The Bedfordshire commissioner (Labour) failed to secure extra funding when central government imposed suffocating conditions on his efforts to make a local case for a tax supplement. Others did try to get through to the public. David Jamieson, the crime commissioner for the

West Midlands, highlighted the loss of over 2,000 officers since 2010. Shoppers at Sainsbury's in Lytham St Annes encountered Clive Grunshaw, the Labour commissioner for Lancashire, trying to persuade them to pay an extra 46p a week to provide an extra eighty officers. Both were ignored.

Crime evidently failed to disturb the public enough for them to want to pay more. Former Metropolitan Police commissioners warned in 2019 that with resources drained to dangerously low levels, there was a public perception of 'lawlessness', amid perilously low expectations of what the police could now do. Yet in the long-running Ipsos MORI survey crime was the sixth most pressing issue, after Brexit, the NHS, the economy, education and immigration. Despite front-page shockers, people still told pollsters that they felt safe in their area. Or were they becoming inured? 'Policing by consent relies on public confidence, and this is being severely dented,' said MPs. Why bother dialling 999 when the police no longer responded to emergency calls or were invisible on the streets? Inefficacy was evident in the number of summons issued and the time it took to charge an offence – up to eighteen days in 2018. The proportion of arrests on suspicion of a violent offence that resulted in a charge or a summons fell; the proportion of people arrested on suspicion of sexual offences who were charged or given a summons halved.

Unjust Rewards

What happened if suspects ever did get charged was the responsibility of the Ministry of Justice (MoJ). During his one-year tenure as justice secretary, Ken Clarke accepted a drop in his departmental budget of 42 per cent, and its damaging effects worked through subsequently. Clarke said the cuts had to mean fewer prisoners and shorter sentences; the number behind bars had doubled since his earlier stint as home secretary in the 1990s, with no appreciable effect on offending rates. The number of prisoners on remand was reduced, but Clarke's attempt to give sentencing discounts for early guilty pleas led to his dismissal for seeming soft and therefore annoying the *Daily Mail*. So much for the liberal instincts claimed by David Cameron in his memoirs. What Cameron did resulted in more prisoners and longer sentences but less to spend on them, a sure-fire recipe for degradation and trouble.

Clarke's successor at justice, Chris Grayling, embodied dogmatism and incompetence, which in him reached their acme. He would later go on to mismanage road, rail and airports; it was he who let a Channel ferry contract go to a company with no boats and a website cut and pasted from a pizza delivery service. As prisons minister, at first he was merely 'tough' in the way his predecessors from all parties had liked to appear when pandering to the tabloids. He banned books for prisoners (they could not be sent into prisons). Then he fragmented and later sold the probation service – his most destructive legacy. The MoJ used to oversee the supervision of 243,000 offenders through a professional service with a strong *esprit de corps*. In June 2014 Grayling broke probation up into new 'community rehabilitation companies', to be fattened up, then sold a year later. A residual National Probation Service was to deal with the riskiest (least profitable) offenders.

The destruction went ahead, but the profits didn't come. Eight private companies won contracts but couldn't make enough money, partly because they had miscalculated costs, partly because the MoJ had simultaneously extended probation to offenders released from jail sentences of under a year, who are much more likely to reoffend (losing the companies money). Contractual obligations were not met. Magistrates and courts did not trust the companies, and so avoided the community sentences from which they had hoped to profit. In turn, the companies downgraded the riskiness of offenders so they would not have to spend money on supervising them. Working Links, the company running offender supervision in Devon, Cornwall and Dorset, went bust in February 2019, but not until the chief inspector of probation found 'professional ethics compromised and immutable lines crossed because of business imperatives'. With less money, the prisons could not do the resettlement work prior to release that was necessary to speed up rehabilitation. Grayling had claimed there would be savings of £12 billion, but despite the companies' efforts to switch their costs and risks to charities and councils, they simply couldn't make the sums add up. The NAO said reoffending had increased as a consequence; savings had not materialised; pushed by Grayling, civil servants had done shoddy work and had paid the companies more than they needed to (to the tune of £467 million). And so on.

The chief inspector of probation, Dame Glenys Stacey, found tens of thousands of offenders – up to 40 per cent of the total – being supervised only by telephone calls every six weeks instead of face-to-face meetings. White noise was being used to stop private conversations between probation officers and offenders being overheard in open offices. Many of the ever-more visible homeless population were ex-prisoners, released with £46 in their pocket and nowhere to go. Unusually for a public servant in this era, Stacey had the guts to come out and say it: probation wasn't suitable for outsourcing. Public owner-ship has to be the safer option. Eventually, the Grayling scheme was scrapped, leaving the shards of an essential public service scattered across the land.

Big talk was heard about 'social impact bonds', through which private investors would receive a return on their invest-ment in prisons and probation. Despite Whitehall obfuscation, they were exposed as a con, and pilot projects in Doncaster and Peterborough fell through. Prison itself got worse. Inmate numbers rose, fuelled by offenders serving short sentences – magistrates preferred them to Grayling's probation regime. We asked to visit Bedford, one of the jails getting hair-raising inspection reports. We were directed to neighbouring Woodhill, a high-security prison in Milton Keynes, which housed one of Lee Rigby's killers. Its governor, Nikki Marfleet, was dedicated and enthusiastic, and as such portrayed a paradox. Despite austerity, despite bullying and dogmatic ministers and rule by a government that despised their work and the taxation it depends on, the public service could still boast exemplars, passionate believers in collective provision.

But impressive as she is, this governor had a daily mountain to climb. HM Chief Inspector of Prisons had just reported a significant deterioration in safety and activity and chronic staff shortages at Woodhill. A 'restricted daily regime has been in place for three years, with half the prisoners locked in their cells'.

Built in the 1980s, HMP Woodhill smelt of stale cabbage: fresh air is always in short supply in prisons. At a maximum allowance of £2 to feed each prisoner three meals a day, the food could hardly smell good, and inspectors had rated it as poor. Overcrowding meant two prisoners in cells built for one, with barely room for two men to stand up at the same time. The frame of the top bunk was bent and sagging; the cell's open toilet sat alongside.

Ofsted rated the prison inadequate for learning and skills, its training facilities underused due to a lack of staff. A third of prisoners felt unsafe, with an increase in victimisation and violence, and a high number of assaults against staff. Nineteen prisoners had taken their own lives in the seven years to 2018. We watched as one high-security prisoner, briefly out of his cell in a communal area, was encircled by no fewer than six officers. He knocked on the glass when he saw the governor in the next room and signalled that he wanted to talk to her, so she stepped in to meet him. A stream of complaints followed, from the trivial to the serious, disconnected, not making much sense from this compulsive talker as he paced and fidgeted. Sentenced to three years, he had served ten because of his violent behaviour in prison, but now he was due to leave next month. What would he do? He claimed to have a wife and family, and a tree surgery business to return to, though the thought of him with a chainsaw might make anyone uneasy. But out he would go, with £46 in his pocket, utterly unfit for ordinary life, likely to be back within days, the officers reckoned.

Some of Nikki Marfleet's prisoners would manage to stay out, but prisons are largely peopled with reoffenders. She said what so many we met kept saying: 'Start at the beginning. It's Sure Start we need, to help families from the day a baby's born or before. Damage is done so young, that's where I'd put all the resources. That's what makes most difference, saving people at the start.' But here she was, trying to cope at the very end of the line, far too late.

Labour had courted public approval by locking up ever more prisoners on longer sentences. After 2010 things got worse: spending in real terms fell by 16 per cent, while prison numbers stayed at their all-time high of around 84,000. Officer numbers fell by 26 per cent, until riots, suicides and shameful inspection reports forced the government to promise another 2,500; that still left 15 per cent fewer than in 2010. Assaults on staff tripled, and the far more frequent assaults by prisoners on one another doubled, while self-harm rose by 88 per cent. A new generation of laboratory drugs, such as spice (synthetic cannabinoids), became more lethal and harder to detect. They came in by drone or, at Woodhill, soaked into clothing and paper: one sheet of spice-soaked A4 could yield £300 inside. As for rehabilitation, the number of prisoners nationally gaining a basic level 1 or a GCSE level 2 qualification in English fell by 43 per cent, in maths by 38 per cent.

Unlike health or social services, prison is one of the few services where the government has immediate control over demand: by fiat it could change sentencing guidelines and cut prison numbers. Instead, since 2010 the government increased the number of crimes punishable with prison and lengthened sentences. One (sole) improvement was a sharp drop in the number of incarcerated children. The Howard League for Penal Reform, together with the Sainsbury Foundation, persuaded chief constables to send children elsewhere, keeping most of them out of the criminal justice system, which they otherwise risked flitting in and out of for life. The numbers of young people locked up had fallen, but the Independent Monitoring Board condemned the staff shortages, lockdown and violence at the young offenders' institution at Cookham Wood. Cost-related lapses were also recorded at the Medway Secure Training Centre, run by the contractor G4S. Prison inspectors reported disturbingly high levels of self-inflicted harm, which were increasing year on year. By 2019 – we have seen this pattern before – the Elastoplast was being unrolled and staff recruitment had begun for youth offender institutions, but going nowhere near replacing the 25 per cent of staff lost.

Eventually, the MoJ got back to the future. A more sensible minister, David Gauke, expelled from the Conservative Party by Johnson, echoed Clarke in deploring the expense and ineffectiveness of custodial sentences. His suggested remedies

– tough community orders and tagging – depended critically on the probation service that Grayling had smashed. Yet Gauke was far from resistant to media hysteria. The Parole Board ordered the release of a convicted rapist, John Warboys, but the ensuing storm of protest from victims' groups and the media led into panicked revision of its terms of reference. Victims of crime would acquire the right to challenge the release of violent offenders.

Prospects for justice were diminished by a combination of budgets and dogma. The Theresa May excuse was deployed. Crime was falling, so there would be fewer court appearances. Some 295 crown, county and magistrates courts, along with tribunals and family courts, were shut, according to the House of Commons Library. Half the magistrates courts in England and Wales closed, many sold off in a desperate attempt to raise funds for maintaining what remained of the estate. Defendants, plaintiffs, victims and witnesses now had to travel long distances, and they often found that the swollen backlog of cases had caused hearings to be postponed or adjourned to another distant court. HM Courts and Tribunals Service (HMCTS) – its own staffing budget cut by 40 per cent – said that everyone should be able to reach a court by 10.30 a.m. if leaving home at 7.30 a.m. and travelling on public transport; a total of six hours travelling to and from court on an attendance day. An academic study found that local court closures led to increases in the number failing to attend hearings. Since 2012 legal aid had gone down by £950 million a year in real terms (pushed through by the Liberal Democrat justice minister

Tom McNally, who recanted once he left office). A review by the MoJ acknowledged that those savings might have merely shifted costs to other departments.

The MoJ dressed spending reductions up as new IT and digital modernisation, but, unsurprisingly, it did not go well. As with Universal Credit, ministers made bland assumptions about poor people's access to and ability to handle the internet. IT project management was poor, investment inadequate. Lawyers raised the question, too, of whether remote links, video screens and self-service websites served the wider aims of justice. Simultaneously, the government severely restricted access to legal aid, leading to a four-fifths reduction in the numbers receiving it. The 2012 Legal Aid Act disqualified even those on the minimum wage. Law centres shut and legal aid solicitors vanished: the official aim was to cut the number of criminal lawyers doing legal aid work from 1,600 to 500 or so. In a remarkable reversal of English legal practice, those wrongly charged and found innocent would no longer get their reasonable costs repaid. Among them was a Tory MP, Nigel Evans, who found himself falsely accused of a crime and had to fork out many thousands of pounds; regret for his support of the legislation was perhaps a form of justice.

Judges found themselves dealing with more and more 'litigants in person', who tried to make their own case in ignorance of the law and their rights. Those evicted from their homes no longer got help to defend themselves against landlords, nor when housing benefit was unjustly withheld. People were left to represent themselves in cases of debt, unfair dismissal, clinical negligence, immigration and schooling. Among the victims were parents left to struggle alone in the family courts. Coram, the children's charity, was grant-aided to offer parents advice – but only in the form of a single telephone conversation, not face-to-face and certainly not in court. We listened in at its Colchester call centre. Staff were under intense pressure, the phones ringing non-stop. A thousand calls a day went unanswered.

One mother was panicking. The court had given her Iranian ex-husband visiting rights, and she feared he would steal their children because he had possession of their passports. Here was an emergency where previously legal aid would have paid for a solicitor to take urgent action; now, she risked losing her children for ever. 'I went to the police, but as he hasn't committed a crime yet, there's nothing they can do. I'm completely broke, I can't afford a solicitor. I'm supposed to go for mediation with him, but it's in London, and I can't even afford the train ticket or to take the time off work. I'm a nurse and I can't change shifts.' The Coram advisers could only tell her: Go to mediation, or you will look obstructive. Like all family cases, it was complicated, and the adviser talked her through it several times, calmly, kindly. Unsurprisingly, the mother sounded distraught, as this was her only chance of advice and support. If she called again, she probably wouldn't get through.

Security at Home and Abroad

But most people were not victims. Here's a characteristic of public services: few are experienced directly by 'the public'. What happened in prison took place out of sight, out of mind; ditto the courts. The majority could usually comfortably ignore the unfortunates – the victims of crime, welfare recipients, minorities, the foreign casualties of war and disaster. This was an era of inwardness, of hunkering down, averting the gaze. Even before the Brexit vote, the UK had become more parochial, less interested in the wider world. Events touching on foreign affairs came and went without eliciting more than transient attention with respect to their causes and contexts in the Middle East or Africa – or, indeed, the rest of Europe.

As Brexit fever raged, a posse of ex-diplomats spoke up about the UK's 'weakened standing in the world [and] threats to national security and loss of influence'. They were preaching to deaf ears. The very possibility of Brexit sprang from a retreat from the world and its problems – mass migration across the Mediterranean, Russian pressure, Isis, Chinese hacking. Reaction to the Skripal poisonings in Salisbury was oddly muted in both right-wing media and among the public. Even aggression in a cathedral city in the heartlands failed to provoke an outwards-directed, adult response – which might, among other things, have raised questions about the capacity of the UK to deal with Russia alone. The Russians should 'just shut up and go away': the puerile foot-stamping by defence secretary Gavin Williamson suited the hour. Perhaps childishness was his qualification for later being appointed to the education brief in Johnson's Cabinet. When Putin attacked, no Aeroflot flights were grounded, no significant freeze imposed on Russian finance or energy operations. Russians could interfere in UK elections with impunity, including the EU referendum, making a mockery of leave's posturing on national security. Russian submarines, meanwhile, had a free pass to threaten the trans-atlantic cables carrying most of the world's internet traffic; the UK had lacked airborne submarine monitoring since the 2010 retirement of its Nimrod patrols. European security crumbled from within as populists in Italy and authoritarians in Hungary paraded as pals of Putin.

The UK did not – could not – just disengage. It remained a great power in terms of its military and nuclear capability, economic strength and diplomatic reach; warship(s) still patrolled in the Straits of Hormuz, even though there were not enough of them to accompany oil tankers; it still occupied that prized if worthless seat on the United Nations Security Council. Cameron had buffed his liberal credentials by committing to an aid budget pegged to 0.7 per cent of GDP every year, but even before he left office it was being raided to cover gaps – for example, to pay for military peacekeeping. Most of the Brexiters saw 'global Britain' as one without any commitment to development aid, a view taken by the majority of Johnson's Cabinet appointees.

Centripetal forces still converged on London in sufficient strength to make Johnson's keening after former greatness all the more poignant. The UK could still undertake military engagements, but half-heartedly; new foreign interventions were few, to the relief of many. RAF jets flew sorties over Benghazi, and Cameron had a photo call with Nicolas Sarkozy after Gaddafi was removed, but their celebration of the liberation of Libya was short-lived. The UK subsequently abandoned all responsibility for a disunited, desperate country that quickly became a staging post for migrants and refugees. An investigation by MPs found that planning for the aftermath was minimal and ham-fisted.

Big Defence, or the even Bigger Defence fantasised over by some, had to mean more spending and a Big State. The Tories had problems there. Similarly, as Christopher Hill argues in *The Future of British Foreign Policy*, post-Brexit the Foreign Office and diplomatic service would need to be mightily expanded in order to do the fabled trade deals and reassert a global presence. Here's another example of the odd decomposition of historic Toryism: once, the warfare state was central to its worldview, but it was also one approved by Labour voters in Sunderland and Strathclyde; now, the pro-military strain was much diluted. The public were not so keen, putting defence well below health and education among their spending priorities. Leave wanted nothing to do with the Continent. So what happens to NATO, with its implied commitment that British soldiers might be sent to die in Estonia, on the border with Russia? Even at home, the faint appetite for muscular action was oddly out of kilter with bellicose Brexiter sentiment.

Policy-makers, like the public, were hesitant and unsure. Syria proved the point. In August 2013 Cameron's bid to bomb the Assad regime was rejected by the Commons. A year later, air strikes against IS outside Syria were approved, and extended within Syria in 2015. To what purpose? The UK then ran away completely from any responsibility for the flood of refugees out of Syria who were lapping up on the shores of Greek islands and, in due course, the Munich railway station – but no, they were not welcome in Dover. UK military operations in the Middle East and Afghanistan were now residual, almost private, out of sight and pretty much out of the public's mind, which was just as well, since the armed forces' performance in the latter country raised multiple uncomfortable questions.

As a former colonial power (today's appendages still including Gibraltar and the tax havens of the West Indies), the UK had particular reason to understand that domestic life was inescapably bound up with actions abroad, but it turned out that it was keen to deny the connection. Retreat from empire had involved tawdry decisions, especially over former colonial citizens who had the right to come to the 'mother country'. Mother not only did not love Ghurkhas or Farsi translators or children of the old empire; despite spending lifetimes here – working, paying taxes, raising families – she wanted rid of them. The perfectly legal arrival of West Indians in the UK had been recorded on landing cards that had been lost by the Home Office, which vies with the DWP for the accolade of the worst-run department of the last decade. It wasn't just the cruelty, unkindness or bureaucratic bungling, but the sheer incoherence of ministers and officials. The *Windrush* expulsions (the name came from one of the boats on which West

Indian migrants had arrived in the 1940s) occurred just as the Tories were talking up a fictional 'Empire 2' and extolling the openness that would ensue after Brexit. Since it did not apply to Poles and Bulgarians, or to (black) stalwarts of the Commonwealth, to whom exactly was this openness supposed to extend? After a number of senior citizens had been deported, political pressure forced the resignation of one home secretary, Amber Rudd. Her replacement, Sajid Javid, was the child of Pakistani migrants who became a banker. This showed how equal opportunities worked on the right: why shouldn't British Asians be as reactionary as any other Tory home secretary? It was a question that was enthusiastically addressed by Javid's successor, Priti Patel.

Geopolitical plates shifted, the public oblivious, policy-makers impotent. China rose, treating as insults the feeble UK protests at its subversion of the autonomy and democracy supposedly agreed for Hong Kong. Most predictions about its evolution were well wide of the mark, especially those blandly saying that the country would follow the stipulated trajectory and become more liberal and democratic. President Xi Jinping tightened the Communist Party's grip. Trade deals were talked up by Brexiters at the same time as security chiefs warned of Chinese companies infiltrating defence systems. As with the UK's dealings with Saudi Arabia, a source of finance and arms purchaser, proud sovereignty soon gives way to the begging bowl and the kowtow.

Foreign and domestic kept colliding, without ministers or the system understanding what was happening. Ditto over

Donald Trump. He and his right-wing backers played UK politics through the likes of Liam Fox, Nigel Farage and Johnson, and with a series of direct interventions that formerly would have been regarded as intolerable and – ahem – an infringement of sovereignty. The ousting of the UK ambassador in Washington illustrated the new intertwining and the willing collaboration of UK politicians, journalists and influence peddlers in subversion. What once might have been called treason had become just a move in a game of ideology and power-grabbing – the *Game of Thrones* analogy once again.

The armed forces' purpose and their ability to do anything more than entertain the tourists on Horse Guards Parade grew more and more uncertain. The government claimed its NATO-ordained target of spending 2 per cent of GDP on defence every year could be met if development aid and intelligence spending were counted in. This fancy arithmetic was an austerity-era ruse. But it did make sense, or at least it would have done had the government been capable of thinking in the round, joining defence to foreign policy, based on some wider vision of the UK's place in the world which, in turn, had secure domestic backing. Sir Mark Carleton-Smith, chief of the general staff, argued that peace and war were two increasingly redundant states, with authoritarian regimes (Russia, for example) exploiting the 'hybrid space in between'.

If the world was a more dangerous place, why reduce defence capability 'on a more or less arbitrary basis', asked Sir Jeremy Blackham, former deputy chief of the defence staff. That's the keyword again, 'arbitrary'. The strength of the armed forces fell, with a 2019 deficit of 6.6 per cent between the numbers required and those enlisted. In 2012 the MoD signed a long contract with the outsourcing company Capita to manage recruitment to the armed forces. The NAO found that Capita had consistently missed targets by up to 45 per cent. Army chiefs openly recommended buying in private security companies – mercenaries – to cover for operations, knowing their manpower was deficient.

What was the twenty-first-century purpose of the soldiers, or the Royal Marines and their (small-scale) amphibious assault capacity? Seaborne operations would have to rely on the French Navy – the same navy, presumably, that would be out in the Channel protecting French fishing boats from post-Brexit attack by Paul Joy from Hastings, to whom we talked in Chapter 2, or fishermen from Cornwall (whose catch could be sold only if French ports were open to their exports); the same navy the UK hoped would help out in the Gulf, to avoid utter dependence on the whims of the Americans. Tobias Ellwood, the defence minister about to be sacked by Johnson, bleated, 'If we want to continue playing a role on the international stage – bearing in mind that threats are changing, all happening just beneath the threshold of all-out war – then we must invest more in our defence, including our Royal Navy.'

In theory, a reversion to old-style pro-military Toryism could start to rebuild the fleet and the forces (if the big money involved were found). But defence demanded rigorous thinking, which had to take in ideology and Trump and the skein of international commitments that an ostensibly sovereign

UK could never escape. What was 'national' defence when American planes were needed for our aircraft carriers because there weren't any British ones? And what about our capacity to detect the enemy submarines stalking them, let alone the surface support ships the carriers needed? The UK's nuclear deterrent was owned by an increasingly unpredictable and unreliable US. MPs scoffed: the deterrent was no longer 'fit for purpose'.

Old reflexes still twitched. The UK remained a big exporter of armaments, and a 'defence industrial strategy' existed, if weakly. But the UK was also a huge importer of defence equipment and lacked 'control' of equipment procurement. The marginally UK-owned firm BAE clung to a role in the Eurofighter Typhoon programme, but its completion depended on foreign companies and components; future generations of fighter aircraft would necessarily be built by non-UK firms. Already the American company Lockheed Martin was lead contractor on the F-35, the new stealth fighter, for which the UK had signed up. Austerity had married a fixation with markets, and Brexit had scuppered intra-European industrial collaboration. Analysts said ministers had gone for the lowest-cost options, regardless of industrial capacity and sustainability. Here was information service IHS Markit in 2019: 'This policy led to the end of the vehicle industry and is now set to see the UK's aviation sector lose large segments through lack of domestic offset from foreign manufacturers. Brexit will accelerate this trend.' For example, the construction of Royal Navy support ships was put out to international tender, further jeopardising the future of the remaining UK shipyards.

In the 2018 autumn budget more money was promised to defence, and the IOUs continued to build up during and after the 2019 Tory leadership campaign. But auditors kept pointing to the gap of £7 billion between expected costs and budgets, a figure that would double in the event of any predictable crises happening, let alone unpredictable ones. If medium-sized nation states such as the UK could no longer organise their own defence, logic said they had to cement and cherish the international links and treaties on which collaboration with other states depended. The government claimed to be doing that through NATO, but NATO and the EU were joined in subtle yet essential ways. Besides, Trump was now saying that NATO was finished.

Defence reviews buckled when they hit the question of the UK's place in the world. What was it? The mantra chanted by ministers was that the UK remained a leading power, world-class, with a full military capacity. NATO was the cornerstone of security, anchored in the military might of the US in Europe. The Commons defence committee opined that 'the US and UK are close allies with a uniquely broad and deep defence and security relationship, and a shared understanding of the challenges we face'. Both parts of the sentence were untrue before Trump entered the White House, and became even less credible afterwards.

9

Places

After the recession Chris Hill, the senior partner at Hawsons Chartered Accountants, had seen Sheffield struggle with high unemployment. City centre construction projects were left half built as banks called in their loans and developers crashed. Hawsons themselves only just managed to avoid making staff redundant, but they stopped taking on new graduate trainees.

Since 2015 things had got better. Hill thought the city was on the up; visitors got a sense of its reinvigoration and buzz (if they averted their eyes from the roofless and the drug addicts in city centre doorways). Yes, he mused, clients in retail were having a bad time of it, with shops shutting, mall rents plummeting, but the manufacturing picture had been positive. Sheffield companies sat in the supply chain of Rolls-Royce, Boeing and McLaren.

'Our two universities are turning out highly skilled young people, which itself draws companies here,' Hill told us. 'A lot of digital start-ups, wages increasing. Ability to borrow has certainly improved.' But the day we spoke, he had just attended a gloomy Bank of England seminar on the shortfalls in business investment. Hill, a remainer, believed Brexit was to blame. 'I see companies sitting on hundreds of thousands of pounds' worth of stock, not knowing what might come next, let alone investing.'

All in all, however, his judgement on Sheffield in 2020 was evens: 'We're just about back to where we were before the crash.'

So, overall, no progress. Sheffield and other cities struggled to recover from the recession, struggled with long-term economic trends, struggled with austerity. 'Cities are left in limbo. They have some control over policies, but most feel like they don't have a voice in national government.' So said Cities Outlook 2019. Five years after its fission George Osborne's Northern Powerhouse felt more like the reactor at Chernobyl, silent and empty. The government feared England's cities because they were not Tory, because they voted remain, because they embodied the necessity of an active state. They were penalised. Day-to-day council spending in cities fell by £386 per person a year, compared to £172 elsewhere. Those are averages. Spending per Liverpool resident fell by £816.

Per resident of Barnsley it fell by £688. We talked to council leader Sir Steve Houghton, once a mining engineer at Shafton Colliery. The spoil heaps were long gone, and he was fizzing with ideas about transforming the town centre, installing biomass heating in Barnsley homes, generating conviction that the town did have a post-industrial, post-coal future as a place of exchange, markets and learning. But 68 per cent of Barnsley's population had voted leave. The place had turned in on itself. Long gone were those optimistic days when (out of one eye, when the sun was out) the steep streets leading up to the town hall could be compared to a Tuscan *centro storico*. Old rivalries between the Yorkshire cities had re-emerged, especially between Leeds and – Barnsley in between them – Sheffield. Houghton's complaint was about the distribution of government grants, social need and financial justice. 'If you are an affluent homeowner who also owns a car and computer and has money to spare, I cannot see how that justifies the same council resources as someone who potentially may not have stable accommodation, relies on public transport to get around and on computers in local libraries to access welfare. Not only is it grossly unfair, but it's illogical. Any finance officer will tell you that the cost of providing services in their borough increases in their more deprived areas due to demand and as residents are less able to finance their needs themselves.'

Regional disparities are greater in the UK than in any other European country, and while, as the Resolution Foundation reports, gaps may not have grown over the decade, abiding differences in economic performance are nonetheless locked in. South Ribble in Lancashire had 25 per cent of young people not in education, employment or training; in North Hertfordshire, it was 1 per cent. Evidence of geographical differences abounded: for example, austerity accentuated sharp relative increases in deaths from cardiovascular problems and alcohol and drug misuse in the north.

The government could not be indifferent to place, but for its MPs and supporters place was primarily comfortable, southern and suburban. The nature of places shaped the Brexit vote but subsequently 'played little role' in policy, said a study – in other words, leave places got no reward. Nonetheless, the contenders to succeed Theresa May all pledged their allegiance to devolution and localism, failing to address Houghton's complaint and saying little about revenue support. They stuck Elastoplast here, offered a modicum of support there, leaving the principal causes of distress – austerity and grant maldistribution – untouched. 'Growth deals' were announced – for example, for Grimsby, consisting of £30 million for regeneration and roads. A cynic would say the purpose was to give the local (Tory) MP headlines for a scheme that, at best, would support the construction of a maximum of 800 dwellings a year in the 2020s. Blackpool could apply for a share of a Coastal Communities Fund, invented in 2012, but the total of £170 million was meant to provide for 278 projects in English seaside towns, and they, like Barnsley, were simultaneously having to subsist on sharply reduced revenues. Blackpool had to sell its deckchairs to try to make ends meet. The resort's problems were endemic and paradoxical. The more the economy sank, the cheaper accommodation became – holiday bed-and-breakfasts became bedsits – and the more unemployed, sick and disabled people were attracted to (or pushed into) moving there. Thirteen per cent of Blackpool's working-age population became dependent on welfare benefits, and prescriptions for antidepressants soared.

Place Is Fate

Increasingly, where you were from determined your chances in life. 'Students in Ipswich schools, especially those from disadvantaged families, are not achieving the same school exam results as they would if they lived somewhere else.' So said Clare Flintoff, head of a local academy trust, who – like many educators – put her faith in the classroom. The belief that disadvantage could be overcome by spending more on education and pushing students harder was well intentioned but myopic. Struggling Ipswich students were not doing well because their homes were poor and their parents' employment was unstable, their destiny truncated from birth.

Growing up in Hastings or Portsmouth, your risk of dying from heroin misuse was higher. In poorer areas, GPs prescribed more painkilling drugs, risking US-style opioid addiction. Seven out of ten high-intensity users of A&E lived in the more deprived areas of the country. Infant mortality in the least deprived parts of England was 2.6 per 1,000 live births, but 5.9 in the most deprived. It was 6.4 in Manchester, which was still poor behind the glitz of its successful city centre. Young people could not afford to move on and out, with any extra pay being consumed by higher rent. In 1997 a Scarborough resident on average earnings would have been 29 per cent better off on moving to an average-paying job in Leeds. By 2018 the advantage of moving had shrunk to barely 4 per cent. Moving from Sunderland to York now meant a drop in earnings of a quarter, once rent was paid.

Area rubbed off on children. In better-off places, perhaps because job opportunities were more varied, children from disadvantaged families fared better. Being poor in Paddington was less disadvantageous than struggling in Shanklin; in Westminster, 64 per cent of children eligible for free school meals got GCSE A* to C in English and maths, compared to 27 per cent on the Isle of Wight. Robert Joyce of the IFS said figures showing the geographical concentration of affluence and high incomes in London (the capital had at least a third of the UK's top 1 per cent) 'may be one reason why many of those on high incomes don't realise quite how much higher their incomes are than the average'.

The Golden Goose

An academic geographer, who should have known better, blamed London's 'monstrous predominance'. But the capital was itself hugely divided. Poverty characterised Tower Hamlets, Newham and Dagenham, and to millions of its struggling denizens it did not feel like the streets were paved with gold. London had the highest rate of child poverty of any English region; payday loans were nowhere more rife than in Croydon. The City of London, for better or worse, continued to generate not just a large slice of GDP, but also the UK's external earnings, without which the economy would have looked a lot worse. The ONS confirmed that since 2010, three regions – London, the south-east and east – took in more tax revenue than was spent there, and the gap between them and the rest of the UK was stark. London raised £17,090 per head, the north-east £8,938. Not to put too fine a point on it, leave-voting Tyneside was subsidised, heavily, by remain-voting Londoners, who each paid an average of £3,905 more in taxes than was spent on them. Nottingham had the lowest disposable incomes in the UK: average household income per head, after taxes and benefits, was £12,232 in 2018. Compare that with £58,816 in the London Borough of Hammersmith and Fulham. The figure derived from Nottingham's very high proportion of workless households; in one ward, Arboretum, half of all children were living below the poverty line.

Residual social democracy survived in so far as money continued to be redistributed via tax credits and welfare from one area to another, evening up the material lives of people in poorer places; the national minimum wage also helped here. But in London, productivity, in terms of output per head, was nearly double the level it was in Wales and Northern Ireland (and Cornwall). These disparities, not new, provoked no response from the government. Except in Northern Ireland. To cling to office, Theresa May bribed the Democratic Unionist Party, and Boris Johnson continued the bungs. Theirs was the icing on an already fruity cake – at £14,195, Northern Ireland had the highest public spending per head of all the UK regions and nations.

Devolution Ignored

American states were once called 'laboratories of democracy', where different policies could be tested. Devolution in the UK was a gigantic experiment, too, except no one was in the laboratory or bothering to take any measurements. The centre of government (the prime minister or chancellor) might have tried to compare and contrast, drawing useful lessons. How, for example, were the parliaments and assemblies performing, in terms of gender, scrutiny, turnout, public support and so on? To have sought an answer implied interest in the *quality of government*, but it did not exist, so differences between parts of the UK grew and shrank at random. English NHS spending grew faster, though Scotland still spent 8 per cent more per person and Wales 3 per cent.

Brexit was a misnomer; it was never a *British* exit. Studies showing the differential impact of Brexit – the north-east would be severely hit – were ignored, both by government and leave voters. Leave's tally in Scotland was 12 percentage points lower than in England. Whatever it was that England wanted, Scotland didn't, and First Minister Nicola Sturgeon staunchly opposed Westminster's claim to have a UK mandate. Her nationalists, in government since 2007, only just failed to secure independence in 2014 and were determined to try again, even before Johnson arrived gift-wrapped as a generator of dislike of what the UK had become. A majority in Northern Ireland also voted remain, though turnout was nine points lower than the UK average. Ireland, north and south, received marginal attention before and during the campaign; afterwards, the border became central. Conditions ripened for centennial reversal of the 1922 partition. In its pro-Brexit vote Wales was a pathological case of self-harming; meanwhile, it became more autonomous than ever before.

Ministers, along with officials, chatterers and corporate chiefs, paid little heed to acceptable levels of divergence and inequality within an ostensibly unified state. An example was the ban on abortion in Northern Ireland. Pressed by women MPs, a Tory minister said Northern Irish women could go to NHS clinics on the mainland. The DUP said there could be no variation in policies between Northern Ireland and the UK, except when it came to abortion and gay marriage. Westminster MPs were not the only ones to spot the contradiction and they legislated to give women in the province the same rights as elsewhere, taking their chance when the Stormont parliament had put itself out of business. While Stormont still operated, up to 2017, the newly fissiparous future of the UK was signalled when the four governments were led by the SNP in Scotland, Labour in Wales, the DUP and Sinn Féin in Northern Ireland and the Tories in England.

Citizens in different parts of the UK now faced different tax demands and spending patterns, in unexplained asymmetries: for example, Scotland and Wales now had higher thresholds for paying stamp duty land tax, which had not been devolved to Northern Ireland. The IfG concluded that the 'financial relationship between the UK's four nations increasingly lacks coherence or any guiding principles'. Some of this stemmed from the relative generosity of the Barnett formula, which was used by the Treasury to distribute funding mainly according to past spending. Scotland, Wales and Northern Ireland got a spending allocation in proportion to their share of the UK's population, but the formula did not reference socioeconomic need, and so did not compensate Wales, where 25 per cent of the population was now over sixty-five, compared with 22 per cent in England. Austerity was replicated in the budgets allocated to Scotland, Wales and Northern Ireland. Their governments could pick and choose priorities within these block grants, and differences did emerge; broadly, however, austerity was a UK phenomenon, even if, for example, Scottish prison and police budgets were relatively protected.

The momentum of Labour's radical programme of devolution carried the Cameron coalition unthinkingly along, and it approved more powers for Edinburgh and Cardiff. The Welsh assembly gained legislative powers in 2011 after a referendum, in which approval was granted by residents warming to self-government. The nationalists commanded Scottish politics, and David Cameron, without giving much thought to its timing or principles, was pushed into an independence referendum. With a turnout of 84 per cent, it was a pretty comprehensive display of what Scottish residents then thought. The union was saved, by 55 to 45 per cent, thanks in part to last-minute promises and campaigning by Gordon Brown – which turned out to be the last instance of significant Labour influence on Scottish politics. The size of the separatist vote was an indictment of how badly the UK had been curated. The margin of the unionists' victory was insufficient to put independence to sleep, and Brexit jerked it back into angry feasibility.

Scotland

Even if the SNP had been unable to convince enough voters that they had a worked-out plan for currency, trade and finance, they established separatism as a permanent feature of the UK set-up – as long as the UK lasts. Despite losing seats to the Tories in the 2017 general election, the SNP contingent in the House of Commons was forceful, coherent and united in representing its remain nation. But Scotland's problem was, and will be, money and small-country fiscal viability.

From tax, Scotland raised some £312 less per person than the UK as a whole, yet because historically the baseline had been set higher, public spending in Scotland was £1,400 per head above the UK average. The Tories had traditionally accepted this as the price of union, a point made by Gordon Brown. In addition, the cap on the Scottish council tax was less tight, so some public services were relatively more generously provided for. Councils had 8.3 per cent less to spend, a much smaller reduction than in England. So although Scotland could not escape austerity, it generally felt better to live there. It was certainly better to get old in Scotland. In 2010, 32 per cent more was spent on adult social care per person than in England; that rose to 43 per cent by 2018. However, those with critical or substantial needs still had to wait more than six weeks for the care they required, Age Scotland complained. Budget reductions for the police, courts and prisons were proportionately less north of the border. Scottish prisons were less violent than in England, though no causal connection was proved. Scotland had no police commissioners; in fact, the eight regional police forces were merged into a national force. No identifiable improvements ensued from the centralised arrangement.

Edinburgh acquired control over parts of social security, worth about £3 billion: council tax rebates, discretionary grants to poor households and the ability to alleviate the bedroom tax. By 2020 the country had its own Social Security Scotland office, with 300 staff. The introduction of Universal Credit in Scotland was lubricated with extra cash and appeared to have created less hardship. In 2019 the SNP increased by £10 a week the payments to children in families receiving welfare benefits, with 400,000 likely to receive the increment. Poverty in Scotland registered as lower than the UK average, if measured after housing costs, thanks to more generous provision of council and not-for-profit rentals. Right to buy for social housing rents was ended for new tenants in 2011, and in 2016 abolished altogether. Subsidies for building new social dwellings increased – to twice the English level. Over the five years to 2018 Scottish councils built more housing than English ones, despite the disparity in size between the countries. In 2016 legislation by the Scottish government greatly increased security of tenure in the private sector, regulated lettings agencies and introduced a new framework for rent regulation; early evaluations talked of a 'fundamental' alteration in the landlord–tenant relationship. Moves to deal with homelessness, reiterated by the SNP, contrasted with what was happening in England.

Scotland gave priority to education, and overall spending fell by half as much as in England. Some of this supported university students, who faced lower fees. Scottish schools avoided the distraction of academy status imposed in England but shared problems with the rest of the UK over teachers' pay and morale. Improvement in pupil performance slowed down; in 2015 England scored higher in international rankings of fifteen-year-olds, reversing previous results. Worries were expressed about the poor educational attainment of school-leavers in deprived parts of the country and the continuing sectarian divide in Scotland's schools. The effects of a poor background on a Scottish child's ability to do well at school were just as pronounced as south of the border. Just like Belfast and cities in England, central Glasgow was repaved, spruced up and reinvigorated, and against the odds in Britain's rainiest city, pavement cafés sprouted. Shocking figures for drug-related deaths, however, showed there was still much more to be done to reverse the historically high levels of deprivation.

The NHS in Scotland escaped destructive reorganisation but not financial pressure, problems in recruiting and retaining staff or backlogs in capital spending. In 2019 nursing and midwifery staff numbers reached a record high, but the vacancy rate was up, together with spending on agency staff. Still, spending on health was about £250 per head higher than in England, which meant Scotland could afford seventy-six GPs per 100,000 people, against the UK average of sixty. Audit Scotland, the watchdog, said waiting times were getting worse. Though Scotland's arrangements for linking the NHS and social care looked closer knit than in England, they were not delivering better results.

The big questions were: what was there to show for the extra money? To what effect had the SNP used devolved powers in their decade in power? If Scotland escaped the dogmatism imposed in England, it was only latterly that the SNP had done much that was identifiably *different*. Scottish towns such as Kirkcaldy in Fife faced a grim present and a dim future. The birthplace of Adam Smith had forged an industrial identity from textiles, linoleum and the local coalfield; in 2020 the biggest employers were the council and the NHS. Some of its housing schemes were rated as the most deprived in Scotland, outside Glasgow. As enterprise and capacity is concentrated in Edinburgh, the big city nearby, is the only future of this town of 49,000 as a dormitory? The same questions applied not just in the old industrial areas of Scotland, but in a host of other places.

Public services faced the same problems as in the rest of the UK. Scotland's GPs felt as overwhelmed by patient demand as their colleagues south of the border. The idea, cultivated by Nicola Sturgeon, of social democracy being able to flourish in at least one part of the UK was borne out only to a limited extent. Surveys failed to find Hibernian distinctiveness in attitudes to inequality. It was 'remarkable how little has actually changed' in Scottish public services, said Martin Sime of the Scottish Council for Voluntary Organisations.

The big question was, and will always be, tax. The annual gap between spending and revenues was spotlighted in the independence referendum: it was 10.1 per cent of GDP if North Sea oil and gas proceeds were excluded, and 9.5 per cent if they were counted in. Moves towards getting more tax in were gentle. The 2012 Scotland Act provided for income tax to increase by 10 per cent more than the UK rate, with a corresponding reduction in the block grant. Edinburgh had its own stamp duty land tax, plus some control over council tax rebates and discretionary housing payments. Council tax bands had been reformed, making local taxation in Scotland a bit less regressive. After the referendum, additional control over income tax was transferred. From 2019 the Scottish government received 50 per cent of the VAT generated in Scotland, although rates were still set in London. By 2020 a third of the tax revenue raised in Scotland had been repatriated.

SNP reforms cut income tax for low-earners, but those earning over £27,000 a year paid more. At over £43,430 a higher rate of 41 per cent set in (compared with the UK higher rate of 40 per cent starting at £50,000), with a top rate of 46 per cent (45 per cent for incomes over £150,000 in the rest of the UK). The result was that Scottish income taxes were marginally more egalitarian, but the IFS pointed out that they were precariously balanced. Scotland would lose as much as 10 per cent of its tax revenue if fewer than twenty people changed their residency status. Scottish public finances became riskier. The country now had its own version of the Office for Budget Responsibility, and in 2019 it projected a £1 billion black hole between spending and revenues, based on a pessimistic assessment of growth prospects.

Scotland did innovate, restricting sugar in soft drinks before the Westminster government got round to it; banning the smacking of children; and routinely vaccinating against human papillomavirus for twelve- and thirteen-year-old girls, administered in school. Scottish sixteen- and seventeen-year-olds got the vote. Alcohol sales in Scotland fell after the introduction of minimum prices in May 2018: a promising start to tackling the country's difficult relationship with drink, said Jeane

Freeman, the health secretary. Scotland got greener, with thousands more hectares of trees planted (11,200 in 2018) than in the rest of the UK. But over a third of its electricity still came from its two nuclear plants at Hunterston, on the Clyde, and Torness, on the Firth of Forth, which were in their dotage as power generators.

Wales

Wales remained substantially dependent on transfers from London. The Wales Act 2014 devolved partial powers to set income tax, usable from 2019 on, together with stamp duty land tax and landfill tax. But the Labour-controlled Welsh government was wary. Too much depended on whether the block grant to Wales was going to be reduced pro rata to any variation in Welsh tax rates. Outgoing Labour first minister Carwyn Jones said in January 2019 that the 'scope for using income tax as an economic tool by varying rates was going to be very limited'. He called instead for a UK-wide 'solidarity tax' to help what remained the poorest part of the UK. Solidarity was in diminishing supply. Theresa May had regularly done her bit by lambasting the performance of Welsh hospitals and doctors in order to score points against Labour. After 2012 the block grant to Wales gave more recognition to social needs but, of course, it also reflected UK-wide spending plans. The Welsh government chose not to use its additional powers to improve social security and left the bedroom tax in place. The assembly did, however, legislate to end right to buy, and while the Welsh government's target for affordable dwellings was less ambitious than the Scottish one, it compared favourably with England's.

Welsh schools had opted out of the testing regime followed in England since the Labour era, but they were not emancipated from problems of performance and accountability. 'Devolution conferred no evident benefits' on Welsh education, said one disinterested observer. Schools were told to adopt cheaper, gender-neutral uniforms to help families meet their cost. The Welsh went ahead with imposing a levy on plastic carrier bags. Dame Shan Morgan, permanent secretary in the Welsh government, doubtless consulted widely, but all she could light on as examples of devolution in operation were an opt-out scheme for organ donation and the Well-Being of Future Generations (Wales) Act, which prompted public bodies to use data and think harder about the state of local areas. These weren't trivial, but they weren't, as she claimed, 'ground-breaking'. Caution was the watchword on infrastructure. It was the Welsh secretary in May's government who announced the end of tolls on the Severn bridges, accomplished in December 2018.

Northern Ireland

Any sense that devolution was a one-way street was firmly scotched by what happened in Northern Ireland. Trust between the unionists and Sinn Féin, never great, disappeared, and a murky local financial affair became the pretext in 2017 for the collapse of power-sharing (more accurately, power-splitting) in the Northern Ireland assembly, a centrepiece of the Good Friday Agreement. The region's status and prospects are unclear; sensible people have now joined the extremists and former terrorists in talking about the practicalities of an all-Ireland political union.

Before the collapse at Stormont, the Northern Ireland government had been allowed to vary air passenger duty on long-haul flights, and the Tories at Westminster were keen to let it cut corporation tax. The idea was to match the 12.5 per cent levied by the Republic. But such a cut could not be made while the assembly was suspended, and the Treasury had insisted losses were deducted from the block grant. Discussion showed how little Westminster now cared about consistency across the UK or the knock-on effects of measures taken in one part on another. The Edinburgh government angrily pointed out how a corporation tax cut could severely disadvantage Scotland.

After the collapse, formal direct rule was avoided and instead the region was administered by civil servants exercising ministers' powers, relying on a succession of minimally debated Westminster acts. Ineffectual secretaries of state came and went through the motions, one of them, Karen Bradley, so clueless that she hadn't realised the Northern Irish voted along religious/tribal lines. She evidently hadn't noticed the DUP procession in and out of Downing Street. The DUP badly misrepresented the people of their remain-voting country in many ways, and not just over Brexit. They did not pretend to represent more than their tribe.

None of the material or existential questions facing Northern Ireland had been addressed before 2016, and Brexit sharpened them to cutting point. Northern Irish public services were undergoing 'slow decay' and 'stagnation', according to the head of the Northern Ireland Civil Service, as a result of the political vacuum and an absence of strategy and planning. Economic fragility was exemplified by the decision of Canadian aircraft-maker Bombardier to pull out, a victim of changing markets and Trump. It was followed by the owners of Harland and Wolff, the iconic shipbuilders, filing for bankruptcy, leaving the yard highly vulnerable. The future of Northern Irish enterprise depended, like so much else, on Brexit and whether manufacturing could continue outside suitable customs and trade agreements. Not all was bleak. The computer-maker Seagate announced expansion at its site at Springtown in Derry, thanks to assistance in the form of government investment. On the ground, Northern Irish life improved. Belfast attracted visitors to its late-Victorian centre – more pavement cafés in the rain – and growing list of attractions, the *Titanic* experience among them. Northern Ireland had become famous as the backdrop to *Game of Thrones*, while the 2019 British Open at Portrush gave a further fillip.

The 2011 census put the Protestant population at 48 per cent, just 3 per cent more than Catholics. More recent figures showed that among those of working age, 44 per cent were now Catholic and 40 per cent Protestant. Demography isn't entirely destiny, but the conditions for a public vote on Irish unification were stacking up. In 2019 the fiftieth anniversary of the arrival of troops at the start of the Troubles was noted. For the past ten of those fifty years the government in London had been indifferent, ignorant, bewildered and complicit in varying degrees.

England

On the morning after the referendum vote in Scotland, David Cameron made grand promises about English votes for English laws. It was a typical gesture, both partisan – to placate Tory backbenchers who feared 'concessions' had been made – and half-baked. It was unaccompanied by any wider consideration about England, English government or how such a gesture would fit in terms of the UK as a whole. 'English votes for English laws' was a rare example of a procedural change for the UK parliament made as a result of devolution, said the IfG. But it was never more than a parliamentary detail; it made no 'significant difference in practice'.

Perhaps if it had, those inchoate feelings about 'control' in Brexit might have been assuaged, albeit by erecting border controls at Hay-on-Wye and Berwick-upon-Tweed. Strong, if unfocused, English nationalism was certainly a strand in leave sentiment. But if Englishry was now omnipresent, it was also evanescent, like one quintessentially English writer's Cheshire cat. The only extant state in which to express English identity was the UK, which was a lot more than England but also different from 'Britain' (because it encompassed a region with a land border with the rest of the EU). St George's flag never quite caught on, whatever was happening to the hatchings on the Union flag. A certain version of England leached out in the various public conversations about, for example, the empire (English, glorious; British, shameful?). It also surfaced in local identifications, with 'the north', Yorkshire, Cornwall and other individual places. Some of these constituted a needy, deprived England. Another England could be sighted in Essex and Kent, and in aged, affluent, fervently leave territories from Devon to Hampshire. This comfortable England, predominantly Tory, was unlikely to be willing to transfer significant funds to the poorer one, even to relieve its leave compatriots.

That was partly because under austerity, place had become disposable. The Tories occasionally burnished their 'localist' credentials, but also deliberately and continuously downgraded the capacity of English councils – even though their party ran many of them. Heartland county councils struggled as demand burgeoned, but they would not increase the council tax and central support fell. Some were badly run. In Northamptonshire, ideologues insisted on outsourcing contracts, which proved inefficient and failed to bring the promised savings. The county became insolvent. Embarrassed, the government did away with it. A proud tract of England that could trace its administrative lineage back to the Saxons was simply dispensed with. After minimal public consultation, the county was abolished and two so-called unitary councils, imaginatively named North and West Northants, substituted for it, simultaneously killing off the local authorities that had given Corby, Kettering, Wellingborough, Daventry and Northampton an element of their identity as towns and places. Mucking around in this high-handed way must have an effect on people's sense of belonging and identity, even if we lack firm evidence about the coordinates of such attachments. With Brexit, belonging somewhere and relating to terrain, urban form, history and boundaries were probably more important than ever. But not, it turned out, to the government. Except later, when ministers at the communities department decreed a celebration of England's traditional boundaries and flew county flags in Parliament Square. Never had the comedians' punchline been more apposite: you couldn't make it up.

Cameron and Osborne favoured business rather than councils and diverted funds that had previously gone to Labour's regional economic agencies to a set of unelected, unaccountable local economic partnerships, led by self-appointed business people. Their boundaries were not the same as those of the councils, which inhibited collaboration. Some £10 billion was given to them, but try as they did – several times – auditors could find little trace of what it bought or how it was spent.

Left Behind

Places within places in the south of England felt as left behind as any northern town. The city of Cambridge was prosperous and future-orientated, but in Abbey ward deprivation was rife: a third of the children there lived in poverty. Away from the villas and the yacht clubs on the Isle of Wight were people on the margins who depended on depleted social services, with a high incidence of learning disability and adolescent mental health problems. In Cornwall, a beloved holiday destination and location of second homes, one child in five went to secondary school without breakfast, relying on free lunches to see them through the day.

In the Somerset constituency held by the reactionary Jacob Rees-Mogg, the government said the area west of Taunton, including Minehead, was a social mobility 'cold spot'; it was to share a twelfth of a special opportunity area fund worth £72 million. Pay was low; job opportunities revolved around retail, restaurants and hotels, health and social care. Houses were bought by retirees and second-homeowners. Buses were scarce, and those without cars were often trapped. Courtney-Paige Pugh of Minehead worked part-time as a waitress: to get to college in Bridgwater, twenty-six miles away, her bus left at 7 a.m., for a journey lasting ninety minutes each way. West Somerset's £6 million was not going to punch through these structural barriers, which had been raised higher by austerity.

Some places fared better. Preston became a pin-up for the Left, as it sought to expand the supply of goods and services from within the district, reducing the outward flow of money (and people). Manchester talked up its 'educational–industrial complex', along with its trams and football teams; stable and long-lasting (Labour) local government leadership was also part of the formula, attracting TalkTalk and Amazon, among other incoming employers. But the former company shut up shop in nearby Warrington, a reminder that the fate of peripheral areas could be the obverse of central business district success. The collapse of Bury Football Club amid the (foreign-owned) success of Manchesters City and United was all too expressive.

'Cranes on the skyline indicate overbuilding, which threatens a price crash in the next downturn,' warned Professor Karel Williams.

Every day twelve people emigrated from London to Bristol. 'The best city to live in Britain,' newspapers declared, citing housing choice, history and heritage, transport and creative energy. Graduates of the city's two universities stayed on to work in tech, aeronautics, film and TV.

But the city had two tales to tell. Bristol West had more degrees per capita than any other constituency in Britain, but Bristol South had the lowest number of school-leavers heading for university. Marvin Rees, the elected mayor, was brought up in poor and predominantly minority-populated St Paul's and was keenly aware of plural identities. In his spacious office in Bristol's commanding 1930s city hall, he lived twin stories. Since he took office in 2016 Bristol had lost 50 per cent of its government grant, and yet he felt he needed to talk positively about the social programmes, housebuilding, growth and urban renewal.

Duality marked Rees's own story as a mixed-race Bristolian. 'When I was growing up, there was plenty of abuse,' he remembers. But now he suits Bristol, a healing symbol in a city that was made wealthy by black enslavement. In the teeth of austerity, the city had managed to keep children's centres going, along with holiday food programmes and libraries, by drawing down reserves and putting up council tax to the maximum. But, says Rees, 'We can't go on. There will be far deeper cuts after 2020, and we need to make sure everyone understands where the pain is coming from.' The council used its land to make deals in which developers were obliged to build genuinely affordable homes. 'We commercialise the parks. We rent them out when we can at a good profit. Our national dog festival brings in tens of thousands of pounds a year; so do our music festivals, and they are very popular. Yes, we had a row over parking charges, whacking them up – but people pay!'

Bristol was 62 per cent remain, and Rees set up a response group to deal with the Brexit fallout. 'There's a real risk Airbus will go – that's 4,000 jobs, 10,000 with its spin-offs. It's nothing but loss for us.'

Ranking places according to gross value added per head, patent applications or qualifications showed London, Milton Keynes, Slough, Reading and Bristol towards the top, Doncaster, Blackburn and Blackpool towards the rear. Some of those places became – to amend the phrase coined by José Mourinho about Arsène Wenger – specialists in self-harm. Here was a builder from Middlesbrough trashing southerners: 'The fact you won't get enough euros for your pounds when you go on holiday in Europe, we don't give a fuck about that.' But sterling depreciation increased the price of imports, including feedstocks, critically important for Teesside's remaining industrial base.

Right Behind

In places such as Boston in Lincolnshire, Brexit was the accident waiting to happen. We had gone there in 2010 and found discontent was rife. Agri-business ruled the rich loam fields of the Fens. The growers and packers had once bussed in workers from the Midlands and bussed them out again. Now, the field-workers stayed. Labour's commitment to ultra-flexible employment helped the gangmasters who recruited in eastern Europe, bought up terraces and crammed migrants in, charging high rents. 'How do you begin to control that situation?' the council leader asked plaintively. But local political consciousness was weak. Tories or independents ruled in the town, and the county would not spend to mitigate social stress. Which grew.

Everyone now knows about Boston, so maybe Brexit should be credited with engendering a new awareness of the hinterland. This was of a paradoxical piece with the growth of class consciousness, in a decade when so much was done to exacerbate disadvantage and inequality. Reporters and authors set themselves up as bringers of enlightenment to the metropolitan 'elite' about conditions in Salford, Northampton, Birmingham, Stafford and Stockport. In Nuneaton, a pro-leave retired factory foreman told the author Mike Carter that if as a result of Brexit, 'the economy goes down the toilet, at least those bastards [in London] will finally know what it feels like to be us'. If this was an expression of English nationalism, it didn't show much solidarity.

But that is to fall into the trap of tarring entire places as leave, forgetting both their numerous remainers and the embarrassed efforts of their councils and chambers of commerce to project a different image. After the vote, businesses and the council in Cornwall rushed to produce a plan, shamefacedly acknowledging that the EU had paid to reconstruct the harbours and the airport, to build roads and digital connections, and hoping that London (a longer journey by train than Brussels by plane) would step in. 'European support has enabled us to put in place the foundations for growth,' said a report by the Cornwall and Isles of Scilly Leadership Board. 'This investment has helped our economy to become more productive, our people to develop higher skills, and our local wages to increase.' Two-thirds of Cornish exports went to the EU, including fish; the various strands of the Common Agricultural Policy were worth around £100 million a year. But that still left 44 per cent of Cornish households with total earnings below £20,000 a year, along with a lack of affordable housing, vanishing buses and fewer GPs.

On the streets of Stoke-on-Trent, extreme and often ill-informed views were easy to find, and it became one of the go-to places for pundits and pollsters. Stoke's plight was pressing. It was the debt capital of England and Wales, its high rates of insolvency matched by Plymouth, Hull and Scarborough. What they had in common was the inadequacy of UK central government efforts to sweep up or apply a bandage after the retreat of industry, tourism and big defence. Austerity had made life even more difficult. But Europe was apparently to blame.

The leave vote in Dudley in the West Midlands reached 71 per cent. It was classed as one of the ten most 'left behind' places in England. A local observer was Stuart Turner, a former deputy Labour council leader. It was a by now familiar tale: 'There was so much industry here – the steelworks, the foundries, even mining. These were well-paid, secure jobs.

But all of that has gone, and there was nothing to replace it.'
With remarkable imagination, the rightwards-inclined Centre
for Social Justice think tank proposed 'enterprise zones'. The
same tax-free zones had been tried, and had largely failed, after
the decimation of industry in the West Midlands in the 1980s.
Resentment and unhappiness followed economic dislocation.
In a district with only 7.1 per cent of the population born outside the UK, 'There is this belief that immigrants are some-
how the reason for all the area's problems,' Turner said. By
'immigrants' people often meant settled ethnic minorities. The
West Midlands had a large population that was unquestionably
British by birth, but brown-skinned and Muslim or Hindu.

*We first met Simon Topman, the Birmingham whistle manu-
facturer, in 2010, when he was president of the Birmingham
Chamber of Commerce. He had been critical of Labour's neglect
of manufacturing. Since then, things had got worse. He especially
deplored the abolition of Advantage West Midlands, the regional
development agency.*

*Brummie born and bred, devoted to the city and a member of
countless committees, he had a special vantage point on decline.
Until 2010 he was the head of Aston Pride, one of thirty-nine
special New Deal for Communities projects set up in the most
deprived places. A cheque for £54 million had been handed over to
the community, which would decide how best to regenerate Aston,
employing the right people to help. He showed us round the derelict
park that had been restored, a newly built sports pavilion and
a revived local museum. A new health centre made care more*

accessible; schools had extra help, with a hot breakfast for every child. An emphasis was put on training and job-finding. The results were positive: lower crime, better school results and employment, and a fall in antisocial behaviour.

Aston Pride was killed off in 2011. 'What upset us, all the volunteers and local people who worked so hard, was that they got no recognition, none,' says Topman. 'The health centre is closing. Birmingham council is in deep financial trouble, and they may sell off the pavilion and cricket ground. The cuts hit every service in Aston pretty hard.'

10

What Next?

The stage is littered with unfinished plotlines, discarded props and bad actors. But surely the next act can't continue with the same charlatanry of sham rainbows and unicorns led by some Westminster version of Elmer Gantry. At least, not for long. Reality will obtrude, forcing action to be taken on accumulating crises, the greatest of which is the climate calamity. On its heels come the social dislocation caused by gaping inequality and the fracturing of the UK and its constitution. Add in ageing and care for the elderly, connectivity and the fate of railways and 5G, plus a score more derelictions festering in the national in tray. The wreckage left by austerity will not be mended by electioneering eye-catchers.

The Verdict

Nonetheless, Boris Johnson's splashing of the cash was deeply instructive about what had gone before. Here was a covert admission that austerity had not only been deeply damaging, but unnecessary, a mere expedient, a prolonged exercise in what they could get away with in pursuit of their core ambition of shrinking the state. Once the polls turned and an election loomed, the Tories dissembled.

WHAT NEXT? [313]

Their ministers, their prime ministers came and went, but this remained the Right's time. The Tories only just held on to power – from 2010 in coalition, from 2017 to 2019 with no majority – yet theirs still amounts to a historic achievement. The contours of policy preoccupation shifted, and after Brexit they pursued populist nationalism, sacrificing principles and people. As they ejected their most distinguished senior politicians and others resigned in disgust, they abandoned honesty, the national interest and our international reputation, but retained power and barred the way to progressive alternatives (such as they were). Throughout all this, a consistent theme was antagonism to government as a positive force for social good and opposition to decent levels of tax and spending. Representing the wishes of (at most) four out of ten of the voting population, weighted towards the south of England, they were able to impose a starveling worldview on the rest of the country.

Before 2010 David Cameron and Iain Duncan Smith had wallowed in 'broken Britain' and its social ills; they and their successors left it more distressed and fragmented than at any time in its post-war history. Brexit harms aside, the UK economy has performed indifferently; growth has been meagre in aggregate and barely registered in terms of household income. Its international reputation blackened, internally fissiparous, the UK is beset. Come 2029, will there be another 'lost decade' to chart and regret?

It's not that the Right won what passed for the battle of ideas. Labour's 'Marxism' over the renationalisation of utilities grew in popularity: corporate performance in water, energy, railways and urban transport reduced the appeal of privatisation, even among Tory voters. People never stopped demanding and expecting a strong health service, good schools and a robust welfare state. Labour-era concerns about inequality still dominated the conversation, even when mutated into 'social mobility'. Awareness of class distinctions grew amid a slanging match in which each side accused the other of being the elite, the Establishment, tussling for the right to be the outsider, the voice of the people. Democracy weakened, party politics fractured, public confidence in institutions ebbed away: such is the legacy of the political winners.

The Task Ahead

But ahead lies reality, which might be our salvation. The era of idealism is ending – Brexit asserted the supremacy of notions about identity over the hard facts of trade and growth – and the age of practicality begins. People have shown themselves capable of denial, but when the rain falls and river water comes flooding through your front room, it's going to feel real. Most pressing of all, with the young increasingly intolerant of further inaction, is the genuinely existential question: how to survive on these islands, on this planet. Tools for tackling the climate emergency exist. We can take heart from what can be done.

Beside the River Medina on the Isle of Wight stands a gleaming modern factory that has been expanding at dizzying speed. Vestas makes blades for offshore wind turbines, enormous sails taller than the London Eye, which are lowered onto a barge and taken down the Solent to be ferried to arrays around the coast. This is the future of industry, though, typical of UK manufacturing, Vestas is a Danish company.

When we visited in 2015, it had 200 employees. Five years later, the payroll was 724, all of them islanders, trained on site. When the company opened a second production line in 2019, they advertised 300 jobs, and 1,000 people turned up, on an island that lacks good education and job opportunities. Production director James Luter is a Vectian born and bred; he showed us round the factory with evident pride – a missionary, passionate about his climate-saving job.

Wind is certainly filling Vestas' sails. 'We work 24/7, there's so much demand,' Luter said. Ships take the concrete and steel towers, along with the blades; they have legs that they fix on the seabed which lift the whole ship up out of the water. The towers and turbines are built on the Scottish coast. Vestas are supplying a wind farm in the Moray Firth, due to open in 2022, which will have the potential to power a million homes, or 38 per cent of Scotland.

The targets for renewable energy could be met well in advance. The UK already has huge offshore wind capacity; the costs of construction have plummeted, the need for subsidy falling. But even as the price drops, the industry needs assurance that government policy won't suddenly veer off like a yacht in a squall. Solar power learnt about ministers' fickleness the hard way.

To survive means changing the way we live, how we move about, what we eat, how we build and occupy our houses . . . the list is long. If none of this featured in the 2019 hustings for the Tory leadership, and concern wove in and out of the general election campaign, new awareness was becoming palpable as people put climate alongside health and Brexit as their top three concerns.

Deniers have lost the argument, though financed by big oil they will keep trying to obfuscate, delay and deride. Even the anti-state Right has ceased to pretend that markets or private enterprise will be any more than marginal contributors. Withdrawing from the EU will prove, yet again, how puny single-country efforts are.

Climate Crisis

The Intergovernmental Panel on Climate Change warned starkly that from 2019, there were only eleven years left in which a programme to limit global warming to $1.5°C$ might succeed. Tipping points are visible in the form of melting glaciers, shrinking ice packs, lethal and unpredictable flooding, droughts and forest fires, from California to Australia, Africa to the Amazon. 'Our house is burning,' was environmental activist Greta Thunberg's message. The joint endeavour of households, business and the state urgently has to alter how we drive, how we build and heat our homes, as well as our eating habits, water use, air travel and more. In places, and in patches, the work has begun.

Take one example: in September 2018 the Highways Agency and local authority began upgrading a three-kilometre stretch of the A421 into Milton Keynes. The new dual carriageway is to have a pavement and cycleway surfaced so as to capture solar energy. In summer, heat will be stored and used to power streetlights and road signs. In cold weather, water pipes laid just below the surface will use geothermal energy and surface heat pumps to warm the road, preventing ice and mothballing the gritting lorries. New technology trialled in Sweden makes the road surface itself a transmitter of power to the vehicles using it. More of them are electric; more of the electricity they use will come from renewable sources.

Late in the day, the May government accepted targets from the Committee on Climate Change that commanded near universal assent: greenhouse gas emissions to fall to zero, with petrol and diesel cars phased out. But much ground, littered with errors of political judgement, has to be made up. Cameron bears a heavy responsibility, for it was his ministers who banned onshore wind in a partisan gesture to their English shire supporters. Just as solar panels were taking off, the VAT on household battery systems was hiked by 15 per cent. (The government tried to blame EU rules, wrongly.) Grants for hybrid cars were abolished, leaving the subsidy regime for green vehicles in disarray. The haulage industry said any move to batteries and hydrogen power for lorries in the 2020s was 'simplistic'; that transition, too, needs to be underwritten. The absence of fast charging points was inhibiting the take-up of electric cars, whose prices were falling.

The climate committee recommended that no new home be connected to the gas grid after 2025. By 2020, 1 million homes were already off it and using biomethane produced from food and plant waste. Only some 26 million households still to go. But imagine if conversion became a great national crusade, with *Bake Off* leading the way on ovens and housebuilders shamed and bribed into replacing hydrocarbon gas with alternatives. A modest 20 per cent cut in beef, lamb and dairy consumption by 2050 was proposed, giving us a while to get used to occasional Quorn. Smoking-cessation programmes show behaviour can be amended and opinion-led, even to countenance a new tax regime; there's public demand for more vigorous action.

Carbon capture creates jobs and commercial and export opportunities. The reuse of the coalfields of South Wales, central Scotland and Teesside for storage of the pollutant is in prospect. That is, provided the pace of technological progress is increased through publicly funded research and costs and benefits are equitably spread. The Nimbys of the shire who rejected wind turbines but won't object to Welsh valleys being overlaid with carbon capture pipework will have to do their bit. Greening policies show once again that gross inequality hampers progress on all fronts, endangering the haves as much as the have-nots.

There's a rich political opportunity here, linking climate survival to investment and better life chances. The Green New Deal on renewables and energy efficiency secured cross-party support, along with programmes to insulate buildings and move to more sustainable farming. There's action here for the communities that have been 'left behind'. The UK is already a leader in offshore wind; the Scottish government's attempt to out-green Westminster makes for benign competition.

The carbon generated per unit of electricity has been dropping. A third of UK electricity now comes from renewables, which could easily grow. Only 800,000 homes and businesses had solar panels on the day the government pulled the plug on feed-in tariff incentives in April 2019. Installations dropped the next month by 94 per cent, with 26.5 million households to go. That shows the powerful effect of government policies. The promising start can be improved upon.

The state will always carry ultimate responsibility for energy supply. Privatisation did not end this fact and climate emergency confirms it; attitudes towards state intervention will necessarily determine action. The North Sea, running dry, is now a net drain on the public purse as oil and gas companies demand tax relief and their redundant rigs moulder offshore. The Nuclear Decommissioning Authority consumes £3 billion a year but earns only £1 billion from reprocessing spent fuel. Its budget will have to grow, with seven reactors due to be decommissioned during the 2020s. If nuclear has any future, it must be properly accounted for and publicly owned. Coal is to be phased out entirely by 2025, so to keep the lights on and computers running the UK must erect more wind turbines. Some 800 projects already have planning permission, but they will generate only two-thirds of the electricity the (highly uncertain rebuild of the) Wylfa nuclear plant in Anglesey would produce. Wind capacity needs to grow by a factor of nine, which means a lot more turbines, both on- and offshore. The possibilities are hotly disputed; the equation has to include back-up generation and storage, which awaits better battery technology. Cue massive public investment.

Land, Sea and Air

Markets don't work alone. The need for the state to shape the energy transition is echoed in other spheres, if necessary overriding individual owners of property to secure the greater good. The planning profession has suffered grievously, especially in town halls, and needs to be remotivated. Victoria Hills, chief of its institute, said, 'Places that put planning at the heart of their corporate strategy are successful places to live, yet our research uncovers a prevailing sense that council planners face huge challenges to their ability to plan effectively in the public interest.' In controlling development and making the best use of land – brown and greenfield – planners have to balance competing needs, holding the ring between the rights of those alive now against the yet-to-be-born, between markets and the public interest, between climate and commerce, between beauty and survival, between one neighbour and another.

Empowered planning is needed for the 5.4 million properties in England – one in six – that are at risk of being inundated by rivers, surface water and sea. Yet if there is too much water in some places, there is too little elsewhere. Private water companies were severely under-regulated and allowed to degrade water quality and waste stupendous amounts: fixing pipes didn't pay dividends, so a third of the water supply is now lost to leakage. The Environment Agency says England will run dry within twenty-five years unless the holes in the pipes are fixed, reservoirs built and water transferred through a grid between regions and watersheds. Population increase plus climate change equals ever more precious water.

The People We Will Be

You don't need a crystal ball to know how many we shall be by 2030. Demographers put the UK population on a path to 70 million, then to 80 million-plus by 2065. Those extra people will not spread evenly across the land. London and the south-east have been growing twice as fast as the rest of England and will gain a further 1.17 million in the ten years to 2024. Additional bodies need energy, water, sewerage, roads; either more dwellings house them or they squeeze in tighter, with less space per person. Their extra energy will have to be sustainably generated. In Oxford, a community battery is being built to serve Blackbird Leys and the Cowley motor plant, but it is as big as a tennis court; space for it has to be planned. Along with energy, transport must be reprogrammed, or else population growth brings more jams, more congestion and decreased speed.

The decennial census will take place in 2021, this time mostly online. Accuracy demands a 94 per cent response rate and vigorous chasing of those who don't respond either because they can't cope with websites or they fear their migration, tax or benefit status could be exposed, despite strict privacy assurances. Questions will be asked about gender and identity, yet important facts about income will not be collected. Citizens are more willing to reveal information about their sex lives than their bank balances, so asking about money reduces response rates, according to research on the last census. But omitting finances leaves a cavern in our knowledge about ourselves, when inequalities press on every policy front.

The governments of 2010–20 did perilously little by way of foresight, analysis or anticipation of the future. They were almost a caricature of the short-termism that prevails in financial and other markets. Repairing the decayed state they have left behind will demand higher levels of technical and statistical literacy. Facts, facts, facts and expertise – a better future depends on them, but also on a political class that can convey them trustworthily to a sceptical populace. The measles outbreak of 2019 shows the prevalent danger of misinformation and stupidity. It's a tall order, but restoring confidence in honest information is crucial to the functioning of markets and public services.

Tomorrow's Young

In 2018 the OECD marked the UK bottom of the class in basic literacy, behind all other European countries, except Spain and Italy. Academic achievement here was more strongly determined by social background than elsewhere. To avoid falling yet further behind, it's once again education, education, education: first to repair the damage caused by shrinking school and college budgets; next to improve the national skill set at all ages. Lives and livelihoods depend on schooling, and so does the quality of democratic decision-making. The Brexit result was a wake-up call: older and therefore less educated generations swung the vote away from better-educated, better-informed, younger cohorts. All the evidence shouts: start young. If the early years are missed, catching up gets harder – but we already know what can be done.

St Stephen's School and Children's Centre in Newham is outstanding, says Ofsted. Yet 98 per cent of children arrive here with English as their second language. Many mothers don't go out to work and live in flats or are crammed into privately rented houses, sharing with other families. But at St Stephen's there are midwives to look after them in pregnancy, health visitor sessions and a clinical psychologist. Stay-and-play sessions encourage timid mothers to drop in with their young babies to meet other mums, with groups and classes offering help and encouraging friendship and communication: baby bounce and rhyme, a sensory room, storytelling, messy play, Zumba for parents and children. Gardens, courts for ball games and table-tennis areas are all immaculately kept up, in a district short of public spaces. Parenting groups help with everything from bedtime routines to toilet training, bottle weaning and book reading. There is careers advice and help with seeking work.

Head Neena Lall has been here for nineteen years. She is a blend of warm and firm, an energetic inspiration who draws Teach First graduates to the school, nursery trainees, too, and once they come, they stay. She expects high scores in arithmetic from all her children. She shows how fast they can learn to read and write within a few months of reception class, the exercise books proving her point, soaring up from faint shaky letters to whole sentences and stories within a couple of terms.

She succeeds partly by having children here from birth, with any problems sorted out very early, drawing in parents and relatives to share in the children's lives and learning. Quality depends on teachers: many nurseries have virtually no professional staff, the children being minded by low-paid young assistants who themselves failed at school. Here, it's different. In the hall, the choir of mixed ages is belting out songs. The year 6s, ready to move on from primary school, are reading out their stories, many of remarkable sophistication – and all in the neatest handwriting. In the baby and reception classes, they are playing gently with fluffy baby ducks; there is an egg incubator so the children can watch them hatching.

Lall pinches pennies, marries support from Newham Borough Council with revenue from the nursery, the funding streams brought together under one roof, the costs shared. Parents such as Aminah are part of the story. Highly articulate and well spoken, you would never guess that when she first came here, she spoke not a word of English. More remarkable still, she has taken a pre-degree course in law, passed her driving test and is now on track to qualify for a paralegal job. 'I could never have done all this without St Stephen's. They helped me at every stage – and I depend on the wraparound childcare here, where they can do breakfast and tea to help mothers work. This place is my home! My family!' A

visitor's heart soars at this oasis in a national system under stress,
with most children's centres closed or stripped bare of such support
services. You can't help beaming at the pleasure parents and chil-
dren take in being there, at the warmth with which it embraces
whole families.

Why not a centre like this everywhere, not just in deprived
areas, but for all families, better and less well off, as Sure Start
was originally meant to provide? Behind the net curtains of
respectability, maternal depression, drugs, alcohol, gambling
and violence touch all social classes. 'Troubled families' are
not going to self-pacify, so what happens when even the existing minor programme of grants offering social support comes
to an end in 2020? Three out of four of England's councils
have cut the help they offer children in early life. That sets
the trajectory of damage for the 40 per cent of two-year-olds
who will fall below the poverty line in 2020 – the largest number of poor children recorded in modern times, according to
the Resolution Foundation. The extra cash promised for local
authorities in the 2019 election would all be swept up for older
people's social care, leaving children bereft.

Going back to the future, we have to recapture Every Child
Matters, the Blair-era plan to merge care and learning, along
with the means to flag up family problems early to doctors and
teachers so that no child slips through the net. An OECD study
established a clear link between social spending and levels of
inequality and immobility twenty years on. Cuts in benefits and
education are guaranteed to darken the chances of children

from poorer families, and on into their futures. The IFS ana-
lysed the health of eleven-year-olds who had been through
Sure Start and found they went to hospital ill or injured less fre-
quently, strongly suggesting that closing centres had contributed to today's rising rates of hospital attendance by children.
If growing anxiety about young people's mental health is well
founded, that's bad news for them as adults, and for everyone
else. Disorders can be hard to treat and recovery may take time,
assuming the necessary psychiatric and psychological services
exist. By 2030 an additional 2 million adults are projected to
face mental health challenges, adding to human misery, as well
as causing lower productivity and earnings, thus dragging on
GDP growth.

Despite the turmoil of academisation and the drop in per
pupil funding in England's schools, GCSE passes at grade C
or above (renamed grade 4) were at worst steady and at best
showed some improvement, at least in core subjects. (The same
could not be said of pupils in Welsh and Scottish schools.) But
the rate of improvement had risen sharply between 2000 and
2011, and that momentum was lost. Now, school places are
lacking: in London, by 2023 there will be 64,000 more children than there are available places. In England, this springs
partly from administrative havoc, as the war on councils prevented them from planning ahead. Another dismal legacy is the
decline in subjects deemed peripheral. Music entries dropped
by a fifth or more at GCSE and A-level as classes and teachers
were cut, along with dance, art and drama: these were deemed
frivolous, which was an error both culturally and economically.

Entries for French and German also fell and were not compensated for by small increases for Arabic, Mandarin and Spanish. Even school study of computer science shrank, diminishing the potential pool of home-grown programmers and IT specialists. As of December 2019, school funding in England is supposed to grow back to its 2010 value by 2021, offering nothing to replenish lost resources.

Yet university enrolment is set to expand further, lifting the prospects of reasoned, informed public understanding and debate, as graduates tend to have more open and enquiring minds and progressive attitudes. The number of eighteen-year-olds in the UK is set to increase by 27 per cent by 2030, by which time some 320,000 eighteen-year-olds in England could be entering higher education each year, 115,000 more than in 2018. Whether they go to universities or take degree-level apprenticeships or other higher courses, the longer education augurs a smarter, more resilient future population.

Tomorrow's Old

Despite this youth surge, our average age will still rise in the years ahead. The UK may be greying less dramatically than other countries, but the quarter of the population aged sixty-plus in 2020 will rise to a third by 2050. Not only has government prevaricated over how to pay for their social care, business has yet to seize the opportunities presented by this cohort with higher than average incomes. Already the over-fifties account for nearly half of consumer spending, yet at

£320 billion a year, the grey pound still hasn't really registered in advertising or retailing.

Much turns on the relationship between age and political preference – tomorrow's old may not vote in the same right-wards direction as yesterday's. Older voters, courted ever more avidly at elections, might further impose the strange Brexity mixture of nostalgic conservatism and recklessness about the future. But the 2010s may turn out to have been a peak period for wealthy retirement; the people who had benefited so much from occupational pensions and enjoyed the effortless rise of property prices will give way to those with less generous schemes who have not seen their housing wealth increase quite so spectacularly. In the 2015 election forty-nine was the age after which the majority voted Tory; by 2017 that had moved up to fifty-one, so each retiring cohort may be a bit more pro-gressive than the last. The old are better voters in terms of turnout: 84 per cent of the over-seventies vote, but only 59 per cent of the under-twenty-fours.

The old will certainly need the young: to care for them, do their repairs, drive their buses and taxis and generate the GDP growth from which their pensions are to be paid. Rejuvenation of the working population has come to depend on migrants, and it's largely thanks to incomers that the ratio of older people to those of working age is less unbalanced in the UK than elsewhere. The numbers needing help to wash, feed or clothe themselves will double between 2010 and 2030 to 2 mil-lion. Will these face-to-face, human jobs be paid well enough and enjoy sufficient status and professionalism to make them attractive? Even would-be privatisers of the NHS admit markets don't train people or anticipate tomorrow's health needs. Today's deficit of doctors, nurses, assistants and allied health professionals will grow unless governments start immediately to plan, train and incentivise recruitment. Even if the joint recommendation by the King's Fund, Nuffield Trust and Health Foundation for a £900 million increase in NHS training were met, courses take years. The district nurse workforce has itself been ageing, and it's ever harder to recruit the dedicated, able women the NHS has traditionally relied upon. There will be a million people living with dementia by 2025, and 2.8 million over-sixty-fives. For many it's too late to start jogging and doing Pilates, and nearly half of those now aged fifty-five to sixty-four are insufficiently physically active to stave off disease and decline. But illness in older age can be prevented by starting younger, so closure of those tennis courts and football pitches has to be stopped.

A New Intergenerational Compact

Keeping venues for playing sports open depends on council budgets. So much hinges on whether affluent older people will pay into the public purse by consenting to taxation of their income and property. Tory councils in England, ever reluctant to increase taxes, have been confining their spending to services tilted towards politically influential older voters. The upkeep of roads, parks, leisure centres and libraries was overwhelmed by the share of budgets allocated to adult social care, with a

Local Government Association 'graph of doom' predicting that virtually all spending would soon be consumed by the old. To maintain social care services at 2019's (inadequate) levels, councils in England would need an extra £4 billion a year in grants, and £18 billion a year by the mid-2030s, according to the IFS. Alternatively, council tax could rise, but even increases of 4 per cent a year – twice the inflation rate – would still leave a yawning gap between revenues and demand.

It's lurid to call all this 'intergenerational strife'. But look at housing: older people possess it and younger people don't – unless they have affluent parents. To help them and sustain society and nation, the state and older people have to agree a domestic treaty: to share a portion of accumulated housing wealth and free up restraints on development in their back-yards. A mighty realignment of people and dwellings is in sight, for the sake of older citizens as much as anyone. Across the UK, only 750,000 dwellings are classed as retirement housing, under 3 per cent of all homes. Two million people live alone, half of them over seventy-five, and many would be better off downsizing. They need sheltered homes with steps they can manage, built in their own familiar neighbourhoods. Others could use the space in these larger family homes. The market won't make the exchange, so the state needs to facilitate the construction of adapted housing and lubricate the swap, free-ing up hundreds of thousands of family houses.

Today's retirees are mostly (70 per cent) homeowners, but by 2030 three times more of those over retirement age will be living in private rented accommodation than in 2020.

Scottish Widows said that non-homeowners now in their fifties should have already started saving an extra £6,000 a year just to afford the rent they will be obliged to pay in retirement, but many haven't saved because they can't afford to. Today's state pension plus a little extra in savings just don't add up to the likely average rent of the 2020s. Earlier, we were sceptical about predictions that the politics of housing would become fraught. We'd heard it before. But the conditions for major disturbances among angry private renters are ripe; soon it will be older renters who demand the government intervene and regulate rents – and they will have the political and lobbying power to enforce it.

Before she fell off the Westminster scaffold, Theresa May seemed to have got the message that subsidising private landlords through housing benefit instead of building long-lasting council homes was short-sighted and wasteful. In one of her last acts she lifted the cap that had prevented councils from building new housing and timidly dusted off long-mothballed schemes. Cameron had threatened but not got round to killing off the Labour-era quango charged with buying up hard-to-develop sites, Homes England. One example: it acquired 250 acres of a 605-acre site at Fairham in Nottinghamshire to develop as new homes and employment space, in collaboration with Rushcliffe council and private companies. The council's target of 13,000 new dwellings by 2028 will contribute towards the 300,000 a year target as England's minimum. A coalition of housing groups put a figure on what it would take to end the housing crisis: £14.6 billion a year for ten years to build 1.45 million dwellings for social rent or shared owner-ship. That is well within reach, since governments can borrow capital cheaply against property assets that stay on its books.

Glories of the Garden

Some signals are green/amber. 'Declinism' is a British tradi-tion, and Ipsos's Bobby Duffy and other surveyors of opin-ion deplore a tendency to overdo the gloom. The UK retains strong emotional unifiers in the NHS and BBC, as well as the armed forces, sporting allegiances and the national pageantry around the monarchy. We visited Fort George, near Inverness, constructed after Culloden to solidify British rule and now the headquarters of the 3rd Battalion, Royal Regiment of Scotland, and we watched units heading out to take part in exercises on Salisbury Plain, a picture of Scottishness and Britishness com-bined. At the fort, the regimental museum of the Queen's Own Highlanders weaves a rich and complex history of empire, glory, trench warfare and policing operations in Aden (Yemen) and Northern Ireland, a portrait of Britain-in-Scotland, with much pride and shame shared. You can find parallel, compet-ing narratives of the past and future, things that still unify the country, in the universities, ancient and modern, research insti-tutes, stadiums, art galleries, theatres and music venues.

'Nothing short of a miracle,' said reviewers of the Royal Shakespeare Company's *Matilda the Musical*, the blockbuster playing in the West End and all around the world since 2011. The Arts Council England contributes a quarter of the RSC's funding; the rest comes from donations, sponsorship and ticket sales, which in turn depend on the imagination and skills of actors, producers and theatre staff. *Matilda*'s difficult seven years in development were possible only because seed funding from the state permitted long-term planning that no commercial producer would have contemplated. Now, the show's brilliant success yields rich returns, from which the exchequer and the company benefits. The devolved governments readily see this, but so much more could be done UK-wide to encourage the arts as generators of cash, culture and pride – and challenge, when they pose difficult questions about how we live.

Gordon Brown saw the growth potential of film production in 2007, using tax relief as subsidy (to the justified alarm of all those who want to see the tax code cleansed and clarified). In 2013 George Osborne relaxed the qualifying rules for film tax credits and became the first chancellor to earn a credit in a Hollywood movie, *Star Wars: The Force Awakens*. Production spend in the UK doubled after 2009, reaching a record £1.72 billion in film in 2016 and £7.9 billion across all screen industries, including television and computer games. UK studios mushroomed, producing blockbusters here partly because a falling pound made it cheaper, but also because of the availability of technical skills. It was not just Pinewood and Shepperton, the old studios; what amounted to an 'industrial policy' for film pushed Channel 4 into a symbolic move out of London, while Manchester and Salford are now a production hub, helped by the BBC, as are Belfast and Cardiff. Optimism marked our visit to Bottle Yard Studios in Bristol: that verve, prompted by positive government intervention, is what is missing from the still-declining manufacturing industries.

But it is alive and kicking in science and technology. Austerity left research relatively unscathed, even if the UK remains way off the international benchmark of investing 3 per cent of GDP in R&D: in 2017 the UK spent only 1.69 per cent. The growth potential of the economy has been reduced by that gap, which the May and Johnson governments pledged to address. The Francis Crick Institute, which opened in 2016 adjacent to the British Library, was a grand gesture; mostly charitably and university financed, it brought together leading life-sciences researchers under one spectacular roof, led by geneticist Sir Paul Nurse, former president of the Royal Society. In an arc from Oxford to Cambridge to London, and in pockets of Tayside and Greater Manchester, UK biotech is in excellent shape, its success pump-primed by public spending. Beneficiaries include profitable pharmaceutical and biotech companies; the BioIndustry Association reckons that to the 482,000 existing jobs in life sciences 33,000 could be added by 2025.

At Astex Therapeutics, with its 140 scientists in Cambridge (plus 110 more in California), there's not a lot to see beyond the banks of computers and automated systems working through thousands of permutations of mutations, using genetic data to identify targets in cancer cells that could be treated with small-molecule therapies. Founded in 1999 by three professors, including Sir Tim Blundell, one of Nobel laureate Dorothy Hodgkin's team, the company's rise shows how well UK science has done.

But the 'valley of death' between lab and stock exchange claims many victims. Harren Jhoti, Astex's chief executive, knows the risk: 'About 95 per cent of biotech start-ups will fail, usually due to their idea not working. That makes finance very difficult.' Astex struck lucky, attracting £50 million in venture capital, a rare sum at the time. 'Early is difficult, but so is middle stage, when you need more investment to scale up.' They have leveraged in more funds, are now part owned by a Japanese company and partner with others. It has taken twenty long years. 'Our first drug approval in 2017 was for Kisqali for breast cancer, and our second was in 2019 for Balversa for bladder cancer. Here's how rare this is: only one in a thousand drugs get to late-stage development, and of those only one in a hundred gets to market.'

Venture capitalists lack patience, demanding a return within seven years, at the most. Launching an initial public offering on the stock market is also a problem. 'It's a cultural issue. They don't understand biotech. They're afraid of it.' UK-based biotech companies find it easier to launch on the American Nasdaq exchange. 'In the US, they have a rule that pension funds must invest half a per cent in new high-tech industries. Britain should do the same.'

Here's a door to the future, in which the UK already has a foot. But the industry worries that it will be overtaken: competitor countries are more generous with tax credits and grants, none more so than China. So much of the UK's attractiveness to foreign research collaborators is Brexit-dependent. Paris, Berlin and Lisbon are vying to turn themselves into technology hubs. Anticipating problems, Oxford is setting up joint programmes with German universities, while the Wellcome Trust opened its first overseas office in Berlin in 2019. A third of the staff in the digital sector in London are non-UK EU citizens whose future in the UK has been jeopardised.

Internet Income

A 'strategy' for UK industry could join together bold policies for investment, training and productivity and include the cultural, service and public sectors. Action has to involve reforms to boardrooms, corporate governance and remuneration. This need not require much ideological sacrifice, even for the Right: the state is already a player, procuring defence equipment, building infrastructure, funding research and development and (often ineffectually) applying some regulation to corporate governance and finance. What has been missing is a conviction that government must intervene, as Michael Heseltine once promised, at 'breakfast, lunch and tea'.

Nine out of ten households had internet access in 2018, up from eight out of ten in 2011. The UK moved ahead on access to public services online. (But forcing applicants for Universal Credit to claim online was brutal. Although the government claimed that 98 per cent applied that way, the boast obscured all too many instances of poor people struggling to register for a benefit that had been introduced dogmatically and meanly.)

A downside of the popular enthusiasm for online shopping has been the demise of the high street. But its regeneration could be financed by challenging the tech giants to pay the equivalent of business rates, levelling the playing field. The head of Tesco, hardly a left-wing firebrand, demanded an 'Amazon tax' on goods sold online; the strongly pro-business German leader Angela Merkel thinks similarly. Taxing the technology giants to pay for better broadband was one of the less controversial commitments in Labour's 2019 election manifesto. Amazon has grown too big, a monolith that sucks in half of all e-commerce. Google hogs 81 per cent of all search engine activity. Foreign agents try to use Facebook to meddle in elections; Instagram is blamed for mental health problems in adolescents. Government needs to step in and revise the categories: these internet giants are publishers and must take responsibility for the content they carry. Regulating the behemoths is a challenge that should appeal to leavers, since it demands the reassertion of UK sovereignty over the multinationals. However, that requires a reassessment of transatlantic relations, with Donald Trump showing how resistant the Republican-dominated US is to allowing any effective taxation or regulation of its giants, especially by foreign governments.

Would these internet companies disinvest if the UK required them to pay fair taxes? London remains a significant draw, even post-Brexit, securing most of the £5.5 billion invested in the technology sector in the first seven months of 2019; the digital sector increased its share of GDP to 14.4 per cent, up from 8.7 per cent in 2013. Facebook said it chose the UK as a base because it attracted a multicultural workforce that hailed from many of the countries where WhatsApp was widely used, such as India. The Chinese company Tencent decided to work in the UK on an AI-based diagnostic tool for Parkinson's disease, with the size and research-friendliness of the NHS a key factor. In the 2020s students will fill PhD places dedicated to studying artificial intelligence, a new £100 million initiative that was announced in 2019. And it's not just London. 'We could be a "California of the UK", a place with a fantastic natural environment and the power to attract,' said Lorna Carver, head of the Dorset Local Enterprise Partnership, a paid booster, but her vision is not implausible. Bournemouth/Poole is a growing conurbation, and the local university is entrepreneurial and has avoided being dragged down by the area's reputation for its heavy concentration of conservative retirees.

One gap is the lack of strong regional champions. The local enterprise partnerships created by Cameron are feeble, underfunded vehicles, with civil servants assessing a third of them as 'requiring improvement'. Accountable local councils would be better. Nor should anyone give up on manufacturing, as the UK still harbours engineering excellence that needs fostering: one example is Rolls-Royce moving ahead with building an electric-powered aircraft. Professor Mariana Mazzucato from University College London said a new 'technological, economic' paradigm lay within our grasp; she is the chronicler of the extent to which almost all leaps forward in technology spring from government investment, including the invention of the internet itself. Markets follow on.

During 2019 the CBI appointed as its new president Karan Bilimoria. He was different, not just in coming from an ethnic minority, but because his business was making something:

beer. Food is now a principal manufacturing sector (though, like everything else, Brexit-afflicted). Among Bilimoria's familiar and reasonable complaints was the UK's perpetual lack of skills; a lack of foreign languages has been estimated to cost 3.5 per cent of GDP. But business is partly to blame, failing to create apprenticeships and develop staff skills. Boardrooms need a severe shaking up. It's high time they freed themselves from the stale old anti-planning, anti-tax, anti-regulation mindset that often pervades the Institute of Directors and the CBI. As the state grapples with the climate emergency, skill shortages and risks to trade, business needs to step up as a credible partner, not as a whinger from the sidelines. To win public credibility, grotesque rewards for mediocre directors will have to go, which will require an outbreak of investor activism.

Business should be more British and, yes, patriotic. That's not in the protectionist or mercantilist sense intended by Brexiters; it means boards committed to their workforce, to taxpayers and to rebuilding Britain. Chief executives, chairs and boards will have to take the public stands they have shrunk away from, publicly naming and shaming colleagues who draw UK privileges but live abroad and avoid paying UK taxes. Business leaders eager to accept honours and access in exchange for political donations are often the first to invest outside the UK, grabbing short-term profit and forsaking long-term growth. Too many keep their money offshore. Ian Fraser's chilling account of the demise of RBS quotes one of its people as saying, 'We're investment bankers, we don't care what happens in five years.'

Reclaiming Ownership

Brexit exposed the hollowness of 'sovereignty'. How far does it reach when vital infrastructure and prized assets are controlled by shadowy, unaccountable corporations? Other EU countries' state-owned rail and energy companies have taken over our badly privatised utilities. By the end of the decade even Tory ministers were parroting Labour lines on nationalisation and the promise of coordinated long-term planning and investment. Ahead lies recalibration of ownership and national security. What price the security of the UK when Hinkley Point, a pivotal power plant, is run by companies answerable to Beijing? By upping data speed and capacity, 5G technology would add £164 billion to GDP by 2030: this is by definition vital infrastructure. But the Chinese IT company Huawei – answerable to the Chinese Communist Party at various points – secured a leading role in the UK's 5G telecommunications network, cleverly recruiting former Tory politicians and lobbyists to dangle temptations in the government's face, such as a promised new microchip research and development factory employing 400 people to be built outside Cambridge.

The UK, unlike its EU neighbours, has long been cavalier about foreign owners and controllers of crucial industries. Nothing has been more damaging to the nation than Margaret Thatcher's breaking of the media ownership laws to allow a massive agglomeration of media under foreign ownership that has swayed our politics and culture, especially in disseminating anti-Europeanism. The American-based Murdoch dynasty exerted persistent, *Sun*-inflected right-wing influence on Westminster and public policy, all the while pretending to espouse national interests over those of 'foreigners'. Not just foreigners but any citizens fallen on hard times, ripe for being despised when, as Claud Cockburn observed back in the 1930s, 'the greater part of the press, daily and periodical, had been at work on an image of the unemployed and their situation, their relation to the rest of the community, designed to counter-act humanitarian sentiments'. That same thread ran all the way through the dominant newspapers, none of whose owners lived and paid taxes in the UK: the Murdoch press owned 40 per cent of readership, alongside the *Mail* and *Telegraph* groups' non-resident owners, whose influence and agendas leaked into broadcasting.

Ready for Robots?

As with 5G, AI and robotics also depend on collaboration between the state and private or foreign-owned companies (whose ownership must be validated). The effects of automa-tion could be seismic: Credit Suisse says the car industry could produce the same output as now with 18 per cent fewer work-ers. Vehicle manufacturing only has a future if the vehicles in question are electric. Ralf Speth, chief executive of Jaguar Land Rover, says UK development of power storage is essential: 'If batteries go out of the UK, then automotive production will go out of the UK.' Brexit has already pushed companies such as Honda out. The OECD reckons that about one in seven existing jobs could, in principle, be subject to full automation, with a further one in three materially altered. Any response needs the same three ingredients: planning, public resources collaborating with companies, and investment in education and training. International evidence shows that in countries where the government intervenes most in the quality of jobs, the workforce performs best.

Taking Back the Streets

Shops will go on closing, with one in ten shop fronts void in 2019, according to the British Retail Consortium; a further 20 per cent of retail space will be lost by 2030. Even sites in Queen Street in prosperous Maidenhead are being boarded up, as town centres everywhere decline. Marks & Spencer was once a mainstay of the 1950s England many Brexit voters pine for, but over a hundred M&S stores are due to close by 2022, disappearing from Barrow-in-Furness through an alphabet of places to Sutton Coldfield and Weston-super-Mare. Commerce, councils and government must find welcoming ways to keep the high streets public places, sites of sociability.

It's not just vanishing shops that presage decline. A pub was closing every twelve hours in 2018, with thousands gone across towns and villages. The Gordon Arms still sits on a pivotal site in High Wycombe, but the weeds multiply on its frontage, paint peels, its signboard is blank. It used to be owned by Greene King, founded in 1799 in Bury St Edmunds and long a prime identifier for the East Anglian town, but in 2019 the brewers sold up to a Hong Kong company more interested in its property assets than a pint of Abbot Ale. Less alcohol consumption might be welcomed, but pubs have been much more than drinking dens: the fictional Queen Vic in *EastEnders* points to the way communities revolve around meeting points, shared spaces. The rate of decline in pubs halved after 2018, when the government gave them business-rate relief and revived Labour-era planning laws to allow community groups to designate their local as an 'asset of community value', making it harder for property owners to redevelop. Community pubs have shown the way, combining retailing, coffee and traditional pub-going. Look how the hard-pressed Moulsecoomb community in Brighton sprang into action to keep their pub open, turning it into a cooperative, The Bevy, which has become a local hub for all ages and for community projects.

Better-funded councils could reverse the disappearance of gathering places – the 760 youth clubs and 130 libraries gone in a single year in 2018, hours cut for those that survive. Sports centres and playing fields closed, and parks and playgrounds were sold. Everywhere communal space shrank, sending a subliminal message not to meet and mingle, but to stay at home, shut the door and stick to your TV. Cameron naively believed his Big Society would spring up in the midst of individualism, but community initiatives need public nurturing to spread and thrive. Local authorities, given the powers, could make grants, set up projects, redesign streets and public places, compulsorily purchase eyesores and re-let empty shops; in other words, they could be given the local power to interfere with market forces in the best interests of what their local people want and need.

Instead, the local legacy is all too visible in uncut grass, rough sleepers in doorways, threadbare local transport, vanishing trading and environmental standards officers, and shuttered libraries and museums. Even if councils raise council tax to the maximum permitted, the gap between what should be spent and likely revenues will become a £30 billion black hole by 2025. That is only the cost of maintaining services as they were in 2019, not improving or restoring them to 2010 levels.

Active Places

Carnegie Trust research showed that disadvantaged regions and towns would be worst affected by the loss of EU trade and European regeneration funds. A painful experiment may be unfolding in Mansfield, Nuneaton and other places where immigrants as a share of the local population increased by over 350 per cent in the ten years to 2015, contributing to Brexit sentiment. If migrants leave or are pushed out, they will not be replaced by locals like for like, so already stressed local economies will suffer. Tourism contributed a high proportion of the economic output of leave-voting Wales and the south-west, but their hotels, restaurants and attractions are highly dependent on migrants, especially EU nationals.

Before it imploded, the Social Mobility Commission said the state had to push public resources into 'left behind' areas. Those populations were ageing and unfit, with available employment primarily in low-skilled and marginal sectors, so bright and motivated young people left and did not return. May and Johnson tried to fend off the charge of indifference with, for example, a minuscule 'stronger towns fund' and various 'deals' offering bits of money to areas such as Borderlands, a new proto-region centred on Carlisle. Ad hoc handouts won't prevent structural financial problems pressing on places such as Derby, where the demand for services will ratchet up in the 2020s: the city's population aged over sixty-five will increase by 42 per cent by the 2030s, with pensioners over eighty-five up by 80 per cent.

However, if given freedom, power and funds, places can find their own solutions. Local authorities, health trusts and voluntary organisations working with businesses can experiment and innovate. Sheffield Hallam University evaluated Rotherham's £500,000 experiment in social prescribing, whereby GPs urged patients to do yoga, arts, fitness and similar activities: it cut A&E visits, saved doctors' time and reduced hospital stays, aided by contacting and staying in touch with lonely older people and providing financial advice.

People are self-organising, given the chance. But some councils will stick in the mud. 'Localism' must be matched by monitoring and funds from central government. Volunteering needs the same attention and support, but its monitor, the Charity Commission, went off the rails as Tory ministers ordered it to scourge and discourage charities that dared to speak up on behalf of those suffering under austerity. Volunteers went on trying to do good, within the framework of new charity laws that sought to gag them, with a new anti-loneliness initiative and the heroic organisation of food banks, which sprang up spontaneously, paradoxically displaying the best of social involvement, made necessary by harsh government policies.

In Preston, cooperative energy surged, new enterprises thriving under council encouragement; they even made an icon of the town's monstrous bus station. Manchester, Leeds and Sheffield forged post-industrial identities, some enthusiastically led by newly elected mayors. Croydon, hurt by the 2011 disturbances, regrouped. In the midst of austerity, some councils took courageous steps: Birmingham expanded pedestrian zones in the centre; Edinburgh announced monthly car-free days; Nottingham put a levy on workplace parking; Bath and Bristol moved towards congestion charging, Oxford towards a central-area car ban.

Raising the Take

Civic renewal has a long way to go. So much depends on reforming another legacy of the 2010s: the rickety financial underpinnings of councils. Tory policy forced them to rely entirely on what they could raise through council tax and their shaky business rates. But places differ markedly in their prosperity and taxable capacity, so, as Peter Kenway of the New Policy Institute warned, this policy would break the link between a place's need and its ability to raise funds. For poorer cities such as Newcastle and Hull, 'There are no guarantees that ability to raise business rates will match needs in the most deprived areas,' while Westminster would wallow in cash from business.

All recent governments have dodged reform of council tax, dumping it in the too-hot-to-handle box, terrified of levying a fairer charge on domestic property. Tax should aim to capture the increased worth that comes from just sitting on a piece of land that inflates in value. As often as not it's the state that causes increasing local house prices: a railway station or a good new school can send the surrounding land values soaring. It's the state that should recover that unearned increment to help pay for services and further improvements – a principle that is already recognised, but only in ad hoc deals between councils and developers, not in the foundations of the tax system.

To repair the damage done, let alone improve the public realm, the 2020s need tax realism. The base is being eroded. Taxing petrol produces diminishing amounts as cars become more fuel-efficient or switch to electric. If the Treasury were not so obsessed with central control, we might already have experimented with marginal but locally significant taxes on tourists, hotel nights and similar. Brexit will, one way or another, push changes in taxation and tariffs at the border and possibly create space for reforming aspects of VAT. No serious strategy for climate change should tolerate VAT exemption for domestic energy supplies. There is hope that countries around the globe will get a grip on the big tax avoiders, as in 2019 the OECD and the G20 panel on profit-shifting agreed a framework for taxing multinationals.

The UK 'tax burden' is less than in other European countries that score higher both on growth and equality, such as Germany and France. Although straightforward comparisons are difficult since both countries have far higher productivity, that proves the anti-state brigade wrong in pretending some universal economic law prohibits higher tax rates. Already, due to a heavy reliance on consumption taxes, on average the poorest fifth of UK households pay 35 per cent of their gross income in tax, far more than the richest fifth. It's true that the great bulk of income tax is paid by those at the top of the income distribution, causing more cautious reformers to suggest limits to increases in top tax rates beyond the 50p in place in 2010. But that leaves plenty of room for putting corporation tax back to its 2010 level and taxing capital, property and asset wealth, along with council and local business tax reform. The not impossible trick is to mobilise potential winners in order to drown the complaints of the minority of losers. Public opinion is on the side of fairer taxes of many kinds, such as online business paying its share relative to the high-street retailers.

On tax the ideological push from the anti-state right was bolstered by a common or garden reluctance to pay more. But attitudes are mixed and malleable. People have had enough of austerity; by a two to one majority they tell pollsters they are now willing to pay more to secure higher spending on schools and the NHS. The British Social Attitudes Survey shows a marked shift, with support for higher spending reaching heights previously seen in Labour's glory days. Even Theresa May endorsed 'fair and balanced' increases, as did a majority of Tory voters. Taxation for a specific purpose wins approval, as with Gordon Brown's raising of NI in 2002 by 2 percentage points, promised for the NHS. Surveys say people increasingly now acknowledge that a better settlement on public services would have to be paid for. The crunch point is taxing wealth. It has to happen; it's a matter of when and who dares.

Queen of Where?

For a symbol of ageing Britain, look no further than Buckingham Palace. Unspoken in public, the reigning monarch is now in her tenth decade, while the son who will succeed her is already in his eighth. With Charles, the mood music around the national figurehead suddenly changes key. Amid outpourings of royalist loyalty, the Elizabethan age will end. It actually fell apart when nationhood, founded on weak but consensual social democracy, was cracked by Margaret Thatcher's revolutionary individualism. Elizabeth II (Elizabeth I in Scotland) may be the last monarch to rule over the UK; a post-Brexit King Charles III might have to preside over Scottish independence and some kind of Irish reunification. Such moves should force fresh thinking about the nature of monarchy, not just in the UK, but in the Commonwealth, prompting a bout of constitutional and cultural rethinking in Canada, Australia and elsewhere. (The idea that Brexit would reinvigorate this loose, divergent band of countries was another of the era's nonsenses.) The accession of Charles (and later, who knows, his son) might be the beginning of the end of the posturing and pretence that precipitated Brexit. The monarchy keeps in place an institutional apparatus of honours, Westminster flummery, lords lieutenant, armed forces' mysticism and so on that might not survive long.

The Brexit crisis in Westminster caused the brutal exposure of the constitution as a gossamer tissue of breakable conventions, in which the role of the Queen, obliged to permit a rogue pro-roguing of parliament, revealed the weakness caused by the lack of a proper constitutional elected head of state with some power as arbiter in such emergencies.

For the Windsors, as for the rest us, the question is, 'Whose country?' Yawning divides are painfully open and explicit, across income, wealth, age, place, partisanship, prospects and beliefs. Brexit exacerbated all dimensions of conflict: on migra-tion, Europe, international alliances and the divide between embracers of modernity versus that old English ache to return to an imagined 1950s. The United Kingdom has become an oxymoron, united not at all on anything. Some – not just Scots – have drawn the conclusion that it has run its course and must now be replaced by some entity that can contain either independent or more radically devolved administrations. Over Brexit, Westminster has already broken away to become the government of little England, but that has not stopped angry St George's flag wavers pitting themselves against parliament. The nature of that cherished England is far from clear, let alone how it should express whatever its identity is. There are the traditional images – cricket, the fading Anglican church, the now disappeared maritime tradition, the familiar landscape of patchworked fields – but they abide alongside the modern facts of multicultural cities with a plethora of outlooks, identities, incomes and lifestyles. How do Bradford and Bridport com-fortably belong to the same country?

No wonder England seems to care so much less than it did about the territorial integrity of the UK. The impact of Brexit will not be symmetrical as regional differences become emphasised – for example, the Scottish government's open-arms approach to migration, while England shuts its borders. Brexit proved that material considerations easily take second place to emotional perceptions and assertions of identity. Will the prospect of Scotland going it alone, inside or outside the EU, depend on questions of money – or nationalism? Government Expenditure and Revenue Scotland gives no quarter: there is a persistent and giant gap between what is spent in Scotland and the amount of tax it brings in. How much would Scottish residents be willing to pay for independence?

The same gap confronts proponents of Irish unification: how much are taxpayers in the Republic willing to pay for the north, and how much are its residents prepared to forego? The cosseting of the Democratic Unionist Party by Theresa May obscured the parlous state of Northern Ireland, political, economic and fiscal. It is as clear now as it was throughout the nationalist insurgency that the Republic of Ireland will have to be heavily involved in the future arrangements for the north. Patient statecraft will be needed to rebuild the bruised relationship between London and Dublin. Together they have to confront the economic marginality of Northern Ireland, its lopsided economy, the threats to what remains of its manufacturing sector. As for the border, the futile search for 'alternative arrangements' to customs checks may soon become a search for arrangements that recognise the de facto unification of the island of Ireland, with its customs border in the Irish Sea – but would residents in the north still get their UK bonus?

The government and constitution of the UK are decrepit, in need of thorough spring-cleaning. The decanting of MPs and peers when the decaying Palace of Westminster is renewed could be a prompt. It's time to correct the corruptions of lobbying and peerages, but most pressing is electoral reform for the House of Commons, now that first-past-the-post is so demonstrably incapable of representing a fragmenting country. Brexit exposed the unfitness of electoral law in the age of social media, hostile foreign intervention and unwarranted use of private data.

Some Reasons to Be Cheerful

In the bowels of the Tate is Richard Caton Woodville's watercolour of General Wolfe heroically scaling the Heights of Abraham to take Quebec City; it was much viewed when the Brexiter generation was at school and world maps on classroom walls still showed great daubs of empire red. That was how Boris Johnson hazily conceived the battle of Brexit – swift and surgical (though, of course, he, unlike Wolfe, would not be killed on the field). He would be gracious in victory and collect the laurels from a gratefully united nation.

It won't happen. Ahead lies a protracted tug of war over the identity of the country. On one side is the belief that open, exporting, green, devolved, educated, public-service and redistributionist states of mind can muster public support against the backward-lookers. Look at how Brexit and the climate crisis have both provoked new political activism. A poll from 2019 found that 63 per cent thought Britain's system of government was rigged 'to advantage the rich and powerful': that's a large constituency for fairer sharing of power and tax. The LSE's Professor Patrick Dunleavy noted that the 2010s did not support the conventional wisdom that political parties were in decline: membership has gone up as well as down, and the aftershocks of Brexit may yield new configurations. The need for electoral reform is more pressing than ever, as there is a present danger that some of the disaffected misidentify problems with our current badly configured democracy as problems fundamental to democracy itself. People of good will, reviewing the era, sometimes long for unity, for citizens to come together on common ground. But what if the field is fissured and on one side there's our tribe, with theirs on the other?

In this chapter we pointed to reasons why policies, parties and political leaders will have to flex and change. Young people will grow in number, with greater expectations of fair treatment, each cohort better educated, more aware. An upcoming political generation cleansed of Brexit mania has every good chance of starting anew. Events, climate, economic trends will press down hard on old free-market ideologies. As the planet continues to overheat, reducing the burn depends on state, communal and household action. Pressure to work together internationally will have voters soon looking back in astonishment at the 'single stupidest thing any country has ever done', in the words of ex-New York mayor Michael Bloomberg.

'Apart,' he added, 'from the election of Donald Trump as US president.' Recovery from both these insanities is possible.

People everywhere are calling for more help from the state, the OECD reports. They want governments to do more for their economic and social security, not less. This comes not just from those on low incomes: two-thirds of those with high incomes want more and better public services. Thatcherite individualism has now run its course and think tanks on the right, sniffing the air, talk of the end of austerity and the need for security of all kinds. As the pendulum swings, the 2020s could see a chance for a renewed and reinvigorated state. Despite growth in expectations and demographic change, UK tax rose only from 30.1 per cent of GDP in 1965 to 33.3 per cent in 2017, the smallest increase among the G7 – showing scope for more. Extra tax need not come from incomes when the UK VAT regime is so unique in its eccentric exemptions, and there is the chance to harvest the giddy rise in untaxed land wealth.

What matters most? When people list their hopes and concerns for the future, for family or for society, the remedies they call for rely on collective action – local, national or international. Jobs and prosperity depend on markets, commerce and capitalism, but those thrive only under the conditions, regulations, infrastructure and encouragements of a democratic state. After the survival of the planet on which we live, what matters most are the things we can only provide together jointly – good health and education, a decent working life, safety. Ask what gives most pleasure, and the response, after family and home, tends to be beautiful public spaces, well-kept parks, stadiums, sports centres, museums, treasured heritage and public buildings to be proud of. If pessimism is often the easy default, optimism is inborn, with that underlying belief in common progress, the expectation that things can, must and will get better.

The lost decade took many of those things away, damaging the common realm during fractious, bitter years. Austerity was heedless and needless. The destruction set alight by Brexit has yet to meet a firebreak, but it will burn out. What emerges from those ashes need not be some new politics, but the recovery of an older, robust national confidence – call it social democracy – that trusts in common purposes, with a fairer sharing of prospects and wealth. Much of what was lost can be regained.